Agriculture Marketing

Edited & Compiled By

Ramesh Chand

Educational Publishers & Distributors

291, Bank Enclave, Laxmi Nagar, Delhi-110092.

Published by:

Educational Publishers & Distributors

291, Bank Enclave, Laxmi Nagar, Delhi-110092.

Ph.: (O) 011-65190343, 43551324, 42564726
(M) 9811088729, (Fax) 42564726, (Res.) 47091605

E-mail: *khelsahitya1@rediffmail.com*

Web: *www.khelsahitya.com*

I.S.B.N. - 978-93-80873-39-8

PRINTED IN INDIA

Laser Typeset by:
JAIN MEDIA GRAPHICS
Delhi-110035.

Printed by:
ASIAN OFFSET PRINTERS
Delhi

Price: Rs. 650/-

Contents

Chapter 1

Agricultural Marketing and Rural Credit: Status, Issues and Reform

Introduction

This article is a part of a larger study aimed at strengthening policy reforms in the area of agriculture, food security and rural development. In countries like India, strengthening of agriculture is critical for facing the challenges of rural poverty, food insecurity, unemployment and sustainability of natural resources. But, there is a need to redefine agriculture as the science and practice of activities relating to production, processing, marketing, distribution, utilization and trade of food, feed and fibre, which implies that agricultural development strategy must address not only farmers but also those in marketing, trade, processing and agri-business. In this context, efficient marketing and rural credit systems assume added importance. Agricultural marketing system is the critical link between farm production sector on the one hand and non-farm sector, industry, and urban economy on the other. Apart from performing physical and facilitating functions of transferring the goods from producers to consumers, the marketing system also performs the function of discovering the prices at different stages of marketing and transmitting the price signals in the marketing chain. The issues and concerns in marketing relate mainly to the performance of the marketing system, which depends on the structure and conduct of the market. An efficient marketing system helps in optimization of resource use, output management, increase in farm incomes, widening of markets, growth of agro-based industry, addition to national income through value addition, and employment creation. Rural credit system assumes importance because for most of the Indian rural families, savings are inadequate to finance farming and other economic activities. This, coupled with the lack of simultaneity between income and expenditure and lumpiness of fixed capital investment, makes availability of timely credit at affordable rates of interest, an essential pre-requisite for improving rural livelihoods and accelerating rural development.

The specific objectives of this paper are to review the existing status of agricultural marketing and rural credit systems; to document the policy framework for functioning of agricultural markets and rural credit; and to identify the areas of further policy reforms for strengthening Indian agriculture. The paper has been divided into eight sections. Current status of agricultural marketing system and emerging issues are discussed in the second section. Current policy framework of agricultural marketing is analysed in the third section. This section also includes recent initiatives in the areas of domestic marketing reforms. Areas of further policy reforms and priorities are brought out in the fourth section. The current status of rural credit system is reviewed in the fifth section. The sixth section brings out the issues and emerging areas of concern in rural credit. Suggestions for policy reforms and strategic initiatives for improving rural credit system are identified in the seventh section. Some concluding observations are given in the last section.

Agricultural Marketing System Status

Current agricultural marketing system in India is the outcome of several years of government intervention. Agricultural marketing scenario in India has undergone conspicuous changes during the last 50 years, owing to the increased marketed surplus; increase in urbanization and income levels and consequent changes in the pattern of demand for marketing services; increase in linkages with distant and overseas markets; and changes in the form and degree of government intervention. While the policy framework that influenced the structure, conduct and performance of agricultural marketing is discussed in the third section, some basic features of the system are presented here.

Marketing Channels

In India, agricultural commodities move from the farm gate to consumers through several channels. Marketing channels for agricultural commodities vary from commodity to commodity but can be broadly divided into four groups viz., (a) direct from farmers to consumers; (b) through public agencies or cooperative organizations; (c) through private wholesalers and retailers; and (d) through processors. Some important characteristics and changes in marketing channels witnessed during the last fifty years are as follows:

(i) The proportion of total marketed surplus going directly from farmers to consumers continues to be small.

(ii) The role of transporters and processors in the marketing channel has considerably increased.

(iii) Specialization of traders in agricultural marketing, both in terms of commodity or marketing functions, has shown an increasing tendency.

(iv) The length of marketing channel has tended to increase due to increase in demand for value-added services and geographic expansion of markets.

(v) The share of private trade in handling marketed surplus has continued to be large. Taking all agricultural commodities together, the marketed surplus handled by cooperatives has been estimated as 10 percent, and by public agencies 10 percent. The private trade handles around 80 percent of the total marketed quantities of agricultural commodities.

(vi) Realizing that the marketing channels for perishable fresh farm products should be as short as possible, and to eliminate intermediaries, direct marketing by farmers has been encouraged during the last one decade. Several states took initiative and established farmers' markets like Apni Mandi (Punjab), Kisan Mandi (Rajasthan), Hadaspur Vegetable Market (Pune), Rythu Bazaars (Andhra Pradesh) and Krushak Bazaars (Orissa). The establishment of such farmers markets helped both consumers and farmers. The success of such markets depends on the kind of infrastructure and facilities provided at these places and upkeep and maintenance of premises. Nevertheless, this is certainly a better alternative system and needs to be encouraged and promoted.

Market Yards and Market Places

Actual buying and selling of commodities mainly takes place in market yards and sub-yards primary and secondary wholesale markets and rural periodic markets haats spread throughout the country. At present, there are 2354 main market yards, 4807 sub-market yards and 27294 rural periodic markets in the country. These are managed by either Agricultural Produce Market committees representing farmers and other stakeholders local self-government institutions or government departments. The users of these markets, mostly buyers, have to pay a fee to the managers of these market places. Facilities in these market places vary extensively.

Nearly two-thirds of market yards and sub-yards were laid out on vast land area with such facilities as auction platforms, shops, godowns, rest houses and parking lots. However, studies have shown that facilities available in these yards are considerably short of the requirements. Further, nearly 85 percent of 27294 rural periodic market places have very little or almost no facilities for trade to take place efficiently.

Market Structure

Market structure is the size and design of the market and refers to those organizational characteristics which affect the conduct and performance of the market. Important structural characteristics of agricultural produce markets include concentration of market power, conditions of entry or exit of firms, flow of market information, degree of product differentiation, and degree of integration - both vertical and horizontal. The market orientation of Indian farmers has, during the last fifty years, increased manifold both in terms of forward and backward linkages. The marketing system is now required to handle large volumes of agricultural products on account of both increase in output as well as increase in marketed-surplus to output ratios. The overall MSOR is estimated to have gone up from 33.4 percent in 1950-51 to 64.1 percent in 1999-00 and is expected to have increased further to around 70 percent in recent years. The marketed quantities in 2000-01 were ten times of that in 1950-51 for cereals, 4.6 times for oilseeds, 5.3 times for milk, 15.4 times for poultry products and 7.4 times for fish. The marketed surplus in 2000-01 was valued at Rs. 4037 billion.

Notwithstanding the direct intervention by the government, the markets for agricultural products in India have remained dominated by the private trade. As already mentioned, nearly 80 percent of the marketed surplus of agricultural products is handled by the private trade. Even in the case of cereals, where government intervention is perceived to be quite high, the share of private trade in total marketed surplus was 72.5 percent during triennium ending 1982-83, 74.0 percent during TE 1996-97 and was 71.1 percent during 2000-01. The private trade during 2000-01 handled more than 100 million tonnes of cereals. With larger quantities required to be handled by the private trade, the size and structure of the market have considerably expanded.

The wholesale assembly and trade in foodgrains is handled by around two million wholesalers. In the area of retailing, there are around five million private retailers and more than 4.10 lakh fair price shops under public distribution system. Nearly three-fourths of the fair price shops are in the private sector. On an average, there is one retail shop of foodgrains for a population of 200. Apart from the traders, processors play an important role as they also enter the market as bulk buyers and sellers. The demand for value-added services and processing has considerably increased the role of processors in the market structure for farm products. In the case of foodgrains, there are 104704 hullers and shellers and 34688 rice mills for paddy processing; 812 roller flour mills and 2.66 lakhs flour-units for wheat processing and 10000 pulse processing units. For oilseeds processing, 131600 cottage level crushers ghanies are giving way to 20000 expellers, 130 oil-refining units and 145 hydrogenation units. For sugarcane processing, there are 408 sugar factories, besides several khandsari units. However, the state of processing and value addition in the food segment continues to be grossly inadequate. Only 16 percent of country's milk output is processed in the organized sector as against a world average of 52 percent. Out of total milk production in India, 33 percent is retained at the village level and 51 percent is handled by traditional unorganized sector. Considering the entire food segment, processed segment accounts for 10 percent, semiprocessed 15 percent and remaining 75 percent is still fresh food market. Further, the food processing is dominated by unorganized small and even tiny sector. The value addition to food production is estimated to be only seven percent in India as against 23 percent in China, 45 percent in Philippines and 188 percent in United Kingdom.

The processing segment of food market including fruits, vegetables and livestock products is growing rapidly and attracting investment since the launch of economic reforms in 1991. The pace can be accelerated further. The multiplier of food industry in India is estimated to be 2.4, which is considerably higher than even power and telecom sector. Expansion of food processing industry can trigger growth in transport, packaging and refrigeration. It also has a strong impact on farmer's incomes and rural employment. Every investment of Rs. one lakh in food processing can generate an employment of 1.8 persons directly and of similar magnitude indirectly.

The agro-industry in India is dominated by the unorganized sector other than those employing more than 10 persons, using power and more than 20 persons, not using power, comprising of small and micro-enterprises. Between 1994-95 and 2000-01, the number of agro-industrial units went up by 4.5 million, expanding the sub-sector's share in manufacturing sector from 65 percent to 82 percent.

By and large, the structural characteristics of market for agricultural products emerge as (a) the market size is already large and expanding; (b) it is dominated by the private sector; (c) unorganized small segment is much larger than the organized sector, but the share of organized sector is increasing; and (d) despite market being large, due to infrastructure bottlenecks and excessive regulatory framework, the efficiency is very low, adversely affecting both the farmers and consumers.

Marketing Institutions

Another important structural characteristic of market structure for agricultural commodities is the institutional infrastructure created promoted by the government for improvement of marketing system. Depending on the objectives and role, the marketing institutions can be grouped into public sector organizations, cooperatives and other formal informal bodies. Public sector organizations include Food Corporation of India Cotton Corporation of India; Jute Corporation of India; Commodity Boards; APEDA; STC; MPEDA; Commission for Agricultural Costs and Prices; Directorate of Marketing and Inspection; Departments of Food and Civil Supplies; State Agricultural Marketing Boards; Central and State Warehousing Corporations; and Agricultural Produce Market Committees. The role and functions of each of these differ and include policy formulation, implementation, supervision, facilitation and direct entry in the market. These apart, a large number of farmers' cooperative organizations have been promoted for undertaking marketing and processing functions on behalf of the farmers or members of cooperatives. By and large, marketing cooperatives in India is a four-tier structure consisting of primary marketing societies, district or regional cooperatives, state marketing federations and national level marketing cooperatives. The main marketing cooperatives include National Agricultural Cooperative Marketing Federation, Tribal Cooperative Marketing Federation, State Cooperative Marketing Federations (general as well as commodity specific), district level cooperatives or unions of cooperatives, and primary agricultural cooperative marketing societies general as well as commodity specific. In addition, the government has established some public sector organizations to promote cooperatives. These include National Cooperative Development Corporation and National Dairy Development Board. In quite a few commodities and regions, the cooperative organizations have played an important role in improvement in the performance of the marketing system by increasing competition. They have contributed in not only marketing and processing of farm products, but also in supply of inputs, including credit to farmers.

NAFED was established in October 1958 as an apex organization of marketing cooperatives. Its primary objective is to strengthen cooperative marketing structure in the country. Specific objectives of establishing NAFED include (a) to coordinate and promote the marketing activities of affiliated cooperative institutions; (b) to promote inter-state and international trade in agricultural and related commodities; (c) to make arrangements for the supply of agricultural inputs required by its member cooperatives; and (d) to act as an agency of the government for purchase, sale, storage and distribution of agricultural products and inputs. To fulfil its objectives, NAFED has been undertaking internal trade, exports and imports, price support and market intervention operations, production and marketing of inputs, promotional activities, developing cooperative marketing of tribal produce, and processing and marketing of fruits, vegetables and other agricultural commodities. As the basic objective of NAFED is the promotion of cooperative marketing, the direct intervention in the market by NAFED has been insignificant. However, it has been playing the role of national nodal agency for price support operations for oilseeds and pulses and in the implementation of market intervention scheme for fruits, vegetables, copra and other commodities as and when assigned by the government. By and large, NAFED has effectively worked on its set objectives.

Marketing Infrastructure

The availability of marketing infrastructure affects the structure, conduct and performance of the market. Studies have shown that owing to considerable expansion in infrastructure, there has been significant increase in both horizontal and vertical integration of agricultural markets, which improved the process of price discovery and transmission of price signals from deficit to surplus area. However, the existing situation is far from adequate. Nearly 51 percent of the villages are still not connected by roads. Grading at primary market level is grossly inadequate. Only around seven percent of the total quantity sold by farmers is graded before sale. The scientific storage capacity is only 30 percent of the required capacity. Cold storage facility is available for only 10 percent of fruits and vegetables. As already mentioned, processing capacity is inadequate and inefficient. Physical infrastructure in market yards is inadequate. Most of the rural periodic markets including livestock markets have no infrastructure. Nearly 41 percent of the villages have no telephone facility. Due to lack of proper handling (cleaning, sorting, grading and packaging) at the village level, about seven percent of foodgrains, 30 percent of fruits and vegetables and 10 percent of spices are lost before reaching the market.

These apart, there is considerable and continued inter-regional disparities in infrastructure for marketing. The index of infrastructure at state level compiled by the Centre for Monitoring Economy shows that the infrastructure is relatively well developed in the state of Kerala, Tamil Nadu, Haryana and Gujarat. But it has continued to be weak in Madhya Pradesh, Bihar and Rajasthan. This is, obviously, reflected in the inter-regional differences in efficiency of agricultural marketing.

Contract Farming

Contract farming is emerging as an important mode of procurement of agricultural products by agribusiness firms (private, public or cooperatives). This is an advance arrangement contract between the farmers and the firm wherein farmers produce an agreed quality and quantity of the produce which is purchased by the firm at the agreed price and time. The contract can be a pure buying arrangement or can extend to supply of inputs and kind of production practices adopted. Contract farming is beneficial to both the farmer as well as contractor. To the farmer, contract farming reduces price risk, to some extent production risk, marketing costs, and uncertainty of credit and helps in acquiring inputs. To the contractor, it helps in ensuring supply of quality product at the right time and at relatively lower cost.

Despite several hurdles, some initiatives, though at small scale, have been taken in recent years in this direction. The Escorts Krishi Sansar, Mahindra Subhlabh, Satnam Overseas and Tata Chemicals have been involved in contract farming in some selected areas but the total coverage is reported to be only 16000 to 40000 hectares. In addition, Coimbatore hatchery, NAFED (mushrooms in Sonepat), ITC Agro Tech Punjab Agro Industry Corporation and some exporters bulk buyers have tied up with farmers for assured purchases of such products as babycorn, tomato, chilies, garlic, onion, potato, banana, gherkins, barley, durum wheat, basmati rice, soybean, mustard, oil palm, coriander, grapes, pomegranate and raw cotton in different areas. Though, these initiatives are in the right direction, there are some reported inherent dangers like over use of natural resources, violation of contracts and introduction of undesirable seeds. Keeping the pros and cons in view, the Union Ministry has drafted a model contract farming agreement and a supportive legislation for insertion in the APMR Acts. The model provides for compulsory registration of contracts, dispute settlement mechanism, settlement of claims within three months, and a ban on agreement on farmer's land.

Market Information and Use of IT in Agricultural Marketing

The system of market information has continued to be far from satisfactory. While the traders and processors use their own informal sources, farmers depend both on formal and informal sources. Though, both market news and market intelligence are important, farmers are more interested in market news. The market news of interest to farmers is collected compiled by APMCs, SAMBs, state departments of agricultural marketing, field staff of Directorates of Economics and Statistics and Department of Food. The information is disseminated through display boards in market yards, announcements during open auction, newspapers, radio broadcasts and some TV channels also. Farmers also gather information through personal contacts with other farmers and traders. However, the market news is able to provide only a broad overview to the farmers due to several defects in the system. The price quotations are not backed by grades and the information is available with considerable lag. This information is not linked to local grade standards. Quite often, the price range is made available, which is of little use to farmers. There is also a serious misconception about the buying and selling price, which are distinctly different.

The development in information technology has great potential for integration of agricultural markets. The Directorate of Marketing and Inspection, Government of India, has set up an Intranet based system for market information networking across the country. The Market Research and Information Network which has already connected 735 wholesale markets, is aimed at catering to the diversified demand for information from all the stakeholders.

The information technology revolution, aided by the revolution in telecommunication has the potential to help in not only market information system but may also change the nature of market functioning altogether by making several intermediaries redundant, reducing the cost of information, lowering the transaction cost and increase of competition. The e-commerce ushered in by the IT revolution has led to enhanced market access and better information and has the promise of circumventing established marketing networks. The model of E-choupals promoted by ITC is the use of e-commerce in procuring agricultural commodities and selling inputs and other goods to the farmers.

The ITC's E-choupal initiative was launched in 2000 and by the end of 2003, had grown to 2700 choupals, covering 18000 villages and 1.2 million people in five states. The commodities covered are soybean, wheat, rice, pulses, coffee and shrimp. The company plans to extend it to 15 states with 20000 choupals covering 10 million people. The model consists of village Internet kiosks located around company's supply clusters operated by 'Sanchalaks' from among farmers rural youths. The kiosks provide real time information to the farmers on inputs, practices, credit availability, product quality required and expected price. Initially, the company faced several problems but were tackled successfully. The problem of connectivity and bandwidth was tackled through upgradation of BSNL kits through RNS kits, installation of V-SAT equipment and mobile choupals. The problem of irregular supply of power was tackled by providing back-up power batteries charged by solar panels. The problem of illiteracy of farmers was solved by providing information in local language through 24x7 help desks. The issue of contractual laws and regulations was tackled by giving public oath to Sanchalaks, as social contracts are more binding then the legal ones. The model has come out to be beneficial to both the farmers and the company. The procurement cost of company went down by 6 to 8 percent and it could procure improved quality of farm products.

Another example of corporate sector initiative in improving information system and application of e-governance is the Gramdoot project, launched in Rajasthan by Aksha Broadband Ltd., an optical fibre manufacturing company in January 2002. The objective of the project is to link the villages with national and global markets. Each gramdoot kiosk is equipped with computer, printer, scanner, web-camera, UPS, battery and optical nodes and all kiosks are linked to tehsil and district offices. Around 34 application forms, usually needed by farmers, are available on these kiosks. Each kiosk costs around Rs. 2.80 lakhs and can employ two rural youths. The loan for setting up such kiosks is available from the financial institutions.

With the launch of on-line futures trading in foodgrains, pulses and sugar in National Commodity Exchanges the government has permitted banks and Department of Posts to set up bulletin boards in all the rural branches to display future prices for NCDEX on real time basis. This would help the farmers to know the harvest time prices in advance at the sowing time. In near future, this may enable them to sell their product in advance at future prices. The cost of bulletin boards (Rs. two lakhs each) will be born by NCDEX. The NCDEX also has tied up with

Echoupals of ITC for such displays. This will also help banks in their lending decisions. This initiative will help all stakeholders in the supply chain viz:, traders, processors, wholesalers and bulk consumers. The investment potential of this venture is around Rs. 3000 crores.

Marketing Efficiency

The concern for the structure and conduct of marketing system relates mainly to its efficiency. Generally, marketing efficiency is measured either as operational efficiency or pricing efficiency. The former is measured in terms of relative size of marketing costs, net margins and gross marketing margins while the latter is measured in terms of price series correlations and through co-integration analysis. A comprehensive review of studies on marketing efficiency has provided the following evidence:

(a) The GMM accounts for a substantial share of consumer's price. This includes marketing costs, statutory charges and net margins of middlemen. Statutory charges account for 10 to 12 percent of consumer's price. However, net margins appear to have shown a tendency of decline over time owing to increase in competition.

(b) The share of farmers in consumer's rupee is higher for foodgrains, oilseeds and spices compared to that for perishable products. GMM in foodgrain markets are lower than for other products.

(c) The gross marketing margins in agricultural commodities, according to one estimate (Acharya, 2003) add upto Rs. 1009 billion, consisting of Rs. 151 billion as statutory charges, Rs. 207 billion as net margins of functionaries and Rs. 651 billion as cost of performing various marketing functions. About 77 percent of the marketing cost, amounting to Rs. 500 billion is estimated as avoidable loss during handling, transport and storage. Investment in marketing infrastructure can save these losses. For example, if cleaning, grading, sorting and packaging of agricultural products are done in the villages, it can help in avoiding transportation of about four lakh tonnes of organic waste from villages to urban centres every day, avoid pollution in urban market centres, and increase the availability of rich organic manures in rural areas. It has been estimated that in this activity alone, around 2.5 lakh jobs in rural areas can be created.

(d) The degree of marketing price efficiency is relatively low for fruits, vegetables, flowers and other perishable products due to inadequate infrastructure to handle such products.

(e) Foodgrains and oilseed markets are highly integrated both horizontally as well as vertically. The degree of integration of wheat and rice markets has further increased during the nineties.

(f) With a given change in supply and demand conditions, the prices at farmgate are sticky downwards and at retail level are sticky upward due to lack of competition in letter and spirit.

Some Emerging Issues

(i) As already mentioned, while the market orientation of Indian farmers has increase manifold, the improvement in the marketing system has not kept pace.

(ii) Dependence of farmers on purchased inputs has also increased several folds. Purchased inputs now account for 72 percent of total inputs (other than own land and labour) as against 20 percent in 1950-51. During 2000-01, farmers' purchased inputs were valued at Rs. 694 billion as against Rs. two billion during 1950-51.

(iii) The accelerated demand for output and input marketing services is now emerging from increased number of production units (farm holdings), which has gone up to 115.6 million. Further, out of total farm production units, 61.6 percent are marginal operating an average of 0.40 hectares, 18.7 percent are small (1.42 hectares per farm) and 12.3 percent are semi-medium (2.73 hectares per farm), each with a small marketed surplus and demand for small quantities of purchased inputs.

(iv) Despite large quantities of marketed surplus handled by the private trade, it did not substantially invest in market infrastructure, due to excessive regulatory framework.

Notwithstanding the continuing small proportion of total marketed surplus going directly from farmers to consumers, the initiatives like establishment of farmer's markets needs to be pushed further.

There is a considerable gap in the facilities available and desired in the market yard sub-yards. For example, even auction platforms are not available in one-third of these markets. Common drying facilities are not available in 74 percent of markets.

Concerns have been expressed in some quarters about the low utilization of marketing infrastructure by the farmers. Examples of under-utilization of warehouses, cold storage units and grading facilities by farmers are cited in this connection. However, non-utilization of these facilities by the farmers should not be a matter of worry so long as somebody else uses these. If traders store farm products in warehouses or transport these through railways or roads, farmers benefit from the infrastructure indirectly.

Removing obstacles on rapid growth of agro-industrial sub-sector can serve as an important means to expand markets for primary agricultural products, foster greater value addition and generate employment in rural areas. There is a great scope, potential and prospects of growth of food processing sector. One of the important hurdles in boosting value addition in food sector is multiplicity of food-related laws and regulations.

Policy Framework of Agricultural Marketing

Agricultural marketing in India is characterized by pervasive government intervention. The objectives and forms of intervention have, however, undergone substantial changes overtime. The state intervention in agricultural marketing is by definition aimed at correcting perceived market failures. Several instruments of state intervention in Indian agricultural produce markets have their origin in the experience of Bengal Famine. This paper argues that while market failure during Bengal Famine and a couple of later decades occurred due to inadequate state intervention, in the current situation the market failure to handle agricultural surpluses is occurring due to over regulation or excessive state intervention.

The interventions in agricultural marketing system were aimed at (a) ensuring remunerative prices to farmers for inducing them to adopt new technology for increasing the production of food and other agricultural commodities and in turn improving their livelihoods and food security; (b) maintaining supply of essential foodgrains to consumers and raw material to the industry at reasonable prices; and (c) evening out the inter-year fluctuations in supply of foodgrains, mainly cereals, through buffer-stocking operations and operating a public distribution system.

The current policy framework within which agricultural produce markets function can be understood to consist of three broad components viz: (a) Regulation of Agricultural Produce Wholesale Markets; (b) Regulation of other Marketing Activities; and (c) Agricultural Price Support Programme including food policy.

Regulation of Agricultural Produce Wholesale Markets

At the time of independence, the marketing practices adopted by the farmers in sale of their produce and the practices prevalent in trade circles were perceived to cause losses to the farmers in terms of undue low prices, higher costs of marketing and considerable physical losses of the produce. One of the measures taken to improve the situation was to regulate the trade practices and to establish market yards in the countryside. The Centre prepared a model Act and circulated to all the states. It took considerable time for the states to enact the relevant legislation.

Later, most of the states enacted Agricultural Produce Markets Regulation Acts and put these in operation. As of now, 27 states have their separate Acts. All primary assembling markets were brought under the ambit of these Acts. Well- laid out market yards and sub-yards were constructed and for each market area, an Agricultural Produce Market Committee was constituted to frame the rules and enforce them. The APMC, which consisted of more than half the members representing the farmers of the market area, was chaired by the farmer's representative4. The studies on impact of regulated markets have brought out several positive features of the regulation programme. These include visibly open process of price discovery; more accurate and reliable weighing; standardized market charges; payment of cash to farmers without undue deductions; dispute settlement mechanism; timing and sequencing of auctions; reduction in physical losses of the produce; and availability of several amenities in market yards. The number of such regulated markets, which was only 286 at the time of Independence, has now gone upto 7161, which cover more than 98 percent of the identified wholesale markets in the country.

Though market regulation programme has initially served the purpose well, in the emerging scenario, several questions relating to the functioning and even relevance are being raised. In a comprehensive study of agricultural marketing system in India during the last fifty years several problems associated with regulated markets have been identified.

(i) The marketing committees do not allow the traders to buy from the farmers outside the specified market yards or subyards. This adds to avoidable cost of marketing.

(ii) Despite expansion in the number of regulated markets, the area served per market yard is quite high. The national average is 459 square km and in some states like Assam, Himachal Pradesh, Orissa, Madhya Pradesh and Rajasthan, it is considerably higher. The farmers are, therefore, required to travel long distances to reach a market place. With small surplus to sell, most of the farmers try to evade these markets.

(iii) Though the Acts stipulate for the provision of some prescribed facilities and amenities in each market yard,

in several markets, the facilities amenities actually created been superseded by the government and, for long, are being administrated by bureaucrats. They have thus lost the characteristic of farmers-dominated managerial bodies. The staff remains overly occupied in collection of market fees and construction work rather than market development.

(vi) With the expansion in the market arrivals, there is considerable congestion in several market yards. This leads to undue delays in the disposal of the farmers produce resulting in long-waiting periods and frustration for the farmers.

(vii) In several markets, malpractices like late payment to farmers are still prevalent and deduction of certain amount for cash or spot payment and non-issue of sale slips by traders have continued unabated.

(viii) Market functionaries (like traders, commission agents and labourers) in some markets have organized themselves in strong associations and thus have created barriers to entry of new functionaries.

(ix) Market fee, by definition, is the charge for the services provided to market functionaries. But a considerable part of the market fee is not ploughed back. In some states, this has even become a source of income for the government.

(x) By and large, the APMCs have emerged as some sort of government sponsored monopolies in supply of marketing services facilities, with all drawbacks and inefficiency associated with a monopoly.

The matter has been under continuous scrutiny during the last five years. On the recommendation of the Expert Committee for Agricultural Marketing the Inter-Ministerial Task Force recommended for formulation of another model Act for this purpose. The Department of Agriculture and Cooperation, Ministry of Agriculture, Government of India, has in consultation

with state governments, trade and industry has formulated a Model Act and circulated to the states. The salient features of the Model Act are the following:

(i) Permission to establish new markets extended to cooperatives, growers or local authorities;

(ii) No compulsion on growers to sell their produce through existing regulated market yards;

(iii) Establishment of direct purchase centres and consumers farmers markets for direct sale;

(iv) Promotion of public-private partnership in the management and development of agricultural markets ;

(v) Separate constitution for special markets for commodities like onions, fruits, vegetables and flowers;

(vi) Separate chapter to regulate and promote contract-farming arrangements;

(vii) Prohibition of commission agency in any transaction of agricultural commodities with the producers;

(viii) Market Committees to promote alternative marketing system, contract farming, direct marketing and farmers consumers markets;

(ix) SAMBs to promote standardisation, grading, quality specifications, market-led extension and training of farmers and market functionaries in marketing related areas; and

(x) Constitution of State Marketing Standards Bureaus for promotion of grading, standardization and quality certification of agricultural produce.

The Model Act was circulated to state governments in 2003. In 2003, Karnataka permitted National Dairy Development Board to set up, a fruits and vegetable wholesale market. In Bangalore, the NDDB has created all the necessary infrastructure and established its own marketing yard. Based on its experience of

organizing milk producers organizations, the Board has organized several self help groups of farmers who are undertaking cleaning, grading and packaging of the produce at the farm level before supplying to the yard of NDDB. The process was formally launched in August 2004. It is now reportedly handling 20 percent of total arrivals of Bangalore city. The traders and commission agents are handling remaining 80 percent of arrivals in the city in the erstwhile APMC yards. There is no reported loss to the APMC as the NDDB is paying market fee to the APMC.

Some other states like Punjab, Haryana, Madhya Pradesh and Tamil Nadu have partially amended their Acts to allow farmers under contract farming arrangements to bypass regulated markets and sell directly to private buyers and contractors. Rajasthan also announced such an amendment in July 2004, but due to resistance from traders' organization, the state government has put the amendment in abeyance.

Other Regulations

Apart from the regulation of primary wholesale markets, several other legal instruments were enacted by the Centre or the states to influence the conduct of the market. Legal instruments that have virtually influenced the process of agricultural marketing till early 1990s include the Essential Commodities Act 1955 and a large number of control orders issued thereunder. The ECA empowered Central and state governments to impose restrictions on the storage and movement of commodities such as foodgrains and edible oils, thus restricting the scope of private investment in these markets. These apart, regulations were imposed for limiting the agro and food processing industries to small-scale capacities. One other feature of food processing sub-sector, which did not allow to attain its growth potential, is the multiplicity of food related regulations. At present, there are atleast nine laws orders governing food-processing activity, administered by 15 different government departments and ministries. An illustrative list of 222 such Acts Orders is available in Acharya and Government of India. Several of these acts orders have been repealed, rescinded or lifted during the last five years. Some of the recent steps towards deregulation are as follows:

(i) Over the years the commodities included under ECA have been drastically reduced. Even onions have been delisted in the middle of October 2004.

(ii) In 2001, the government removed restrictions on investment in bulk handling and storage by private investors, including permitting upto 100% ownership by foreign investors.

(iii) In 2002, the government lifted licensing requirements, stocking limits and movement restrictions on wheat, paddy rice, coarse grains, edible oilseeds and edible oils.

(iv) Again in 2002, the government removed the restrictions on access to credit under Selective Credit Control Policy.

(v) During the same year, GOI amended the Milk and Milk Products, Order, (MMPO) 1992, to eliminate the restrictions on private investment in new processing capacity. The MMPO was refocused on ensuring food safety.

(vi) In 2002, the Government of India also reduced levy on sugar factories from 15 percent to 10 percent.

(vii) In 2003, the GOI eliminated the ban on futures trading on 54 commodities including wheat, rice, oilseeds and pulses, which were prohibited under the Forward Contract (Regulation) Act, 1952.

(viii) The Government of India has removed the restrictions on plant scale and capacity expansion, as also the licensing requirement for most of the food processing industries.

(ix) The steps to bring out a single unified food-law were initiated by constituting a Group of Ministers at the Centre. This group has drafted an Integrated Food Law.

Nevertheless, there is considerable unfinished agenda of domestic marketing reforms for the agricultural sector.

(i) Despite, deregulation of food processing industry, small-scale low technology firms established under the old restrictive laws still dominate the industry.

(ii) Removal of licensing requirements, stocking limits and movement restrictions for major agricultural products is a temporary measure and not enforced in all the states. Being a temporary measure, private sectors sentiment to make investment has not been favourable so for. The threat of their reimposition discourages both domestic and foreign investments.

(iii) Due to the threat of reimposition, despite the removal of restrictions on investment in bulk handling and storage and provision of investment incentives, the private sector continues to remain hesitant to invest in bulk handling and storage.

(iv) Despite automatic approval of foreign equity upto 100% in food processing, owing to multiplicity of food laws, the full potential could not be exploited so far. The integrated Food Law is yet to be formalized and put in place. This, when brought into force, will help in expediting around 7000 cases filed against the food processors.

(v) Restriction on sugarcane processors in terms of sale of sugar still continue, though at reduced level. Ten percent of the sugar output is required to be surrendered to the government as levy and remaining free-sale part is also subjected to controlled releases in the market.

(vi) Small scale reservation on groundnut and mustard processing is still continuing.

(vii) Restrictions on futures trading in livestock products are still in place.

(viii) Monopsony procurement of raw cotton in Maharashtra is still in place, which comes in the way of free marketing of raw cotton in the country.

Agricultural Price Policy

Agricultural Price Policy has considerably influenced the marketing system of agricultural commodities in India. The policy was basically aimed at intervention in agricultural markets with a view to influencing the level of fluctuations in prices and price-spread from farm gate to the retail level. The objectives, thrust and instruments of agricultural price policy have undergone conspicuous shifts during the last fifty years. Upto the mid-sixties, the main instruments of policy were controls restrictions, food imports and distribution of foodgrains below the market prices.

After mid-sixties, when new seed-fertilizer technology became available, the price policy was assigned a positive role for augmenting the availability of foodgrains by increasing domestic production. The thrust of the policy was placed on achieving the twin objectives of assuring remunerative prices to the farmers and providing foodgrains to the consumers and raw material to the industry at the reasonable prices. The framework of the policy was modified in 1980 and its emphasis shifted from maximizing the production of foodgrains to a diversified production pattern consistent with the overall needs of the economy. Again in 1986, the emphasis of the policy shifted to building into the system the major factors, which in the long run, influence the prices of farm products for making the farm sector more vibrant, productive and cost effective. Some of the important price policy instruments, currently in vogue are as follows:

(i) Fixation of minimum support prices for 25 commodities including sugarcane for which a statutory minimum price is fixed.

(ii) Selective market intervention scheme for some other commodities, not covered under MSP policy fruits, vegetables and spices.

(iii) Fixation of levy prices of rice and sugar and imposition of levy on rice millers and sugar factories.

(iv) Maintenance of buffer stocks of wheat and rice.

(v) Distribution of rice and wheat under public distribution system at subsidized prices the targeted PDS has a three-tier price structure APL households, BPL households and the poorest of the poor households.

(vi) Open market purchases of some commodities by public agencies at market prices during the peak arrival period and their open market sales at the appropriate time raw cotton, raw jute, and oilseeds.

(vii) Encouragement to producer cooperatives to undertake marketing on behalf of the farmers.

The level of support prices is fixed on the basis of recommendations of Commission for Agricultural Costs and Prices. A designated agency works as the national nodal agency for undertaking price support operations. The support prices are kept at the same level through out the marketing year and all over the country. The support level varies according to the variety and grade. The inter-year changes in support prices have always been non-negative.

The assessment of impact of agricultural price policies pursued in the country should be based on the achievement of specified objectives, incentives or disincentives created for farmers, and distortions, if any, created in the marketing system. The impact can be summarized as follows:

(i) The policy has been instrumental in creating a fairly stable price environment for the farmers to induce them to adopt new production technology and thereby increase the output of foodgrains.

(ii) Geographically disbursed growth of cereal production coupled with PDS of cereals helped in increasing physical access to food.

(iii) Supply of subsidized inputs to farmers and subsidized distribution of foodgrains, enabled to keep the real prices of staple cereals declining vis-à-vis per capita incomes, which helped in improving economic access to food. Owing to the decline in the real prices of basic staple food, the organized sector and the industry could keep their wage bills low, as rice and wheat have a considerable weightage in the consumers price index. The benefits of price policy and input food subsidies, have, thus been shared by all the sections of society i.e., surplusproducing farmers, farmers deriving their entitlement from production, other farmers who are net purchasers of foodgrains, landless labourers, urban consumers and the industry.

(iv) The price policy and related programmes reduced private sector incentives for spatial and temporal arbitrage. For example, for rice and wheat, the inter-year price rise has been considerably lower than the storage cost, discouraging private sector investment in storage and related trading activities.

(v) While it is true that the private sector participation in foodgrains trade was reduced due to FCI's operations but whether FCI is operating at the costs higher than the cost of private sector for the same operations. This leads to the issue of the efficiency of Food Corporation of India (FCI) vis-à-vis the private trade in price support operations and subsequent distribution of foodgrains. The efficiency of FCI has been questioned on the ground of its economic cost and consequent outgo on food subsidy. In this connection, several aspects of FCI's operations need to be noted. First, both the grain purchase price support price and the issue price are administered prices and determined by the Government of India. Second, it has been shown that out of the total expenditure of FCI on procurement and distribution, 71.6 percent is on those items over which the Corporation has no control as these are determined outside the system. The High Level Committee on Long Term Grain Policy has put 69 percent of the economic cost of FCI as policy induced costs. These items include mandi charges, purchase sales tax, cost of gunny bags, interest on working capital and freight rates. The private trade will also have to incur these costs unless it is able to evade some of the statutory taxes charges. Third, the losses during storage and transit are estimated at around one percent, which cannot be considered unduly high as compared to the private channels. Fourth, the establishment charges and administrative overheads of FCI are estimated to be 2.8 percent of the economic cost, which are not higher than the net margins of private trade. Fifth, a recent study commissioned by the Union Ministry of Consumer Affairs, Food and Public Distribution has brought out the existing structure of marketing costs of wheat and paddy rice in the open market. The study has shown that for attracting private trade to buy wheat and paddy from the markets in surplus producing states, the retail prices during lean months in deficit states ought to rule at more than twice of peak season wheat prices of surplus states. This ratio was estimated as more than three in the case of paddy rice. These ratios are not less than the ratio of FCI's economic cost of wheat rice to the respective support prices. The findings of High Level Committee on Long-Run Grain Policy are on similar lines. The Committee has observed that the margin required for private trade to move grain from rural to urban areas of the same state is similar to FCI's distribution margin, which involves an average transport lead of more than 900 kilometers. And sixth, the study has suggested for retention of a public agency to handle foodgrains trade on the ground that in its absence, the private trade may turn out to be exploitative.

(vi) During the last 6-7 years, lack of prudence in fixing the level of support prices of rice and wheat led to not only accumulation of excessive stocks but also raising the public cost of foodgrain policy. During these years, the government fixed MSPs of rice and wheat at much higher levels than that recommended by CACP. With coalition governments, the political economy considerations outweighing the rational factors in determining the level of MSPs are likely to be more frequent in the coming years.

(vii) Apart from undue hikes in the levels of MSPs for rice and wheat, frequent relaxation of FAQ fair average quality norms, inappropriate timing of raise in issue prices of grains for PDS, and improper meshing of export-import policy were responsible for accumulation of stocks with the government at some points of time. Currently the stocks are below or almost close to the minimum prescribed levels.

(viii) In the case of sugarcane, the state governments in many states have been fixing what may be called 'state advised prices' for cane, which are much higher than the statutory minimum prices fixed by the centre. Sometimes the sugar industry finds them unremunerative. The SAPs, coupled with the policy of levy on sugar factories has frequently led to the situation of piling up of cane price arrears and ultimately to the phenomenon of sugarcane sugar cycles in the country.

(ix) There is also a problem of ineffective implementation of price support operations for rice and wheat in states other than Punjab, Haryana, Western Uttar Pradesh and Andhra Pradesh, where surpluses have emerged during the last decade, but farmers could not get the minimum support prices for their produce. This happened mainly because the nodal agency and state agencies in the new emerging surplus states are not geared to undertake price support operations. The FCI remains occupied with large volumes of purchases in traditional surplus producing states. Some sort of decentralized procurement and refocusing the operations of FCI to non-traditional states may help in this regard.

Marketing Reform Initiatives

Agricultural marketing reforms have received the added attention of the government during the last six years. Several Committees and Expert Groups were commissioned by the Government of India to suggest the direction of reforms in the field of agricultural marketing. The first was Expert Group on Agricultural Marketing constituted by the Union Ministry of Rural Development in 1998. Following the constitution of this Expert Group, a major structural change occurred leading to the transfer of agricultural marketing division of Union Government from the Ministry of Rural Development to the Ministry of Agriculture. In December 2000, the Union Ministry of Agriculture constituted an Expert Committee on Strengthening and Developing Agricultural Marketing System in the Country. This Committee reviewed the entire system of agricultural marketing in the country and submitted its specific recommendations to the Government in June 2001. The Expert Committee's recommendations include various legislative reforms as well as reorientation of policies and programmes.

Subsequently, Government of India constituted an Inter-Ministerial Task Force in July 2001 (Jain) to suggest measures for implementation of the recommendations of the Expert Committee. The Task Force interacted with various stakeholders and identified nine priority areas. Each of these priority areas was assigned to separate inter-ministerial Working Groups to work out a road map for reforms and development or strengthening of each of these areas. Based on the output of Working Groups, the Task Force in May 2002 suggested the direction of change in policies and programmes. It also recommended an implementation plan along with the identification of Ministries organizations for implementation.

While the Expert Committees and Task Force were on the job, the Union Government launched two other comprehensive studies. One of these was the Millennium Study of Indian Farmers launched by the Ministry of Agriculture. In the Millennium Study, agricultural marketing was an explicit component. This study was aimed at the review of agricultural marketing scenario in the country and changes therein during the last fifty years. The draft of this study report was ready in early 2002 and the main findings were made available to the Expert Committee and Task Force. However, the final report came out in 2004. The lessons for long terms policy of agricultural marketing development, drawn in the Millennium Study, are summarized in Appendix 6. The other comprehensive review launched by the Government was the commissioning of a high level committee on long term grain policy by the Union Ministry of Consumer Affairs, Food and Public Distribution (Abhijit Sen. This committee submitted its report in July 2002.

The status of acceptance of these recommendations by the government and their implementation has been reviewed in the earlier sub sections. As is obvious, several of these recommendations are yet to be accepted and implemented.

Suggestions for Changes in Agricultural Marketing Policy Environment

Since the mid 1990s, there has been an increasing convergence on the need for reforms in agricultural marketing because pervasive regulations have unnecessarily increased marketing costs and risks and uncertainty. The excessive marketing margins have placed downward pressure on farm prices, increased the cost to consumers, reduced competitiveness of exports and depressed demand of local consumers. The indicators for guiding reforms in agricultural marketing should include (a) improvement in marketing efficiency by reducing costs of marketing; (b) better returns to farmers for their produce; (c) reducing farmers marketing risks; (d) availability of quality products to consumers at reasonable prices; (e) improvement in physical and economic access of masses to food and nutrition; and (f) creation of additional employment in agricultural marketing.

Amendments in State Agricultural Produce Markets Regulation Acts

The centre has already circulated a Model Act for adoption by the state governments. The Model Act is quite comprehensive and when adopted, will help in improving the efficiency of the marketing system and in encouraging private sector investment in the field of agricultural marketing. So far only a few states have adopted the model and that too partially. The resistance to the adoption of the Model Act is from both state governments and traders commission agents. The states APMCs have the fear of losing market fee if alternative markets are established. The traders commission agents have the fear of losing their business incomes. It is possible to allay such fears. There are several options available. The contractors under contract farming can assure payment of market fee to APMCs. The APMCs can declare more sub-yards to be managed by cooperatives or private entrepreneurs. In the village sub-yards, private sector companies or associations can create cleaning, sorting, grading and packaging facilities, where rural youth can be employed. The traders commission agents may be persuaded to organize into groups or work as individuals as agents of contractors. It may be recalled that when in the fifties, the original model APMR Act was circulated, it took around 10 or 15 years for the major states to adopt it. However, this time, with adequate sensitization of all the stakeholders, the revised Model Act can be adopted by states in relatively short period. For this, a massive campaign of publicizing the benefits of amendments in state APMR Acts and sensitization of key stakeholders is required.

Improvement in the Management of Agricultural Produce Markets

Independent of the amendments in state APMR Acts, there are certain problems relating to the functioning of APMCs, which require immediate attention. These pertain to bureaucratization of market committees, non-ploughing back of market fees for market development, and cartelization of traders and market functionaries. One other problem relates to the over-emphasis of market committees on collection of market fees rather than promotion of marketing efficiency. These problems can be tackled by the state governments even without amendment in the APMR Acts. This will require state governments to act on the following lines:

(i) To hold regular elections of market committees.

(ii) Compulsory ploughing back of market fees for development of marketing facilities.

(iii) Liberalizing the licensing of traders and market

functionaries.

(iv) Promotion of grading, standardization and quality certification.

(v) Creating cleaning, sorting, grading and packaging facilities in villages and allow traders to buy in the villages by declaring these places as sub-yards.

Simplification and Deregulation of Domestic Markets

The uncertainty created by the lack of stability in the regulatory environment has discouraged private sector investment in supporting marketing infrastructure, agro-processing and agroindustry that could have expanded demand for primary agricultural products as well as generated employment in rural areas.

(i) The potential of growth in food processing sub-sector can be exploited by quickly bringing the Unified Food Law. A Group of Ministers had been working on it and a draft of an Integrated Food Law is reported to have been prepared. This needs to be expedited.

(ii) Despite withdrawal of restrictions on storage, movement, bulk handling and other activities, investment from both domestic and foreign investors is not flowing into the sector. The main reason is the fear of reimposition of such restrictions as the withdrawal is temporary. There is a need to allay such fears. This can be done by either replacing ECA by an simplified Act which empowers the government to impose such restrictions only during the emergency or by widely publicizing the withdrawal of restrictions to clear the fear psychosis prevailing among investors.

Reduction of Farmers' Marketing Risks

Farmers face both yield and price uncertainties. The yield or production risk can be covered by the crop insurance and now weather or rainfall insurance scheme. As regards the marketing risks, three instruments are currently available to the farmers.

One is the programme of minimum support prices. Notwithstanding the defects in the implementation of minimum price support policy, it has helped a large number of farmers in surplus producing states to cover a part of the price risks faced by them. Effective implementation of MSP policy, as suggested earlier, will help the farmers in reducing their price risks.

The other instrument for covering price risk is the emerging scenario of contract farming arrangements, which are in a way future contracts on prices. There are several success stories relating to such arrangements. A pre-condition for contract farming to expand is the amendment in State APMR Acts. This apart, a Model Contract has also been formulated and circulated to states. However, several complementary measures are needed for contract farming to expand on a large scale. It will need (a) organization of farmers producers groups; (b) legislation and effective implementation of a contract law; (c) improvement in the quality of input delivery and research and extension services; (d) training of farmers in maintenance of quality standards; (e) provision of complementary infrastructure including IT kiosks (like e-choupals) in rural areas; and (f) development of an effective land administration system. This will also require identification of a group of villages for each niche commodity and provision of credit and incentives to farmers to shift to the identified commodity.

The third instrument is the farm income insurance scheme introduced on a pilot scale in 18 districts during Rabi 2003-04 and extended to 100 districts of 16 states during 2004-05. FIIS covers both price and yield risks. The scheme is compulsory for loanee farmers but optional for others. If successful, FIIS will replace National Agricultural Insurance Scheme (NAIS) but NAIS will continue in uncovered districts. The government has announced a subsidy on premium up to 75 percent for marginal and small farmers and 50 percent for other farmers. The scheme is nodoubt laudable but its success will depend on the speed with which the estimates of area, yield and prices realized by the farmers are arrived at. These parameters both at area and individual farmer's level are not easy to objectively compile.

Further, the guaranteed level of income is also based on indemnity of 80 percent of moving average of seven years of actual yield. Statistically reliable yield estimates below the district level are not available and special yield estimation surveys at sub-district or lower levels have all the limitations of losing objectivity. The experience of pilot tests of FIIS has not yet been made available. Whatever may be the outcome of pilot testing, the long run solution for the insurance of farmers' risk is an effective FIIS. Till such a scheme is put in place in all the areas, a combination of minimum price support policy, contract farming and crop livestock insurance scheme would need to continue.

Farmers Organizations and Capacity Building

The advantages of de-regulation of markets, minimum guaranteed price scheme, contract farming or crop income insurance will flow to the farmers only to the extent farmers organize themselves in marketing groups, self-help groups, cooperatives or companies and learn skills suited to the new marketing environment. Understanding the quality standards (including FAQ), learning the terms of contract and insurance, and choosing and preparing the produce for the market are going to be essential skills for the farmers. The state marketing departments, APMCs, marketing cooperatives, NGOs and PRIs should pay increasing attention to capacity building and organizing farmers for marketing in the new environment.

Complementary Public Investment for Private Sector Investment in Marketing

Substantial investment in agricultural marketing infrastructure is necessary. The Expert Committee on Agricultural Marketing had estimated an investment requirement of Rs. 2687 billion during the current decade. Nearly half of this is projected to be made by the private sector. For inducing the private sector to invest, apart from the conducive regulatory framework (as suggested earlier), public investment in certain marketing facilities is necessary. While the process of deregulation and amendment in APMR Acts is on going and farmers are increasingly getting organized, the public investment schemes should be put in operation so as to improve the investor sentiment. In this connection, recent announcement of a central sector scheme for setting up of markets and rural godowns in leftout areas is a welcome development.

Policy Framework and Status of Rural Credit System

Indian rural credit system, at the time of Independence, was dominated by the private moneylenders, large landowners, traders, relatives and friends. The interest charged by the lenders used to be unduly high. The land or other assets were kept as collateral. The Rural Credit Survey of 1954 brought out the problems associated with the then prevailing rural credit system and made several suggestions for improvement. During the 1950s and 1960s, agricultural credit cooperatives were encouraged as institutional agencies for *inter alia* catering to the credit needs of rural families. However, their reach to the masses in terms of credit delivery was far from adequate. By 1962, the share of institutional agencies in total debt of rural households increased to only 17.3 percent as against 7.3 percent in 1951-52. Nevertheless, the initiative led to the recognition of the importance of institutional credit agencies in agricultural and rural development. A number of studies during fifties and sixties revealed that institutional form of term lending contributed to private fixed capital formation in agricultural and institutional credit support helped the adoption of high yielding technology. The studies also revealed that due to inadequate flow of institutional credit to small farmers, they lagged in the adoption of new technology. Thus, it came to be increasingly realized that a sound institutional rural credit system needs to be evolved not for just financial inter-mediation but also for playing a catalytic role in achieving the national goals of agricultural development, rural employment generation and poverty alleviation.

The overall objective of the rural credit policy has been to provide an institutional alternative for supply of adequate credit at lower rates of interest, with a view to achieving the objectives of growth and equity. The major strands of the policy have been catering to the credit needs of poor at lower rates of interest, adopting innovative schemes to target certain groups sections, providing insurance for risk and integrating lending programmes with rural development and poverty alleviation schemes. The inherent approach has been a multi-agency system, explicit relationship between credit and input use fixed investment, security remaining no longer a criterion for lending, and using credit planning as tool for serving development objectives.

Some of the landmarks in evolving an institutional rural credit system are:

- 1969: Nationalization of major commercial banks
- 1975: Establishment of Regional Rural Banks
- 1982: Establishment of National Bank for Agriculture and Rural Development
- 1990s: Finance Sector Reforms and Launch of several new innovations.

Several institutional innovations introduced and or tried at different points of time during the seventies and eighties include system wide innovations viz., lead bank scheme, district credit planning, annual action plan, farmers service societies, LAMPS, District Level Coordination Committees, Block Level Coordination Committees and State Level Bankers Committees. These apart, bank level innovations include rural service centres scheme, farm clinics, farm information and exchange clubs, future farmers clubs, satellite branches, rural service volunteers and change agents.

RFI Outlets and Their Share

There has been considerable expansion in the institutional credit outlets in rural areas. These include 33000 branches of commercial banks, 14000 branches of RRBs and around 100,000 outlets of cooperatives, making a total of 147000 RFI outlets. On an average, there is an outlet for a population of 5000 or for 1000 families. The network of cooperatives includes 92682 primary agricultural credit societies for short-term credit and 2258 units for advancing term loans. There are 30 state cooperative banks with 686 branches and 366 district central cooperative banks with

10518 branches. However, 140 cooperative banks are reported to be sick. There are 196 RRBs with 14498 branches in 495 districts. Out of these, 187 RRBs have been provided equity support. Upto March end 2003, their advances stood at Rs. 20700 crores (against deposits of Rs. 48900 crores) with gross non-performing assets (NPAs) of Rs. 3200 crores (14.4% of advances). In 2003-04, around 100 RRBs are reported to have come out of red. The loss making number of RRBs now stands at 20 only.

Despite expansion of institutional credit outlets, the share of institutional agencies in total rural credit (debt of households) was only 61.2 percent in 1982 and around 66 percent in 1991. Still considerable part of the credit by rural families is availed from noninstitutional sources. This is particularly true more for poor households. Rural poor's credit needs are small but urgent and often unpredictable. Their credit needs do not distinguish between production and consumption. As the institutional credit agencies are not able to internalize the peculiar credit needs of poor in their policies and programmes, rural poor continue to depend on informal sources. The lending terms of informal sources may be harsh but are convenient. A study has revealed that the overall flow of institutional credit to the poor is only 16 percent and 63 percent of credit of the poor is used for consumption purposes.

Trend in RFI Lending During Nineties

During the 1990s, the term lending in rural areas has tended to slow down. The growth of longterm institutional loans decelerated from 20.2 percent during the 1970s to 14.8 percent during the 1980s and further to 11.9 percent per annum during the nineties. This happened mainly owing to the deceleration in lending by the commercial banks. The growth of long term advances by CBs came down from 29.9 percent per annum during the seventies to 18.6 percent during the eighties and further to 12.1 percent during the nineties. The investment lending by RRBs has also decelerated during the nineties.

Agricultural sector is an important component of rural credit, accounting for around 85 percent of total rural credit Sharma et al, 2001. The growth of institutional credit for agricultural sector also registered a deceleration during the nineties (Sahu and Rajasekhar, 2002). Over the years, agricultural credit as a proportion of agricultural GDP has gone up from 5.4 percent during the seventies to 8.3 percent during the eighties, 7.4 percent during the nineties and 8.7 percent during 2001-02. However, the ratio of agricultural credit to total bank credit has been declining over the years. This ratio has declined from 20.5 percent during seventies and 20.1 percent during eighties to 14.4 percent during nineties and further to 10.5 percent during 2001-02.

During the nineties, there has been considerable decline in Credit-Deposit ratio in rural as well as semi-urban areas whereas the ratio for urban areas has considerably gone up. The share of rural areas in total bank credit has continued to be lower than their share in total bank deposits and this gap has tended to widen after the launch of financial sector reforms in early nineties. There is, thus, an indication that deposits mobilized in rural areas are being used in urban metro metropolitan areas.

Demand and Supply of Rural Credit

The Working Group on Agricultural Credit for the IX five-year Plan had stipulated a target of lending Rs. 229750 crores for the five-year plan period. Against this the actual institutional lending for agricultural sector was marginally higher at Rs. 233703 crores. The institutional lending exceeded the target during the later years of the five-year plan period.

Against a growth rate projection of 16 percent per year in agricultural lending during the IX fiveyear plan period, the target fixed for the X five-year plan period is 24 percent per year. The X Five Year Plan has targeted a credit flow of Rs. 736570 crores, of which Rs. 381652 crores is the share of scheduled commercial banks. Against this target, actual lending during the first year (2002-03) of the five year plan was Rs. 69560 crores, which was only 84 percent of the stipulated lending of Rs. 82073 crores for that year. The CBs during 2002-03 advanced Rs. 44000 crores which was much lower than their stipulated target. Actual lending to the agricultural sector during 2003-04 was Rs. 80000 crores, which was also considerably short of the stipulated level of lending for this year. Out of Rs. 80000 crores, CBs lended 54.9 percent (Rs. 43900 crores), RRBs 7.6 percent (Rs. 6100 crores) and cooperatives 37.5 percent (Rs. 30000 crores). Concerned about the slackening performance, the GOI has asked the RFIs to increase their lending to Rs. 104500 crores during 2004-05 which includes 30 percent increase for CBs (Rs. 57000 crores) and cooperatives (Rs. 39000 crores) and 40 percent increase for RRBs (Rs. 8500 crores).

Inter-Regional Disparities in RFI Lending

There is considerable inter-state and inter-regional variation in access to credit due to (a) differences in credit absorption capacity; (b) strengths and weaknesses of the credit delivery system; and (c) recovery climate. There are also considerable differences in access to institutional credit across rural social classes. The main reasons identified are (a) insistence on collateral security; (b) complicated administrative procedures; (c) cultural gap between RFI officials and poor; (d) long distance from the village to RFI branches; (e) inflexible lending policies; (f) lack of provision for consumption credit; (g) political interference; and (h) wide spread belief that the poor are non-bankable.

The performance of RFIs is relatively poor in the northeastern region. The share of NE region in deposits and credit upto March 2000 was 3.6 percent and 1.75 percent as against 37.9 percent and 33.5 percent respectively for the western region. Inter-regional differences in access of farmers to institutional sources of credit, brought out by the Input Survey of 1991-92 reveal that on an average, 17.5 percent farmers borrow from the institutional sources. The percentage of borrowers is as high as 97 percent in Punjab. The second group of states according to the percentage of farmers borrowing from institutional agencies includes Bihar (51.4%), Himachal Pradesh (44.1%) and Haryana (41.3%). The percentage of borrowers from RFIs is less than 10 percent in Uttar Pradesh (7.1%), Rajasthan (2.7%) and Orissa (8.2%). Out of total borrowers from institutional sources in the country, more than 38 percent are from Bihar alone. Andhra Pradesh accounts for 10.4 percent, Uttar Pradesh 8.2 percent and Madhya Pradesh 7.4 percent of total institutional borrowers. The share of Punjab and Haryana in total institutional borrowers is only 6.3 percent and 3.6 percent respectively.

Inter-Farm Size Variation in Access to Credit

Farm size wise distribution of institutional borrowers is nearly in proportion to the total number of farms in each size group. Therefore, there does not appear to be any farm size bias in lending from institutional agencies. Out of total borrowers, 51.1 percent are marginal, 20.7 percent are small, 16.9 percent are semi-medium, 9.3 percent are medium and 2 percent are large.

The share of different farm size groups in total borrowings from institutional sources is, however, not in proportion to the number of farmers in each size group. It is not expected also because per farm demand for credit is not the same across farm size groups. The share of marginal farmers in total borrowings is 24.6 percent, small farmers 20.7 percent and of semi-medium farmers is 24.2 percent. Thus, farmers upto two hectares size account for 45.3 percent of total borrowings and upto 4 hectares account for 69.5 percent of total institutional borrowing.

Purpose of Borrowing Lending

The borrowing from financial institutions has traditionally remained concentrated on such activities as farm-machinery, minor irrigation and animal husbandry. Rainfed agriculture, horticulture, storage and processing activities remained relatively neglected as far as lending to farmers is concerned. Advances against stored agricultural commodities were usually made to traders. Advances of commercial banks against stored agricultural commodities in March 2004, stood at Rs. 15771 crores. Out of this, 34.3 percent was against cereals, 26.9 percent against sugar gur khandsari, 17.6 percent against cotton kapas, 10.1 percent against edible oils, 6.7 percent against oilseeds, 2.9 percent against pulses and 1.5 percent against raw jute. The main draw back in the expansion of pledge finance is that the warehouse receipts are not yet negotiable instruments for getting credit.

Recoveries and Defaults

Indian rural credit market is confronted with a paradox. Informal sources charge more than 20 percent interest, keep land or other assets as collateral and yet recoveries are high. But RFIs charge half the interest, do not keep collateral and yet face high defaults in payment. Timely recoveries of loans are an important link in the credit cycle. Poor recoveries or defaults in payments affect recycling of credit, squeeze-up the resources and lead the banks to a state of financial unsustainability. There are several factors responsible for mounting defaults. These include (a) natural calamities; (b) inadequate income generation; (c) high transaction costs; (d) inappropriate financing policies; and (e) poor working of RFIs. Waiver of loans announced by the Government from time to time has a considerable influence on the recovery climate. For example, the Government of India in 1989 announced Agricultural and Rural Debt Relief (ARDR) scheme, under which outstanding institutional loans upto Rs. 10000 were waived. Another important factor affecting the recovery climate is writing off the bad debt, although bad debts are a small proportion of overdues. Gulati and Bathla (2002) have shown that the bad debts in total outstanding were 3.6 percent in 1980, 2.7 percent in 1989, 4.2 percent in 1992 and 2.9 percent in 1997.

During the second half of nineties, while the recovery situation in scheduled commercial banks and RRBs improved, that of cooperative banks worsened. However, the overall recovery situation of cooperative banks was better than CBs or RRBs (Appendix 13). Gulati & Bathla have shown that in the total defaults during 1997, the share of CBs was the highest at 46.2 percent, followed by RRBs 25.1 percent, PACS 20.6 percent and of Land Development Banks was 8.1 percent. Though the share of CBs in total defaults is considerably higher than other RFIs, the non-performing assets as percentage of advances, are relatively large in RRBs. Overall for RFIs, NPAs were estimated as 16.5 percent of advances during 1998-99. Sharma and others have identified external as well as internal factors for poor recovery of loans in RFIs.

There is a considerable difference in the position of overdues across states. During the last 20 years, the states like Andhra Pradesh, Rajasthan, Uttar Pradesh, West Bengal, Punjab and Tamil Nadu have improved their position of overdues. On the contrary, recovery position of Orissa has worsened. In Assam, Bihar, Madhya Pradesh and Maharashtra, overdues as a percentage of outstanding loans continue to be more than 30 percent.

Demand for Credit and Interest Rate

The demand for rural agricultural credit with respect to interest rate is negative but inelastic. The elasticity is positively related to the level of interest rate. However, the demand for credit is highly elastic to input and output prices. The interest rate is nevertheless, of considerable significance to farmers and poorer sections. As regards the cost of credit to the borrowers, as per the RBI policy, the lending rate is linked to the size of the loan. For commercial banks, the stipulation is that for loans upto Rs. two lakhs, the lending rate should not exceed PLR, which by banks is arrived at by adding cost of funds, transaction costs, risk cost and profit margin. During 2002-03, it varied between 9 and 12.25 percent. The lending rate for loans above Rs. two lakhs is at the discretion of the bank. For RRBs and cooperative banks the concept of PLR is not applicable.

Service Area Approach

Several initiatives were taken and innovations were introduced during the last 15 years to increase the lending by RFIs. These include Service Area Approach, mandatory lending system, micro-finance, Rural Infrastructure Development Fund Scheme and Kisan Credit Card Scheme. Service Area Approach was introduced in late eighties. It has served the purpose well but there is a mismatch between the potential and actual lending. Borrowers are forced to go to the branch of designated RFI, even if they are not satisfied. In some states, the villages in the service area are too many. The private banks are not able to operate due to service area restrictions. The branches of non-service area RFIs have to wait and obtain no-objection certificate from the service area branch. RBI, on 26th October 2004, has proposed to dispense with the provision of SAA except for the government sponsored programmes.

Mandatory Lending Scheme

With a view to increasing the flow of bank credit to the areas of national priority, a scheme of mandatory lending was introduced in 1989. It stipulated that 40 percent of net bank credit should go to the defined priority sector including 18 percent to the agricultural sector. The priority sector was defined to include agriculture, small-scale industries and other important sectors. For the foreign banks, the mandate of priority sector lending was fixed at 32 percent. There was not a major problem in fulfilling the mandate of priority sector lending. At the end of March 2003, the priority sector lending was 42.5 percent of NBC for public sector banks, 44.4 percent for private sector banks and 33.9 percent for foreign banks. However, there was considerable and persistent shortfall in meeting the target of 18 percent lending to the agricultural sector. For example, at the end of September 2003, public sector banks could achieve only 15.9 percent and private sector banks only 10.8 percent of total lending to the agricultural sector.

Several new measures were taken during the last two years to bring down defaults NPAs and help in increasing rural lending. RBI in March 2002 announced a one-time settlement scheme for small and marginal farmers with an outstanding loan of upto Rs.50,000, which were nonperforming as on 31-3-98. NABARD has recently introduced some new provisions of lending which include (a) loans for agri-clinics or agri-service centres upto Rs.10 lakhs for individuals and upto Rs.50 lakhs to group of entrepreneurs with an interest of 10 to 12% recoverable in nine years with a moratorium of two years, (b) help to small, marginal and tenant farmers or share croppers for acquiring land of 2.5 to 5.0 acres at an interest of 13-14%, with 20% margin money, recoverable in nine years with a moratorium of one year; and (c) pledge loan to farmers 75% of value of stocks in cooperative godowns subject to a ceiling of Rs. one lakh. In June 2004, the GOI announced a debt relief package to farmers by asking RFIs to reschedule the debt of farmers affected by drought during last five years for payment during next five years with a moratorium of two years and not to count them in NPA. Such farmers have been made eligible for fresh loans. The banks have been also permitted to advance loans to those under distress due to borrowing from non-formal sources.

The RBI has also revised the norms of NPAs. Under these norms, for short duration crops, the outstanding loans will become NPA only if these are not paid for two crop seasons after these fall due and for long duration crops, after one year of their falling due. For helping banks to meet their mandatory lending requirements, the RBI in its annual policy statement for 2004-05, has announced some measures viz., (a) waiver of margin money security requirement for agricultural loans; and (b) coverage of loans for storage structures in rural areas under priority sector.

Conclusion

Attempts to strengthen Indian agriculture must address not only farm production but also processing, marketing, trade and distribution. We must link farmers to markets and in this endeavour, marketing and rural credit systems are extremely important. Indian agricultural marketing and rural credit systems have under gone several changes during the last decade. However, in the emerging environment, these need much more changes for making agricultural sector vibrant and responsive to the aspirations of the rural masses. The suggested agenda for reforms includes revision in the state Agricultural Produce Markets Regulation Acts, redefining the role of state marketing boards and market committees, repeal of ECA except under emergencies, putting in place a unified food law, introduction of new instruments like contract farming and warehouse receipt system and assurance to investors that regulations will not be reimposed. The policy of price support needs to be rationalized and decentralized. CACP and support prices should be given statutory status. Complementary public investment in marketing infrastructure should be made. The system of training of farmers by strengthening marketing extension education network needs to be put in place. Instruments for insurance of farmers against production and price risks should be made an essential component of development strategy. In the field of credit delivery, the financial institutions are under stress, particularly since the financial sector reforms of 1992-93. The credit policy should continue to emphasize small borrowers. The commercial banks have started feeling shy of lending to agricultural sector and rural poor. The provisions of mandatory lending for priority sector and the agricultural activities should continue. The banks should take the help of NGOs and local formal institutions in their lending programmes to reduce the transaction costs. These apart, effective linkages between farmers and processors on the one hand and between processors and credit agencies on the other should be promoted. The inter-locking of credit and product input markets are crucial and should be recognized. For meeting the credit needs of the poor, the programmes like linking of SHGs with lending agencies are important but in these linkages, the role of promoting institutions should not be lost sight of. Marketing and institutional credit systems have always remained critical for agricultural development and their role has further increased in the liberalized economic environment. A set of reforms and strategic actions suggested in the paper will help these systems in further strengthening Indian agriculture.

Chapter 2

Agricultural Marketing and Access to Transport Services

The article describes research relating to the role that road transport has to play in maintaining rural development and food security. From case study material the relationship between accessibility, marketing and agricultural development is examined.

It is argued that transport costs play a critical role in identifying the link between accessibility and agricultural development. It is estimated that replacing a footpath by a vehicle track may have a beneficial effect to the farmer of over a hundred times more than improving the same length of a poor quality earth track to a good quality gravel road. Wide divergences in market prices suggest that food marketing is inefficient and subject to monopolistic practices. From comparative research between Africa and Pakistan it is argued that there is scope for major reductions in Africa's road freight transport costs.

Key issues

- The importance of developing basic vehicle access to areas of high agricultural potential over increasing the quality of access to areas which already have vehicle access.
- Some countries have much higher transport costs than other countries. This impacts on final market prices.

- Marketing systems can be inefficient and suffer from monopolistic practise. This impacts on the final price of products and on the demand for transport services.
- The use of IMT's can significantly improve rural peoples marketing opportunities.
- The positioning and availability of markets has a large impact on the demand for transport services and the type of vehicle used.

Key topic areas

- Transport costs and agricultural development
- Agricultural markets and marketing
- The use of IMT's in agricultural marketing

Introduction

An efficient transport system is critically important to efficient agricultural marketing. If transport services are infrequent, of poor quality or expensive then farmers will be at a disadvantage when they attempt to sell their crops. An expensive service will naturally lead to low farm gate prices the net price the farmer receives from selling his produce. Seasonally impassable roads or slow and infrequent transport services, coupled with poor storage, can lead to losses as certain crops e.g. milk, fresh vegetables, tea deteriorate quickly over time. If the journey to market is made over rough roads then other crops e.g. bananas, mangoes may also suffer losses from bruising; this will also result in lower prices to the farmer. Agriculture is best served by consistent high urban, and international, demand. This is best brought about by an efficient, high volume, transport and marketing system where the transporting and marketing unit costs are low. If the margin between what the farmer receives from the sale of his produce and what the urban consumer pays for his produce is high then the effective demand transferred to the farmer will be correspondingly be reduced. Similarly if internal transport costs in a country are particularly high then the scope for agricultural exports will also suffer in comparison with other more efficient countries. The pattern of agricultural marketing is strongly influenced by the nature of transport services. Many developing countries suffer from monopolistic, low volume and high cost transport and marketing systems. Economies of scale are present in both transport and marketing operations.

In the following we will consider transport costs, the impact of roads on rural development, access to markets and the potential use of IMTs.

Transport Costs

It is generally recognised that transport operating costs, are higher on rough roads than on good quality bitumen roads and generally this will be reflected in passenger fares and freight tariffs. For example in Zambia the route from Chipata to Mpetamai is on good quality gravel road and costs Kwacha 62.5 per passenger kilometre; while the route from Chipata to Mwanga (74km) is on poor quality earth road and costs twice as much per km. However a wide range of transport costs (measured per passenger km or tonne km) have also been found in different countries for similar types of transport operation on similar roads. This indicates that there is substantial scope for improving efficiency of transport operations in many countries. A comparative study of rural transport carried out in Ghana, Zimbabwe, Thailand, Pakistan and Sri Lanka in 1994-5 has shown that Ghana and Zimbabwe have transport charges that are two to two and half times more expensive than for Asian countries for comparable journeys of up to 30km. In this case data was collected from a variety of different types of vehicles including tractors, power tillers pickups and trucks.

In surveys in Tanzania designed to measure the impact of poor road condition it was found that over a 50km distance that an increase in roughness of 50% would increase truck charges by 16% and increase pickup charges by just under double. It was also found that there were large changes in wet and dry season charges on poor quality roads. For example, on one road passenger fares increased by 60% in the wet season and freight charges increased by 65%. Similar figures were also found in Madagascar where on poor quality roads wet season passenger fares on "Taxis-brousses" were 70% higher than dry season fares.

A similar picture emerges for long distance transport where the evidence suggests that freight transport costs and charges in much of Africa are also consistently higher than comparable costs in Asia. In the period 1986 to 1988 long distance freight transport tariffs in Francophone Africa were over five times higher than tariffs found in Pakistan. Similar levels of freight rates were found for long distance traffic in Zambia, Zimbabwe and neighbouring countries in 1989. Similar low rates to those found in Pakistan were found for long distance traffic in Vietnam and in other Asian countries including India. More recently it was found that long distance freight rates in Tanzania were on average three times higher than for Indonesia. However transport charges and costs (per tonne km) by conventional vehicles are not uniform. Not only are there large differences in costs between different countries for the same type of transport particularly between Africa and Asia, there are large differences between rural short haul transport usually carried out by pickups or small rigid trucks) and long distance interurban transport that is more often carried out by heavy tractor and semi-trailer. Research carried out in Cameroon, Mali and Côte d'Ivoire has shown that costs of short distance local transport (i.e. up to 10km) are on average six times those of long distance transport. Similarly in Madagascar freight charges on non-national routes were some three times higher than on national routes.

The Impact of Transport Costs on Agricultural Production

The proportion of transport charges to final market price will vary with a range of factors such as commodity type, the efficiency of the transport and marketing sectors and travel distance. Studies carried out in Ghana demonstrate this variation. As a proportion of final market price wholesale transport to Kumasi were found to be between 3.5 and 5% for maize, yam and plantain with mean distances of the different crops of between 120km to 200km. In another study an average of 7 to 8% were found for Koforidua. A more recent study carried out by the Ministry of Transport found that for Accra the proportion was 11% for maize and 25% for tomatoes. The impact of total transport costs on agriculture will be higher than these figures indicate because the critical factor is the relationship between transport costs and what the farmer receives for his produce at the farm gate. Both marketing margins and transport costs including the high cost of head loading produce to the village or roadside need to be subtracted from the final market price. The results will, of course, vary from country to country and year to year.

The effect of reduced transport marketing costs on agricultural productivity can be estimated using agricultural supply price elasticities. These have been shown to lie in the range 0 to 1.5. If it is assumed that transport costs of moving goods to a major urban market are equivalent to say 30% of farm gate prices and that agricultural prices are set at the urban market then, a reduction of total transport costs by 20%, which is totally passed onto the farmer, will induce a rise in farm gate prices by six per cent. If it is also assumed that the total agricultural supply elasticity is +1 then one may estimate that total agricultural output would rise by about 6%. Road investment has an important part to play in reducing transport costs, however improving short lengths of feeder roads may have little impact if no change in transport mode occurs. It has been calculated that upgrading 5km of feeder road from earth to gravel standard might only increase farmgate prices by about one tenth of one per cent. In comparison bringing new motor vehicle access 5km closer to a village or farm when the alternative was headloading by hired labour could increase farmgate prices by over a hundred times as much.

The above analysis has largely assumed that changes in transport costs will be passed to farmers and not go to transporters, food wholesalers and retailers or the final urban consumers. Competitive transport and food marketing is required to ensure that the benefits from reductions in transport costs are passed on to farmers and to final consumers. Unfortunately in many parts of Africa this is far from the case. Where food prices are not government controlled it is common to find a wide variation of food prices between different regional markets in Africa which cannot be easily explained by transport costs. For example, it was found in the Ashanti Region of Ghana that the prices of cocoyam, plantain and tomatoes varied by more than two to one in different district markets at the same time. In one month the price of cassava was reported to be six times the price in another! Within Ashanti Region to transport produce from the lowest price market to the highest price market would have accounted for around 5% of the price difference for maize and plantain and around 15% for yam. Similarly in Zaire it can be calculated that transport charges account for about 15 to 20% of the total difference in price of cassava for Kinshasa and village markets 260 to 600km away.

Besides transport costs, other factors that can account for a wide range of prices, these include small volumes, poor price information, commodity perishability, differences in storage and retailing costs and a monopolistic marketing system. For example at the village level travelling wholesalers will travel together to a village may collude and set prices to the farmer before they arrive. Individual farmers will often have little choice as to whom they will trade with. More often than not it will be with one travelling wholesaler with whom the farmer has a long standing relationship, this is often strengthened by a credit agreement. For many farmers, indebtedness will force them to sell at peak harvest time when prices are low.

The price of transport is not the only disincentive to increased agricultural production. There is evidence from all over SSA that crops remain un-harvested, or are spoiled once they have been harvested, because of an inadequate supply of vehicles at harvest time. For example, Gaviria presents evidence from Tanzania that in some regions after the 1987 88 harvest that up to 89% of harvest remained stranded with typical figures in the region of 10-40%.

Agricultural Markets and Marketing

The importance of an efficient and competitive marketing system has been stressed as a complement to rural transport services and infrastructure in promoting development. However, the presence of markets in themselves also constitute a means by which the effective demand for transport can be increased. A market acts as a point where goods and people are amalgamated together and thereby concentrating the demand for transport. Where populations are dispersed markets are also likely to be dispersed with long average distances to market and people less likely to make the trip. This is an important consideration for the demand for IMT's where, if distances become too large, an IMT may not be viable.

In addition, one of the most effective ways that farmers have of getting the best price for their produce is for them to sell it themselves directly to final consumers at rural or urban markets, and thus bypass the normal marketing system. Although farmers do not have the economies of scale of travelling wholesalers it is often recognised by urban dwellers that the keenest prices are often provided by the farmers. Farmers bringing their own produce to market represent a very important way of limiting the power of the marketing cartels. However there is usually little support by the authorities for this type of 'unofficial' trading and farmers are frequently harassed as they attempt to sell. As far as possible facilities should be provided at urban markets, at minimum cost, so that farmers can sell their own produce without being disadvantaged or harassed in the process.

Whether farmers rely on travelling wholesalers, traders, parastatals or large private marketing companies they all reduce the farmers bargaining power, and critically, it reduces demand for transport services and the supply of vehicles available for rural people.

Access to Marketing and Storage Facilities

The following are the results of the analysis from case studies in Ghana, Thailand, Zimbabwe, Sri Lanka and Pakistan looking at the provision of transport services and the impact that marketing facilities may have. The presence of markets and storage facilities play an important role in affecting choice of vehicle. Markets and storage facilities both provide the same role of acting as a place where agricultural produce can be amalgamated. This may be for the purpose of immediate sale or for transportation to the next destination. Access to markets and storage facilities therefore affect vehicle choice in two main ways.

Firstly, the ease of access to these facilities, whether in terms of distance or ability to use the facilities, will dictate the farmer's decision on which vehicle to use. For example, if the storage facility is close he she may decide to buy a non-motorised vehicle which would have been of no use if the facility was beyond a certain distance. Similarly, if once the farmer had reached the facility he was unable to use it either because of its expense or because of exclusionist type practises, the need for a vehicle becomes redundant, and the farmer's produce may as well be sold to the village trader. The farmer will only demand a more advanced vehicle if it is the perception that the vehicle will enable an effective increase in farm gate prices. Secondly, where goods are amalgamated it means that the density of demand for vehicle services increases. The density of demand is of vital importance in determining vehicle choice. The larger the demand the more an efficient and cost effective vehicle can be justified and hence the unitary costs of transport are reduced. The existence of markets and storage facilities are important at any level. For example, at the village level a small grain store may be able to accumulate enough demand from all the farmers to justify the use of a donkey cart for transportation to market. Without the store individual farmers may only be able to justify headloading their surplus produce to market. Similarly, at the district level a market could attract city traders who bring large trucks to transport the produce bought at the market in bulk.

The ease with which farmers and traders have access to markets and storage facilities will be reflected in their distribution costs (transport and storage). If distribution costs are low this will effectively increase farm gate prices which will give farmers the incentive to increase production. One of the factors of production in this case would be agricultural and or transport vehicles. Table 1 shows the characteristics of market and storage accessibility in the five survey sites. It demonstrates that in the

Asian case studies, markets and storage facilities were on average closer to villages than in the African ones. In addition farmers were more able to sell their produce at those markets. In Ghana for example, the multitude of middlemen that are involved in the marketing process means that even if a farmer is able to get to a market he may not have the facilities or contacts needed to sell his produce at reasonable prices. The lack of storage facilities also means that farmers will take lower prices rather than risk not being able to sell their produce.

The Potential of IMTS for Agricultural Marketing

Intermediate means of transport IMTs can play a useful role in agricultural marketing. This section draws on the work of Sieber.

In SSAfrica the marketing of agricultural produce is often restricted by poor transport. Many reports show that harvests are rotting in the fields and at collection points due to a lack of transport to markets.

As this section will show, IMT can significantly improve access to markets and can create new opportunities for farmers. To analyse the role of IMT, it is necessary to distinguish between markets within and beyond walking distance and markets that can only be reached by motorized transport. Agricultural Marketing and Access to Transport Services 4:3:a Rural Transport Knowledge Base 8 Rural Travel and Transport Program 2001

If markets are within walking distance

Headloading can play a considerable role in marketing of agricultural produce. Sieber observed in Makete that more people used a footpath to travel to a local market than were transported by vehicle on a comparable road. Some villages preferred to transport a large proportion of their products by walking instead of selling it to traders with trucks because the traders would pay them less than they receive at the market. A footpath improvement was found to reduce travel times, increase transport loads and diminish accidents. This caused stronger market integration and reduced rural isolation. However, transport by walking is restricted by weight carried or distance to market if more than half-day walk is involved. IMT can increase the carrying capacity and speed, reducing transport costs. IMT create additional economic opportunities; for example. farmers could grow more or heavier crops. IMT enable farmers to sell their produce when road conditions are bad, motor vehicles rare and, therefore, producer prices are high. In Kenya, farmers report that they pass roads in the rainy season with their ox carts, where trucks are stuck in the mud.

If markets are too far to walk

IMT enable farmers to reach distant markets. Three-to-four hours of walking is often regarded as the threshold for access to markets. A pack animal can extend the distance to 20km in hilly areas, a bicycle to 30km in flat terrain and a single-axle tractor with trailer covers up to 50km. Thus, IMT make new markets accessible where producer prices might be higher; new products might be demanded, or inputs might be cheaper.

If markets are beyond the reach of IMT

For long distances the use of motor vehicles is essential. However, an appropriate approach can be applied, if multimodal transport is considered. The conventional approach, focusing mostly on roads and motor transport, has drawbacks that shall be discussed briefly to explain the appropriateness of multimodal transport. Another cause for poor rural transport is inadequate transport services, restricted by road conditions, low demand and short supply with vehicles. In *1988*, only nine motor vehicles per 1000 inhabitants were registered in Sub-Saharan Africa (excluding the Republic of South Africa). Since then this ratio has probably not increased significantly due to the economic crisis and a foreign exchange shortage. Most vehicles are used in big cities and not in rural areas. In rural areas of SSAfrica the static or declining transport fleet has created a situation that favours the sellers of transport services and not the buyers. In many rural areas the competition among service providers is very low and therefore they are not under pressure to transmit cost reductions to their clients. A non-competitive environment might be one of the reasons why transport costs in the Côte d'lvoire are six times higher on rural roads than on major highways. The quasi-monopolistic rural transport market enables operators to charge excessive fares that directly reduce farmers' income.

In the high costs of road freight transport in Africa has been identified. The main causes appear to be a combination of high input costs, low utilisation and poor maintenance and operating practices that are often the result of monopolistic practices. In attempting to solve rural transport problems aid donors have largely focused on the supply and maintenance of road infrastructure. Clearly this approach has major limitations:

- Insufficient provision of transport services, especially during harvest times;
- Low competition of service providers on rural roads;
- High vehicle operating costs on bad roads; and
- Inefficient vehicle operations

Multimodal transport may help solve many of these problems: using the comparative advantages of IMT in the transport chain from the field to the market. IMT can efficiently carry small quantities from the field or storage facility to collection points, where trucks operate to their optimum: fully loaded on long distances and good roads. Assuming free market entry for transport operators, the use of IMT will increase competition because:

(a) IMT operate at low costs between collection point and village

(b) More efficient transport operations between collection point and market will be an incentive for other enterprises to offer their services.

Increased competition will break the monopolies of rural transport operators, forcing transport costs down and, thus, raising the income of rural producers. Additionally, IMT can use low-cost infrastructure, reducing public expenditure for infrastructure provision and maintenance: bicycles and pack animals can operate on footpaths, animal carts and rickshaws on low cost tracks. Low-volume roads can be downgraded to tracks; wooden bridges or fords can be built instead of concrete bridges.

IMT's can reduce transport costs

Next to agro-ecological factors, transport costs have a significant influence on the cropping patterns. More than a century ago Thijnen (1783 - 1850) observed circular structures of the agricultural land use around the market towns; with the intensity of agricultural production decreasing with further distance to the market. More often than not this holds true for the cropping patterns on farms in Sub-Saharan Africa: some authors have found that heavy crops are only cultivated around the farmstead and collection points, whereas high-value crops like cocoa are grown further away from the road network. Often, new fields are not taken under cultivation if' the distance to collection points is long and therefore transport costs too high also indicates that the radius of cultivation can be extended if farmers use IMT to transport their produce. It has been observed that ox carts in Zambia can extend the agricultural area to a radius of 20 km around markets and depots.

The overall role of IMTs in agricultural marketing

Walking, the dominant mode of on-farm transport, can restrict any increase in agricultural production. IMT can improve the efficiency of on-farm agricultural transports by reducing transport costs and time. The effects on agricultural production can be manifold:

- Cultivation of bigger areas;
- Utilization of more fertile, but remote, soils;
- Production of heavier corps,
- Increased utilization of fertilizer and manure;
- Reduced pest damage and spoilage at crop harvest time;
- Reduction of transport time, partly used for income generation;

- Reduced effort and drudgery involved in human porterage; and
- Spill-over effects if animals are used for ploughing and transport

Thus, IMT enable the farmers to respond better to markets by augmenting or changing their production. Additionally, they reduce losses, save transport costs and time. If markets are within walking distance than headloading is important. Transport efficiency can be significantly increased by improvement of footpaths or the use of IMT. If markets are more than half a day's non-motorized travel, a multimodal transport system is a cost-effective solution. Trucks are unbeatable on long distances, good roads and fully loaded, and IMT operate more efficiently on short distances with small loads and on bad roads making a multimodal approach the best solution for rural transport problems.

Chapter 3

Domestic Marketing of Agricultural Products

Marketing of Egypt's agricultural output has been directly and indirectly exposed to government intervention over the last thirty years. The political and socio-economic conditions of the Egyptian society have made it imperative to apply more than one system for marketing agricultural commodities.

Historical Background

A. Cotton

The government's interest in the cotton trade was, until the middle of the twentieth century, confined to the last stage of exportation from the Alexandria seaport. Little attention was given to the organization of cotton marketing which remained for years lacking legislative regulations outlining transactions among dealers on the cotton market within the framework of direct supervision. Before 1961, the cotton trade took place in two types of free markets:

- on-the-spot market;
- future cotton trading.

Prices in both markets were fixed according to supply and demand. Under such a market-oriented system, most producers had to sell their seed cotton just picked at a low price so as to pay their debts, such as rental, government dues and production loans. Large-scale producers, who usually got their cotton ginned and graded, preferred to sell their lint cotton by auction, thus gaining better prices. Among the advantages of free marketing was the multiplicity of trading channels and price determination according to market mechanisms. Cotton trading on-the-spot and future cotton trading depended on organizing a market news and information service to assist the interior marketing operations. Gins used to receive seed cotton at successive periods during the harvesting season and, therefore, there was no stacking of cotton on gins' storing yards. Under this free marketing system, brokers could not control supply and demand. Had this been the case, producers would have been exposed to violent shakes as a result of fluctuation of world prices.

B. Rice

Before the second World War, rice growers used to sell the surplus of household consumption paddy to the local traders, brokers who worked for large-scale merchants, or to rice mills or local hullers. Paddy was stored in the warehouses of the commercial banks. The needs of rice mills were drawn from this reserve stock. During the second World War, obligatory delivery of a certain quota of the per feddan yield was imposed by the government. The legislation exempted holders of less than one feddan from the quota system and prohibited the transportation of paddy from one district to another without prior governmental approval.

C. Wheat

Before the second World War, the government had played no active role in wheat marketing. Wheat producers used to sell their product to the local traders or to brokers who worked as agents of wholesale traders at Rod El-Farag and Ather Al-Nabi markets. Mills secured their needs from those traders under no government controls on the local market. During and after the second World War, the state imposed its control over the local wheat production which was not sufficient enough to fulfill the domestic demand. The Government imposed an arbitrary delivery system whereby producers had to deliver a predetermined quota for rice production to the Agricultural Credit Bank within the framework of a special cropping pattern purposely designed to ensure grains availability in the local market. A certain percentage of the farmer's holding was compulsorily determined by government for wheat plantations. ACB paid the fixed price according to variety and grade. Premiums were given to deliveries beyond the set quotas and fines were imposed on producers who failed to fulfil the requirement. The legislation banned transportation of wheat or wheat flour without permission from the Ministry of Supplies.

In 1954, the Government amended the compulsory quota system in a manner that gave way to private wheat trade. Producers were allowed to sell out their product through their co-operative which transported the crop to the ACB storehouses after weighing and grading. This period has witnessed the initiation of the co-operative marketing system with the enlarged base of small holdings after the 1952 revolution. Co-operative marketing was first initiated in the agrarian reform lands and was later generalized to cover all the country. Delivery was compulsory until 1974. From 1975 to 1983 delivery was optional and turned to be compulsory in 1984 and 1985. It again became optional by the 1987 season to this date.

Development of the Agricultural Co-operative Marketing System

Agricultural co-operatives entered into the marketing domain in the middle of this century. The first cooperative for flax producers was established in Cairo. Wheat and cotton's co-operative marketing was initiated and vegetables and fruits co-operatives came into existence by that time. Sesame, tomato and broad beans, rice, onion and garlic were covered by the co-operative marketing system in the 1960s, whereafter most crops were incorporated into the system. The number of specialized marketing co-operatives increased to cover crops at present. Though the co-operative marketing started optional, it turned to be arbitrary for certain major field crops cotton, rice, wheat, maize and sugarcane during the seventies and until 1987 when the economic reform policies in the agricultural sector were introduced on the basis of liberalizing the production and marketing of almost all crops with the exception of cotton and sugarcane which will be soon liberalized.

The domestic marketing of the agricultural commodities and production inputs was correlated with the co-operative marketing system. The Central Agricultural Co-operative Union represents the top of the Egyptian Co-operative Structure. It consists of three multipurpose co-operatives at national level.

These are:

. The General Co-operative for Agricultural Credit;

. The General Co-operative for Agrarian Reform;

. The Agricultural Co-operatives which are established according to the need and the nature of the activity and finally the General Co-operative for Agricultural Mechanization.

Both GCAC and GCAR represent a national co-operative in their respective areas of activity. CACU performs several functions, such as the planning, co-ordination, and supervision of co-operative training and of the process of establishing the multipurpose and specialized co-operatives in the governorates.

The local co-operative follows up the implementation of the cropping pattern in its area of jurisdiction, decides the required extent of credit, secures loans from the available sources of finance for its production and service projects—in its legal capacity as an independent entity and for its members who seek such facilities in accordance with its constitution and the laws and by-laws that govern credit affairs at village banks. It also falls within its provinces to co-operatively market the crops of its members.

The Marketing System

A. The Quota System

An obligatory delivery system was imposed on certain

commodities of greater demand such as rice, wheat and maize, or export and industrial crops such as cotton, flax, sesame and onion. Producers were obliged to deliver predetermined quantities of these crops to the state at predetermined prices. The quota system aimed at ensuring the availability of these products for the local consumption and for the industrial sector, in addition to securing foreign currencies from export crops. Procurement of the major crops was confined to the state agencies, such as the public sector Authority for Rice Mills, the Public Sector Authority for Wheat mills, Silos and Bakeries and the Public Sector Authority for Cotton Affairs. The Principal Bank for Development and Agricultural Credit, with its vast network, supervised the marketing operations of these crops. To guarantee high productivity, MOALR incorporated the major production areas into a crop rotation system and issued a legislation banning the private transportation and trading of these crops during the production seasons.

The percentages of crop delivery varied from one year to another according to the volume of domestic production, consumption and the appropriateness of importation terms. For example, in certain years, wheat was subjected to the quota system due to the relatively low wheat imports. *Table 1* shows the percentages of obligatory and optional delivery of major crops. It indicates that the average percentage of wheat compulsory delivery reached 7.5% in 1984 and 1985, but the delivery was optional in the other years. The percentage of cotton delivery was 100% of the national production while that of rice was 48%. The percentage of sugarcane delivery was 72.4%–85.7% as the remaining percentage was contracted for sugarcane juice shops.

The crop quota system was characterized by lower procurement prices than the free co-operative marketing system wherein the producer had the liberty to make decision on the area and type of crop he might be willing to grow on the basis of contracts concluded before season to maximize his revenues and secure the subsistence needs of his household. The prices were normally fixed by market mechanisms.

B. The Contracting System

In Egypt, this marketing system is applied to the agricultural crops and livestock products. A written contract is concluded between the producer the vendor and the procurer (who may be an individual or a company), whereby the first party is committed to deliver the second party an agreed quantity of the crop in question at an appointed place and time. The state, through its specialized institutions, often resorts to this system to secure the needs of the industrial sector, taking into consideration the quantity, quality and the suitable time of delivery. Also, the system is applied to consumer goods that need heavy subsidy to producers so as encourage them to maintain production of such commodities as poultry, the marketing of which is controlled by MOS and its agencies.

MOS secured its needs of locally slaughtered chickens by means of a tripartite contract concluded annually between MOS, MOALR, represented by the Public Company for Poultry As-Salam Company and the slaughter-house sub-sector. According to this contract, the company provided 60% of the chicks as well as the feeds to the slaughter house which, in turn, delivered it after being slaughtered to the marketing authority of the MOS.

With regard to the imported chickens, MOS, represented by its Public authority for Food Commodities, concluded contracts with the exporting countries according to certain price conditions and hygienic requirements. The price stipulated in the contracts depended on the extent of the monopolistic position of any of the two parties and on the producer's ability to modify his cropping pattern. If the buyer's monopolistic position was stronger than the vendor's and if the latter's ability to modify his cropping pattern in favour of the crop, subject of contract, the price will be in the interest of the buyer as was the case between sugarcane producers and the Egyptian Sugar and Distillation Company. The contracting system specifies the duration of the contract one production season or more at the end of which both parties have the liberty to discontinue the agreement. Therefore, this system, in the absence of monopoly, is regarded as one of the best marketing systems, especially if the state is committed to implement plans for development.

C. Free Marketing

Many crops, such as vegetables and fruits, are marketed freely. The surplus production of crops that are subjected to the quota system, such as broad beans and maize, is likewise marketed freely. The private sector plays a greater role under this system as compared to the co-operative sector. Wholesalers, their brokers (agents between producers and wholesalers and between the latter group and the retailers) and exporters have specific roles under this system. The private sector performs almost all the marketing functions starting with purchasing, transportation, storing, selling, financing and even risk-bearing.

Following are the salient features of the system which widely applied to horticultural and vegetable crops:

- The commodity is procured by local brokers who may provide producers with finance needed for production. Those brokers are either working independently or representing others at the wholesale market.
- When in bulks to the retailers or through an intermediary agent.
- Retailers may have a direct access to the producers.
- Consumers, at a very limited scale, may purchase their needs directly from the producer.
- Co-operatives have a very limited role under this system. It is confined only to the marketing of potatoes and some other vegetable crops.
- Government intervention is represented in fixing the price at the stages of wholesale and retail trade, with the purpose of protecting the consumer and ensuring the availability of the agricultural products at reasonable prices without ignoring the producer's right to achieve reasonable profit.

Due to the fact that supply at vegetable and fruit market is largely controlled by a limited group of wholesalers, the fixed price lists are, in most cases, not binding. By the beginning of 1987, compulsory delivery and state-fixed prices of almost all crops were terminated with the exception of cotton and sugarcane. Floor prices were laid down for cereal crops for growers who desire to deliver their crops to the government. The purpose was to ensure price stability and avoid the bad effects of sharp price fluctuation on producers.

D. Role of the Private Sector in the Current Marketing Systems

With the exception of cotton and sugarcane, marketing of all crops has been fully liberalized. Floor prices have, however, been fixed for those producers who opt to sell their products to PBDAC or to MOS.

Recently, importation and marketing of chemical fertilizers, seeds, pesticides and agricultural machinery have been liberalized. The public sector's agricultural companies have been privatized and turned into holding companies with subsidiary firms. It is expected that, by time, those companies will be turned into partnerships, the participation shares of which will be open to the public. It is also expected that cotton production and marketing will be fully liberalized as from 1993–94. The problem yet to be solved is the modality of privatizing: cotton gins, export companies and companies for cotton industrialization with their heavy investments. This would depend mainly on the capability of the private sector to finance and manage these assets.

Marketing before the Structural Reform

1. Cotton Co-operative Marketing

Despite the positive aspects of the co-operative marketing of cotton, represented in the limited number of brokers, the undertaking of all the marketing functions by the government, subsidizing production inputs and providing the necessary loans from PBDAC at subsidized interest rates, there exist a number of impediments in the cotton's co-operative marketing system, namely:

1. The system is, in itself, an embodiment of state monopoly represented in the delivery of the entire yield at a depressed administered price. This has left a negative impact on cotton area and production.
2. Selling seed cotton to unlicensed private ginneries although the laws prohibits such illicit practices.
3. Re-classing seed cotton at ginneries after it has been classed at the collection centres, thus adding to the marketing costs.
4. Interrupted flow of seed cotton as the rate of delivery increases at a certain period thus leading to stacking at the collection centres.
5. Facing some transportation problems during the marketing season.
6. Lack of trained manpower at the collection centres.
7. Repeated complaints by the producers of the existence of accountancy errors in their debts to PBDAC or the double deduction thereof from their financial dues.
8. Exaggerated number of committees in the cotton's co-operative marketing system.

Problems of the Rice Marketing System

The marketing of rice, together with the other grain crops, encounters similar marketing problems which are:

1. The high percentage of quantitative loss over the successive marketing operations from farm gate until the product reaches the consumer. This is largely due to the lack of efficient packaging and storing facilities and to the relatively inadequate credit and marketing services.
2. Administered prices, announced at an inappropriate time, did not encourage producers to abide by the quota system.

3. Irrationalized consumption patterns.

4. The absence of indicative studies of the local and world markets in order to make proper decisions on production and future expansion.

5. The lack of co-ordination between local production and domestic and foreign marketing policies.

Problems of the Wheat Marketing System

Wheat marketing encounters the problem of quantitative and qualitative loss during and post-harvest throughout the consecutive marketing stages. To reduce the loss, the storage capabilities have to be improved by building silos at seaports and inland locations. The currently used handling and transportation system need to be reviewed to reduce loss during loading and unloading. The overall marketing system, starting with the producer and ending with the consumer, must be turned into a more efficient system.

Problems and Determinants of Fruit and Vegetables Marketing

1. In many instances, classing and grading are not undertaken at the level of producers or wholesalers. Sometimes, producers perform some of these marketing operations but they lack adequate scientific bases, thus leading to more losses in the succeeding marketing operations. Transportation is particularly important for fruit and vegetables marketing, in which time is a determinant factor. It is a seasonal marketing activity, the demand reaching its peak during September through December which synchronises with the marketing season for cotton and rice. During this period, producers have to resort to the private transport company in view of the transportation load shouldered by the Transport Co-operatives. As a result, the cost increases by 30%–50%. The lack of cooler vehicles adds to post-harvest losses during transportation, especially during the hot summer season. The loss is further aggravated when the roads are not properly paved.

2. The lack of storage facilities for vegetables and fruit at

both wholesale or retail markets. In the traditional methods used for the storage of potato, the percentage of loss reaches 20% while in cooled rooms, mostly owned by the private sector, it reaches 1%-1.5%.

3. Cash or material credit for horticultural crops is not adequately available. Traders and brokers exploit small producers by providing them with loans in advance without much complications. But this directly affects the percentage of commission the wholesalers gain. Though officially set at 5%-8% of the commodity price, it actually reaches 20% due to credit interest rate and other charges.

4. The marketing margins for locally marketed vegetables range from 50%-60% of the retail price. This percentage is distributed between the wholesale and the retail trades which offer very modest services.

5. For example, the wholesalers do not offer such marketing services that improve the product's quality. The wholesale traders conclude their transactions in small shops leased some forty years ago at nominal rental value. They confine their marketing service to unloading and the direct process of wholesale.

6. One of the major distortions of the existing marketing system of fruits and vegetables is the monopolistic position of wholesale dealers. A limited number of large-scale merchants control a large percentage of market transactions while a large number of small-scale merchants deal in a small percentage of the fruit and vegetables produce (in what may be termed as minority monopoly).

7. Small and dispersed area are cultivated with vegetables within the same region, which implies an increase in the marketing costs that include sorting, grading, packaging and transportation due to the absence of vegetables and fruits collection centres where such processes are performed on a large scale.

8. The marketing infrastructures such as wholesale and retail markets, storehouses and brick cooling systems affect the efficiency of the overall fruit and vegetable marketing system.

The existing markets are inadequate as far as capacity, location, hygienic supervision and other services are concerned. Rod El-Farag fresh products market in Cairo is an example of these inefficiencies. This resulted in disorganized markets taking the form of privately owned selling centres subjected to weak surveillance. Many a time, the idea of building new planned wholesale markets for fresh products has been frequently considered but received very little response from the wholesalers. The situation is further aggravated by the lack of sufficient investments in marketing compared to production in view of the fact that investment in the latter directly affects the output and thus has a direct bearing on returns while the former reduces post harvest losses or improves quality.

9. Packaging for local marketing is still primitive, thus increasing perishability during handling until the fresh product reaches the consumers. Primitive packs are still used for locally marketed fresh produce, thus leading to increased post-harvest losses as a result of mechanical damage. Improved packs are mostly used for export produce.

10.The processing companies depend largely on wholesalers for securing their needs of fresh fruit and vegetables and partly on growers; in both cases, the contracted quantities are not supplied in full, thus reducing the operational capacity of these factories. Moreover, the end-products, until recently, were priced below real cost due to subsidization of consumer goods. To reduce their losses to the least possible limit, the companies resorted to produce below their actual operational capacity, thus raising the average cost of the end-product.

11.Inaccessibility to market information such as the size of marketed quantities of a specific product, competing products, market conditions and other details that are taken into account in the decisionmaking process. In the absence of such information, producers are not in position to obtain lucrative returns from their fresh produce.

12.Marketing activities for the purpose of exportation face the problem of inadequate spaces in air freight, let alone the monopoly of these spaces by a limited number of exporters who prefer to use the national carrier which is cheaper than the international carriers, thus leading to an increased demand for a limited cargo space.

13. The lack of sufficient studies on foreign markets: especially consumption patterns and market capacity. Traditional markets have been lost to the Egyptian fresh produce as a result of competition in quality and packaging.

Local Pricing of Agricultural Products

In the past, pricing of some agricultural crops posed a major problem. Administered farm gate prices were fixed for cotton, grains and sugarcane while fruit, vegetable and feed crops were left to market forces. This has eventually led to a contradiction between the national and the individual interests. The administered prices were generally depressed in relation to world or free market prices of crops under quota system. Therefore, farmers became disinclined to grow crops subjected to government control due to their reduced profitability. Cotton was called "the government crop" as it was less lucrative when compared to the alternative rotations. The pricing policy was guided by the production costs plus the marginal profit equivalent to twofold the rental value of the agricultural land which was then fixed at seven times the land tax. The pricing policies of the sixties, the seventies through the mid eighties, were more in favour of the consumer and the other sectors of the national economy, at the expense of the agricultural sector. During the sixties, and partially through the seventies, the state's goal was to support the industrial sector through the contribution of agriculture to the national economy.

These policies led to an uneven distribution of income, in disfavour to the agricultural sector which was burdened with indirect taxes in addition to the overvaluation of the local currency when fixing the farm gate prices on the basis of the export prices of cotton and rice. Until the seventies, the U.S. $ was officially fixed at L.E. 0.70 while its value at the "black market" reached L.E. 2.0 which constituted yet another indirect tax on growers of export crops. Farm gate prices whether for the arbitrary or the optional crop delivery system were thus based mainly on production costs to which the cash rental value during crop season is added to allow a net revenue equivalent to that same rental value.

Farm gate price = Production cost (rental value included) + Rental value – Value of annual production Average production per feddan for the main crops

Where production costs include recurrent costs land preparation, seeds, pesticides, irrigation, fertilizers and other agronomic practices. Production costs comprise labour, seeds, fertilizers, pesticides, machinery and sundry expenses. In addition to production costs, other methods were sometimes used for estimating the farm gate price, such as the net revenues of the alternative more lucrative rotations in order to achieve some degree of balance between return to producers under different cropping patterns. For example, if the net revenue of the wheat rice rotation was more than that of the short season berseem cotton rotation, the difference was added to the cotton-based rotation to make up for the deficit in price to producers.

World prices were also used as indicators in fixing the farm gate prices through applying a border price for delivery. This system, which lasted until 1987, has resulted in structural price distortions which were accompanied by distortions in the cropping pattern. The area cultivated with berseem has remarkably increased at the expense of the area cultivated with wheat as the profitability of the former is higher than that of the latter which was subjected to the obligatory delivery system. As a result, the prices of wheat by-products became higher than that of wheat grains due to their depressed farm gate prices while demand for wheat straws was exceedingly higher under the circumstance of dry fodder's shortage. This situation has led to the negligence of the primary crop (grains) for the sake of the secondary product

Producers sought to grow wheat varieties known for their high straw yield, which, in itself, was an inefficient use of the already scarce land resources. Until the early 1980s, Egypt produced only 20% of its wheat consumption needs.

The enforcement of the cotton area control by the government has deprived farmers from growing more lucrative crops, despite the fact that Egypt has a relatively high comparative advantage in cotton production. The compulsory co-operative system was the only source of providing the farmers with production inputs at subsidized prices. Subsidization entailed heavy burdens on the state's treasury. In view of inputs shortage, especially fertilizers, producers had to procure them from the "black market" at almost double the government price. Some farmers resorted to selling out their quotas to producers of the more lucrative crops such as berseem, vegetables and fruits. This negatively affects the original crops to which fertilizers have been allocated and also the agricultural loans.

The obligatory pricing system of vegetables and fruits at both wholesale and retail markets and the oligopoly of the wholesale market by a limited number of traders have led to either a low quality of the marketed quantities or the control of the supply of the already perishable produce. This has eventually led to a loss amounting to about 30% of the fresh produce. This system has had an indirect effect on prices to producers who paid very little attention to the marketing operations or to investment in the field of marketing which had a negative bearing on the marketing efficiency. The over-valuation of the local currency *vis-à-vis* the U.S. $ constituted an implicit tax on producers, thus leading to the limitation of Egypt's agricultural exports.

In 1987, the government had a propensity towards economic liberalization. With the exception of cotton and sugarcane, the production of all crops was liberalized, and prices were left to market forces. But it is noteworthy that prices during the transition period did not represent a genuine equilibrium of the market force, as the government intervened to favour supply of such commodities as wheat, maize and red meat through importation until 1990. The imported quantities was reduced over the last two years as a result of the increase in wheat production. Until the mid-eighties, almost 75% of wheat consumption requirements were covered by importation. In 1991, this percentage was reduced to 50%-60%. Maize importation for feed industry was reduced from 50% to 30% over the same period.

Marketing Margins Efficiency

1. Marketing margins

A marketing margin is defined as the difference in the value of physical qualities at the various levels of the marketing process. It represents the difference between farm gate and wholesale prices, or between wholesale and retail prices. The total marketing margins constitute price diffusion. The marketing margin includes the marketing costs plus brokers profits. The marketing costs are the actual expenditure born by the producer or the broker plus the recurrent costs, if any, during the commodity's movement from producers to consumers.

But the high marketing costs—which constitute a large part of the marketing margin does not necessarily reflect low marketing efficiency, especially if the increase in such costs implies marketing services required by the community of consumers. On the other hand, the broker's marketing margin increasing without an equivalent increase in the marketing services would result in a reduced marketing efficiency wherein marketing profits would increase at the expense of marketing services supposedly provided by brokers. The marketing process, in such a case, is characterized by the existence of a parasitic group of brokers who gain much for minor services. When the marketing system achieves greater efficiency, those parasitic brokers can be impelled to leave the business, especially in the case of fresh produce marketing wherein the increased number of brokers reduces the producer's share in the consumer's unit of income.

The producer's share in the consumer's income unit ranged between 55%-68% for orange, banana and grapes. In the case of cotton and sugarcane which, until recently, were subjected to obligatory delivery, the marketing margins represent the difference between broker price and the state-fixed procurement price. If the difference between the world prices and the locally fixed prices is negligible, this can be taken as an indicator for an effective local market. But such was not the case for cotton and sugarcane, the prices of which were fixed by a number of economic and political factors previously elaborated. Production costs and revenues of the alternative (more lucrative) crop rotations may be a determinant factor in pricing. The world price is usually used as an indicator for setting a procurement price. In 1990 91 the cotton procurement price represented 55%–60% of the world price. In the past, the cotton procurement price represented 30%–40% of the world price. This indicates that the marketing margin for cotton constituted 40%–45% of its equivalent farm gate world price.

Marketing Efficiency

Due to government intervention in cotton and sugarcane production and pricing, the marketing efficiency was not attained. Similarly, technical efficiency was not realized as a result of the lack of technical expertise and or of appropriate marketing facilities. This may also be attributed to the depressed farm gate prices which eventually led to negligence of such agronomic practices as picking in cotton, thus leading to a detrimental effect on the length of cotton staple; let alone the meagre price differences among the various grades. Among the factors that lead to inability to achieve technical efficiency in cotton marketing is the in-flow of the crop within a short period of time more than 80% of the crop was delivered at collection centres over 45 days. This represents a heavy load on cotton gins beyond its storing capacities. Subsequently, cotton sacks, stored in the open air, are subjected to mechanical and biological loss. Due to synchronization with rice marketing, the marketing costs increase due to excessive demand for transportation services. This also applies to grain crops which undergo quantitative losses throughout the various marketing stages due to insufficient transport, storage, marketing and administrative capabilities, let alone the lack of co-ordination in the local production and marketing policies. As for sugarcane, the present low levels of operational capacity impede the attainment of marketing technical efficiency. The operational capacity of the sugar factory at Deshna reached 64% compared to 72% at Armant. At Nagea Hammadi, the excessive quantities beyond the factory's operational capacity are transferred to Gerga and Isna factories.

With regard to vegetable and horticultural crops, the marketing efficiency has not been attained yet, due to the lack of technical efficiency in handling until the product reaches the consumer. For example, sorting and grading processes are not performed at farm or wholesale market levels, thus leading to mechanical and biological losses in the next marketing stages. As previously stated, transport is extremely important for the perishable fresh produce. But transportation costs increase drastically during the high season of cotton and rice marketing. Vegetable and fruit producers encounter cash credit problems which force them, especially small-scale producers, to establish financial links with wholesalers who provide advance credit well before harvesting. This led to the control of the fresh produce market by a limited number of wholesalers. A glaring example of this form of oligopoly is the present vacuum between this group of wholesalers who refuse to move to Al-Uboor fresh produce market which has been ideally designed and constructed to provide the badly needed facilities; on the pretext that it is remotely located outside consumption areas.

Market information is an important component of efficiency. A large sector of producers, consumers and even brokers lack ample information on supply and demand and prices prevailing in the various markets. But the establishment of an efficient marketing information system requires the creation of a grading and standardization system to be codified and enforced.

3. Marketing Services

Marketing services differ relatively with the degree of government intervention in crop marketing. The obligatory delivery of cotton and sugarcane at depressed procurement prices necessitated the provision of such services as cash and material loans by PBDAC's village branches. A cotton grower was entitled to a picking loan of L.E. 50 per feddan which would be increased at commercial interest rates on request. The General Co-operative of cotton producers specifies the number of collection centres and, in collaboration with PBDAC and cotton companies, the co-operative determines the number of cotton sacks needed by each governorate. Village co-operatives distribute sacks to producers according to the registered area of cotton and the village's average production per feddan. The marketing committee at each governorate announces a time schedule for delivery at collection centres where weighing and classing take place on the same day of delivery in the presence of the producer, the procuring company's representative and the co-operative's representative. The cotton companies, to which the title deed is transferred, transport cotton to the ginneries where it is sorted out according to classes and grades. Final settlement between the village co-operatives and the procuring companies is decided on the basis of the ginning outturn in addition to the secondary products . Baled lint is then moved to the cotton pressing company in Alexandria where fumigation and pressing take place for export cotton. A large portion of cotton bales is also moved to domestic mills.

With regard to sugarcane, the Egyptian Sugar and Distillation Company concludes contracts with producers whereby the latter deliver the yield of the contracted area on the day of harvesting. Almost 90% of the crops is transported from the fields to the factory by means of carts provided by the company. Once arrived at the factory's site, the crop is weighed in the presence of producers' representatives. The price is determined on the basis of the theoretical percentage of sugar (10.3%). A premium is added to price proportional to the increase in the real percentage of sugar (and *vice versa*). With regard to fresh produce (vegetables and fruits), harvest is undertaken either by the producers or the brokers. Packaging and transportation are also undertaken by producers in case they opt to market their produce by themselves. The two marketing processes are sometimes undertaken by wholesalers or brokers to whom the title is transferred. Brokers may also sell out the horticultural or vegetable crops on behalf of producers in return for an agreed commission of the net price after deducting the cost of transport.

In case the producer opts to transport his produce to the wholesale market, the wholesaler with whom he transacts unloads the consignment and sells it for him in return for an agreed commission. No sorting or grading is done in this case.

For exporting fresh produce, sorting and classing are two important marketing processes undertaken by exporters. Crediting is yet another important service done by brokers at the time of contracting. This entails an increase in marketing costs and subsequently a decrease in the producer's share in consumer prices. Storage is a cost-effective marketing service for such crops as onion, garlic, potatoes and, sometimes, grapes. Sorting takes place either by producers or wholesalers for crops having high keeping ability. As for grapes, it is normally stored under cooling conditions.

Future of Domestic Marketing Under the Structural Adjustment Programmes

1. Privileges of SAPs

Under the economic liberalization policy, marketing institutions will work according to production functions that give maximum yield of the available resources, better known as technological marketing efficiency. The macro-economic reforms will make available complete information on new technology, training and incentive systems that raise efficiency. It is also expected that market mechanism, which will determine prices according to supply and demand force, will lead to allocative efficiency at which the marginal costs equates the marginal revenue. The marketing institution that works under both concepts of efficiency will eventually realize what is termed as economic efficiency, which means the efficient use of resources on a cost-benefit basis. It is important to distinguish between market functions and market role in price formation. Market functions such as collection, packaging, transportation and storage will be performed according to criteria of efficiency without necessarily having direct relationship with price formation. However, prices will be a function of commodity quality based on the effective performance of marketing functions which will lead to the reduction of quantitative and qualitative loss. Changes in the cropping pattern will take place in view of price indicators and relative profitability. Similarly, changes in the food consumption pattern may occur in view of new price relationships and the relative costs of foodstuffs. Due to incentives to producers and marketers, quality will certainly improve to meet consumer's requirements, thus leaving a favourable impact on the overall marketing system. This will encourage investment in the field of marketing which will be affected by the world market for exportoriented commodities. The present export systems will be modified to cope with the requirements of the world markets. This will necessitate enhancing the capabilities of exporters unions to assess the world market changes including capacity-competition, requirements and time schedule of exportation. An accurate marketing information system will have to be established to assist in formulating plans for agricultural production, marketing and processing.

Problems of the Free Market Economy

Centrally planned and market-oriented economies have their pros and cons. We have discussed the positive impact of economic liberalization on marketing efficiency. But every economic system has two aspects. The first relates to efficiency and the second to justice which may not be within reach under economic liberalization policies which imply the phasing out of subsidy to producers and consumers, high interest rates on credit to producers, decontrolling exchange rates and exploitation by brokers. As a result, production and marketing costs will increase in a manner conducive to price instability. Producers may experience economic tremors as was the case before the sixties. Sharp fluctuations in cotton prices had resulted in great losses to producers. Such a shift from centrally planned to market economy will lead to an increase in the prices of consumer goods which soared in the last two years especially for law-income groups. But the high, unstable prices are not expected to continue beyond the transition period. Market incentives will increase production and improve its quality in a way that positively affects price stability and improve the agricultural trade and subsequently the national economy and consumer welfare.

The State's Marketing Role Under Economic Liberalization

Economic liberalization does not necessarily mean that the state will divest its role in the market. Even in countries that adopted liberalization policies well before us, the state intervenes indirectly in the production and marketing systems. In the EEC countries, there still exists a system for subsidy to producers and exports. A protectionist policy is applied within the EEC to ensure preferentiality of their products. If this is the case with the advanced countries, it is more befitting for the Government of Egypt to play an indirect role in protecting both producers and consumers alike. It is well known that the international market prices do not reflect the real prices of commodities as a result of distortions attributed to subsidy systems applied in certain countries. This would affect market negatively through wrong indicatives used in orienting production and marketing and would have a direct bearing on the proportional relationship between both.

Therefore, it would be in the fitness of things to exercise a good degree of surveillance on the domestic market performance and the possible emergence of monopolistic or semi-monopolistic groupings. The state intervenes to ensure the application of floor prices if producers are expected to encounter market uncertainty. In the case of price deterioration, producers may deliver all or part of their crops to the government at pre-declared floor prices. The government should maintain a strategic stock of those crops that have strategic importance in order to intervene in times of need and in favour of supply when prices soar. In other words, the government should keep an eye on changes in supply and demand for agricultural commodities to guarantee price stability. It should also levy customs and duties on imports to stabilize the domestic market. However, the structure of price differences will not necessarily be affected by the difference between the local price and the border price of a commodity.

Meanwhile the government should adopt and provide a powerful market information system in order to improve market performance. Nonetheless, the government should provide indirect subsidy to low-income groups. The United States apply a similar system known as "Food Stamps" which give low-income consumers an access to certain commodities at low prices. The government should encourage agricultural marketing co-operatives free from governmental interventions regarding their management. By so doing, the marketing co-operatives will make full use of mass marketing operations which will subsequently lead to the reduction of marketing costs and will help curb the manoeuvres of greedy brokers.

Chapter 4

Agricultural Markets in Developing Countries

The history of agricultural markets in developing countries reflects attempts to establish the appropriate government responses to the inefficiencies created by incomplete institutional and physical infrastructure and imperfect competition. Government intervention in the 1960s and 1970s to resolve market failures gave way in the 1980s to market-oriented liberalization to 'get prices right' and, more recently, to 'get institutions right'. But markets openness may accentuate the latent dualism of a modern, efficient marketing sector, accessible only to those with adequate scale and capital, alongside a traditional, inefficient marketing channel to which the poor are effectively restricted.

Agricultural markets in developing countries

Markets aggregate demand and supply across actors at different spatial and temporal scales. Well-functioning markets ensure that macro and sectoral policies change the incentives and constraints faced by micro-level decision makers. Macro policy commonly becomes ineffective without market transmission of the signals sent by central governments. Similarly, well-functioning markets underpin important opportunities at the micro level for welfare improvements that aggregate into sustainable macro-level growth. For example, without good access to distant markets that can absorb excess local supply, the adoption of more productive agricultural technologies typically leads to a drop in farm-gate product prices, erasing all or many of the gains to producers from technological change and thereby dampening incentives for farmers to adopt new technologies that can stimulate economic growth. Markets also play a fundamental role in managing risk associated with demand and supply shocks by facilitating adjustment in net export flows across space and in storage over time, thereby reducing the price variability faced by consumers and producers. Markets thus perform multiple valuable functions: distribution of inputs (such as fertilizer, seed) and outputs (such as crops, animal products) across space and time, transformation of raw commodities into value-added products, and transmission of information and risk. Per the first welfare theorem, competitive market equilibria help ensure an efficient allocation of resources so as to maximize aggregate welfare.

The micro-level realities of agricultural markets in much of the developing world, however, include poor communications and transport infrastructure, limited rule of law, and restricted access to commercial finance, all of which make markets function much less effectively than textbook models typically assume. A long-standing empirical literature documents considerable commodity price variability across space and seasons in developing countries, with various empirical tests of market integration suggesting significant and puzzling forgone arbitrage opportunities, significant entry and mobility barriers, and highly personalized exchange. Widespread inefficiencies result from incomplete or unclear property rights, imperfect contract monitoring and enforcement, high transactions costs, and binding liquidity constraints. Such failures often motivate government intervention in markets, although interventions have often done more harm than good, either by distorting incentives or by creating public sector market power. The history of agricultural markets in developing countries reflects evolving thinking on the appropriate role for government in trying to address the inefficiencies created by incomplete institutional and physical infrastructure and imperfect competition. The emphasis in the

1960s and 1970s on government intervention to resolve market failures gave way in the 1980s to market-oriented liberalization to 'get prices right' and, more recently, to a focus on 'getting institutions right'.

Past approaches

Agricultural marketing of most major export and food commodities and of modern inputs such as fertilizer, machinery and hybrid seed was historically highly regulated by developing country governments into the 1980s, via input price controls and subsidies, oligopolistic input markets, monopsonistic produce marketing boards, pan-seasonal and pan-territorial administrative commodity pricing, oligopolistic processing industries, and fixed wholesale and retail prices. Commodity prices were generally set below market levels, implicitly taxing producers while subsidizing consumers. Marketing channels were typically very inefficient, with centralized storage and processing facilities and government-imposed grades and standards for product quality, although these were not always and everywhere enforced. Sometimes these inefficient systems provided satisfactory coordination of marketing channels, but that was by no means universal. Heavy government presence, especially pan-seasonal and pan-territorial producer pricing, and fixed retail pricing systems and bans on private commerce effectively eliminated most incentives for private arbitrage or investment in fixed capital by marketing intermediaries. Meanwhile, management by government fiat too often facilitated corruption, which often had a devastating long-run impact on economic governance. In addition to state-run marketing boards, producer marketing cooperatives were prevalent in developing countries at all levels of the marketing chain, ranging from credit unions through farmer cooperatives to wholesale-level cooperatives. Credit unions commonly accumulated funds for input purchase or served as intermediaries for government-subsidized credit programmes. Farmer marketing cooperatives typically facilitated bulk input procurement, price negotiation, and sharing of transportation costs. Wholesale cooperatives mainly assembled bulk commodity lots for sale into government processing and distribution channels. Cooperatives have often worked well in specialized production areas distant from major markets, and with homogenous production of not-soperishable commodities such as coffee. However, due to high administrative and coordination costs, free-rider problems and political interference, cooperative systems have not lived up to expectations in most developing countries, and many have collapsed. In contrast to the major export and domestic staple food crops, smaller-scale food commodities for domestic consumption, such as indigenous fruits and vegetables, have almost always operated on a free market basis, with little history of state intervention or price regulation. These markets are characterized by many cash, spot market transfers of product between intermediaries en route from producer to consumer, many small, nonspecialized and unorganized buyers and sellers, few if any grades or standards, one-onone (dyadic) price negotiations, poor market information systems, and mostly informal contracts, largely enforced through social networks. Such marketing channels depend disproportionately on rural periodic markets prevalent in most of the developing world, arguably the closest one ever gets to a true 'free market': free of government regulation, subsidies and taxes, and lacking public goods such as physical infrastructure, contract law, public market price information systems, or codified product grades and standards. Indeed, they have been termed the 'flea market economy' by Fafchamps and Minten.

The emerging problems of state agricultural market control

Given the inherent variability of agricultural production and the significance of agriculture in economic activity and general well-being in developing countries, price stabilization policies were long considered necessary for economic stability. However, a number of problems emerged. First, the fixing of commodity prices below market levels inevitably created a disincentive for agricultural producers. By the late 1970s, low producer prices had led to the stagnation of production and exports and to increased parallel market activity, including cross-border smuggling, in many developing countries, especially in those areas of Africa and Central America that were largely bypassed by the Green Revolution.

The second major problem was the fiscal and political sustainability of government agricultural market interventions. The inefficiencies of parastatal marketing boards, along with the repression of private market intermediation, led to unreliable supplies of consumer goods for politically important urban populations. Moreover, those inefficiencies, combined with the numerous subsidies and frequent corruption within government-controlled marketing channels, became too costly for central governments, which faced massive pressure from international donors in the 1980s and 1990s to trim expenditures and to eliminate price controls .

Economic liberalization: market relaxation and state compression

Market-oriented agricultural policy reforms were a centrepiece of economic liberalization in developing countries in the 1980s and 1990s, commonly within the context of broader structural adjustment programmes designed to restore fiscal and current account balance, to reduce or eliminate price distortions, and to facilitate efficient price transmission so as to stimulate investment and production. The new focus was on re-establishing a close correspondence between local and world market prices, so-called border parity pricing.

The withdrawal of the state from agricultural market intermediation, specifically price discovery, was seen as a necessary condition in getting prices right, itself a necessary condition for improving market efficiency and stimulating investment and productivity growth.

The market-oriented reforms typically implemented by developing country governments included, on the input side, the liberalization of land and labour markets, decontrol and de-licensing of input production, supply and distribution, removal of input subsidies and price controls, closure of loss-making credit schemes, liberalization of credit markets, and reform of agricultural extension. On the output markets side, reforms included commodity price liberalization, the removal of parastatal monopoly power and commodity movement restrictions, and reduction in tariffs and quotas on imports. The net result of these reforms typically turned on the balance between the procompetitive effects of reduced government interference in marketing operations what Lipton termed 'market relaxation' and the anti-competitive effects of reduction of public goods and services that underpin private market transactions what Lipton termed 'state compression'. Since the two phenomena were typically inextricable in agricultural liberalization initiatives, experiences varied markedly. The empirical evidence suggests that commodity prices generally increased after market reforms, often stimulating an increase in production, especially of export crops.

These price increases also facilitated the emergence of supermarket chains, exportoriented outgrower schemes and export processing zones, and a generalized stimulus to agro-industrialization in developing countries. Increased investment in the downstream marketing channel has transformed the orientation of many agricultural markets from raw commodity towards processed product markets, and with this increased investment came increased competition. In countries such as Chile, India and South Africa, private firms now play a leading role in development of improved seed varieties, producing and distributing inputs, post-harvest processing and modern retailing through supermarkets and restaurant chains. Both formal and informal traders entered agricultural commodity marketing channels as government controls fell away, from rural periodic markets all the way through urban retail markets.

However, market entry has tended to be limited to certain marketing niches not protected by capital, information or relationship barriers, with substantial bottlenecks in other areas such as inter-seasonal storage and motorized transportation. Neither widespread entry into market intermediation activities nor workably competitive markets emerged everywhere, let alone quickly. For example, because long-haul motorized transportation in rural markets tends to involve considerable sunk costs and some economies of scale due to poor road conditions and high vehicle maintenance costs, entry into this sector of the markets has often been limited after the removal of legal and policy barriers to entry. Meanwhile, the end of pan-seasonal and pan-territorial administrative pricing has brought increased price risk, with consequences for investment incentives facing both producers and market intermediaries. The elimination of input subsidies and removal of government monopsony power in crop marketing has also often led to reduced access to input financing and increased input prices. The withdrawal of parastatals from core input marketing activities created a void that the private sector often failed to fill due to underdeveloped physical communications, power and transport infrastructure, credit constraints and continued bureaucratic impediments that increased transactions costs for input suppliers. In addition, periodic state and donor-funded input programmes have often reduced profitability and frustrated private investments. Input credit schemes by processors have been used in the post-reform period in an attempt to overcome the low input use resulting from these access problems, for example in the cotton sectors of Mali and Uganda and horticultural export sectors of Kenya and Zimbabwe.

Although the level of reform implementation differed from country to country, in many cases reform was only partially implemented and policy reversals were common. In important food and export markets, liberalization efforts have been prolonged and incomplete, reflecting the difficulty in relinquishing government control in the face of uncertainty and political pressures to intervene in order to resolve perceived inequities or inefficiencies in market performance. For example, parastatals remain active in the West African cotton sector, the southern African maize sector has not been fully liberalized, and in Indonesia BULOG continues to operate amid private marketing companies. The ebb and flow of market-oriented reforms and the frequency with which governments have engaged in policy reversals has made it terribly difficult to tease out clear patterns in the impact of liberalization measures on the performance of agricultural markets in developing countries.

Post-structural adjustment market reforms

As the weaknesses of reformed agricultural markets in developing countries became evident, development agencies' and governments' focus began to shift from merely 'getting prices right' to 'getting institutions right' so as to address market failures arising from imperfect information, contract enforcement and property rights, and insufficient provision of public goods. Such reforms have used non-price measures in an attempt to develop the public and private institutions necessary for efficient market operations and to reduce transactions costs and business risk.

The post-structural adjustment era has also coincided with international market deregulation through the GATT and its successor, the WTO. Bilateral, regional and global trade agreements have reduced tariff and non-tariff barriers to cross-border flows of raw and processed agricultural commodities, and increased the openness of financial markets, leading to increased capital flow into developing countries, especially in the form of foreign direct investment. Where structural adjustment reforms had substantially reduced state control over input and output markets, trade and FDI liberalization has paved the way for major investment in post-harvest processing and retailing in developing countries since the 1990s. This 'new' capital investment differs from the structural adjustment era reforms in that whereas the focus previously was upstream, in the input, production, and wholesale sectors, more recent emphasis, especially in private investment, has tended to be downstream, in food processing, retail and restaurant markets. The exceptionally rapid diffusion of supermarkets in developing countries, in particular, has also been driven by improved coordination and communication technologies in addition to increased urbanization, lower prices of processed goods, increased per capita incomes in developing countries, as well as saturation and intense competition in foreign firms' home markets. In Latin America, for example, supermarkets currently account for 50-60 per cent of national food retail sale, compared with only 10-20 per cent in the 1980s. The rise of supermarket and restaurant chains has changed the fundamental structure and operations of agricultural markets significantly, directing far more market power downstream, often to chains wholly or partly owned by multinational corporations. Commodity procurement by retailers has become more centralized, with consolidated buying points at a regional, even global, level. It is not uncommon for a major supermarket chain located in three different countries to consolidate its procurement in a few large growers in just one of those countries. Global food chains have also established regional procurement nodes - for example, Walmart throughout Asia and Latin America - and in-country commodity procurement for regional firms such as the China Resource Enterprise has been centralized from individual store level to provincial systems. These structural shifts have increased contract farming and outgrower schemes between agro-industrial firms and farmers in developing countries, and production of non-staple foods has increased.

Increased foreign investment in agricultural markets in developing countries, however, has produced conflicting results. Increased industrialization of agricultural markets has fostered improved market efficiency and competitiveness, integration of formerly fragmented markets, product diversification through differentiation, and value addition and technology transfer. However, the rapid pace of structural change, with some developing countries accomplishing in a few years what developed countries accomplished over decades, has left limited room for adjustment by smaller, less wellinformed and poorly capitalized market actors to new ways of doing business. There is thus growing concern that market openness may lead to the replacement of traditional processors by oligopsonistic multinationals, accentuating the latent dualism of a modern, efficient marketing sector accessible only to those with adequate scale and capital, alongside a traditional, inefficient marketing channel to which the poor are effectively restricted. The tendency towards selection of a few medium- to large-scale firms or producers capable of delivering consistent quality product at large volumes has toughened competition for structurally inefficient producers, and seems to have led to some crowding out of smaller producers. Local informal wholesalers and retailers have found themselves having to compete with bigger firms, both for the more efficient producers offering consistent product quality and throughput volumes, and for consumers seeking more services. The emergence of big, concentrated downstream private marketing intermediaries could also potentially lead, once again, to non-competitive agricultural marketing channels, effectively replacing government with private market power.

Increased contract farming, while offering significant potential for smaller growers in the form of guaranteed markets and prices for their produce often coupled with input credit and extension service, has evidently also reduced farmer bargaining power in negotiating contract conditions. These negotiations now take place bilaterally, between individual farmers and the large contracting firm, rather than via collective bargaining by farmer associations with government parastatals.

Conclusion

Agricultural markets play a crucial role in the process of economic development. Yet, by virtue of the spatial dispersion of producers and consumers, the temporal lags between input application and harvest, the variable perishability and storability of commodities, and the political sensitivity of basic food staples, agricultural markets are prone to high transactions costs, significant risks and frequent government interference. The relative power of developing country governments and private domestic or multinational firms in agricultural markets has varied over time. But the fundamental functions of input and output distribution, post-harvest processing and storage, as well as the persistent challenges of liquidity constraints, contract enforcement and imperfect information, have characterized agricultural markets in developing countries under all forms of organization.

Chapter 5

Organic Farming: Wheat Production and Marketing

Introduction

Wheat is the most commonly grown cereal in Australian organic farming systems. It is adapted to a range of climatic and soil conditions so it suits many of the mixed farming areas in Victoria. Organic wheat production requires attention to soil fertility, rotation, agronomy, and grain storage to ensure product quality and marketability. Cereals comprise the largest export volumes of any certified organic category, growing from 252 tonnes in 1999 to over 1,297 tonnes exported in 2003. Premium prices can be expected for organic wheat and these reflect quality parameters that are similar to conventional wheat. There are approximately 1,511 certified organic farms in Australia, and 14% or 212 of these produce cereal crops.

Production requirements

Current organic wheat production in Victoria is concentrated in the Wimmera and north central regions with smaller quantities being produced in the north east. Wheat is best suited to areas where annual rainfall is between 300-600 mm. Growing season rainfall is critical to achieve good establishment, tillering and grain filling.

Soil management

The National Standard for Organic and Bio-dynamic Produce

provides general principles for the management of soil in an organic farming system.

i. Healthy soil is the prerequisite for healthy plants, animals and products. With organic farming, the care of a living soil and consequently the maintenance or improvement of soil structure, fertility and nutrient cycling, is fundamental to all measures adopted.

ii. Sufficient organic material should be regenerated and or returned to the soil to improve, or at least maintain, humus levels. Conservation and recycling of nutrients is a major feature of any organic farming system.

The basis of a successful organic grain crop is the fertility of the soil in which it is grown. Soil fertility is based on the physical, biological and chemical components of the soil environment. Physical soil fertility in an organic farming system can be promoted by:

- Having an adequate supply of organic matter through green manuring and pasture phases,
- Having good soil structure through minimising cultivation,
- Having moisture retention but also good drainage,
- Having sufficient gas exchange around the root zone, and
- Warmth and moisture at the appropriate time.

Biological fertility refers to the diversity and activity of soil organisms. Soil organisms play a fundamental role in recycling nutrients for plant growth. The soil environment that is most beneficial for these organisms to operate has:

- Plenty of oxygen (needed for aerobic microbes),
- A neutral pH, and
- Organic matter that contains sufficient levels of nitrogen.

Chemical fertility refers to the level of available nutrients required for plant growth. Wheat has a requirement for phosphorus, nitrogen and potassium. The majority of Australian soils are deficient in phosphorus with the amount of phosphorus in the soil depending on the parent material, the extent of weathering, how much has been lost through leaching and the level of organic matter. Options that are available to organic producers to ensure adequate phosphorus supply for crop growth include:

- Maintain soil pH between 5.5 and 6.5 (CaCl2) to achieve maximum phosphorus availability,
- Encourage biological activity with sufficient high quality organic matter *Mycorrhizae* fungi can form symbiotic relationships with plant roots to facilitate phosphorus supply, and some bacterial species can solubilise phosphorus for plant uptake,
- Apply allowable phosphorus inputs (based on a demonstrated need) such as reactive phosphate rock and avian deposits. Generally, reactive phosphate rock is effective as a source of phosphorus in areas that have an annual rainfall of at least 750mm and acidic soils.

In organic farming systems the supply of nitrogen for plant growth comes primarily from the fixation of atmospheric nitrogen via the legume *rhizobia* symbiosis. This can occur during a pasture phase, or by growing a legumebased green manure crop that is returned to the soil. Subterranean clover and lucerne provide the highest additions of nitrogen to the soil. Potassium is also essential for crop growth and is linked to both phosphorus and nitrogen supply. Potassium deficiency can be a problem on lighter textured soils but is not considered a widespread problem in cropping systems. It is important to monitor soil health regularly through appropriate testing to understand nutrient supply, biological and physical health.

Rotation

In organic farming systems wheat is grown in rotation with

pasture or legume phases. Wheat can be grown directly after a pasture phase when soil fertility is maximised providing that adequate management of grass weeds has occurred. Grass weeds can compete vigorously with wheat and can be a source of disease and seed contamination. A break crop such as canola, followed by wheat, is useful to avoid potential disease problems in wheat after a pasture phase. Research has shown that decomposing canola stubble can provide a bio-fumigation effect in soil, decreasing the potential for common wheat diseases. However, canola is a 'nutrient hungry' crop and in an organic system, growing wheat after canola may not be the most productive rotation option.

Weed management

Organic farming systems rely on an integrated approach to weed management, using a range of tools to reduce the impact of weeds in both pasture and crop. The grass weeds, typically annual ryegrass (*Lolium rigidum*, Gaudin) and wild oats (*Avena fatua* L.) are the most important weed species that compete with organic wheat. Management to reduce the seed bank of weed species prior to wheat production has to occur during the pasture phase. A range of options exist for producers to manage weed species in pastures:

- Strategic heavy grazing of pasture to prevent seed set in late spring,
- Cutting hay or silage,
- Green manuring,
- Mowing, and
- Growing a forage break crop between the pasture and crop phases.

Strategies also exist for weed management during the crop year, such as delayed sowing and using competitive cultivars, but these should be considered in conjunction with sound pasture management practices.

- **Competitive cultivar:** choose a cultivar that has good early vigour, a tall growth habit and wide leaves. Some of this information can be obtained in the crop sowing guides.
- **Clean seed:** ensure that wheat seed is free of weed seeds.
- **Delayed sowing:** sowing can be delayed in order to achieve a weed germination that can then be cultivated prior to sowing. Delayed sowing can often result in reduced yield.
- **Autumn tickle:** this light cultivation can stimulate ryegrass germination so that these seedlings can be cultivated prior to sowing.
- **Seeding rate:** this can be increased to reduce the competitive ability of grass weed species

Harvest and grain storage

Organic wheat is harvested in the same manner as conventional wheat. Care needs to be taken to ensure that the harvest sample is as clean as possible of weed seeds and other material, as penalties apply for foreign material in cereal grain. Harvesting equipment that can collect weed seeds through the seconds bin allows for more flexibility in the harvesting process and better weed management. Wheat grain should be harvested at or below the receival limits for moisture; this is usually 12.5% for wheat. Seed cleaning services are available but these will reduce the gross margin of the organic crop. Many organic producers invest in sealed silo technology to store their grain on-farm. This provides flexibility in the marketing of organic grain, gives producers the opportunity to store seed for subsequent years and to assist in drought management by having grain for animal feed. Producers can consult the NSW Agriculture Agfact P3.5.1 On-farm Storage of Organic Grain for further information.

Marketing requirements

Quality

Protein content is critical for export and domestic markets.

For export markets, most wheat is required to be above 12% protein. This is because many European countries have high duty charges for wheat with a lower protein content. It is important to have a good idea of the protein level of wheat grown in your region, as this will affect marketing decisions. For example, the majority of wheat grown in north east Victoria achieves less than 11% protein, whilst in the Wimmera and Mallee regions, higher protein levels can be achieved.

There is emerging interest in some Asian markets for cereal grain for the production of beverages and these may provide future market potential for lower protein content wheats. Some domestic markets require lower protein wheat, but the domestic market is limited and organic stock feed may be the only alternative if wheat is not exported.

Other important quality parameters for some markets include screenings, grain size and variety. The organic standards are similar to the conventional production standards, although this does depend on supply and can be more flexible in some years.

Price

Organic wheat prices vary considerably depending on the market and the quality protein content, screenings, grain size, variety. Premiums vary depending on the season and can vary from zero (occurs rarely) to 100%. In most years, markets offer a premium of 30 - 50% above the conventional price.

Organic prices for wheat do not vary as greatly as the conventional market. This may be due to many producers growing on contracts. Generally the only assured markets for organic wheat with high prices are for the high protein (>14%) organic wheat grain which can be exported. Other markets vary more seasonally (ie. through supply) and as countries implement and change tariff rates. Freight charges vary depending on the market and can be included as a delivered price for some companies, whereas others pay extra depending on where the receival station is.

Chapter 6

The Role and Importance of Branding in Agricultural Marketing

A branding strategy is often employed in the marketing of manufactured or processed food products but many other food products have comparatively lower levels of branding. At the same time there are frequent calls to utilise branding as a marketing strategy for New Zealand's export products. The branding literature to date does not seem to include any studies detailing the validity of branding for such products. In this study the theoretical relationship between the consumer's requirement for branded products and the benefits to producers from branding are explored. Using a simple model developed from a theoretical framework, three hypotheses are tested using data collected from Christchurch supermarkets. The results provide some support for the ability of the model to predict the level of labelling used. However, the results did not show that labelling attracted a price premium for agricultural or horticultural food products.

Introduction

Branding strategies have become an accepted part of marketing activity and it is the norm for manufactured and processed food products to be offered to consumers as branded products. However, as any vigilant consumer would have noticed, there are still a wide range of food products that remain unbranded.

Food products such as meat and horticultural products are often relatively unprocessed and do not have clear brands associated with producers or suppliers. It has become common to find generic brands associated with particular supply regions or varieties of products, but these are normally developed by groups of suppliers, or are merely used as labels to identify particular attributes of the products. In attempting to explore such issues it is often assumed that the lack of such activity is a result of the small firms that exist in the industry, or simply because of the lack of marketing knowledge amongst producers. It appears that an omission from the branding literature is a basic analysis detailing the role of branding strategies in the marketing of these products. Although the lack of branding strategies for such products has been commented on by recent researchers work in this area is limited. In considering this problem it becomes necessary to analyse the most general conditions in which branded products might be used as a part of a successful marketing strategy. This involves understanding both the reasons why consumers might value brands, and the conditions under which producers would find it profitable to invest in brand development.

In this paper a simple model of consumer behaviour is adapted to the information environment associated with purchasing decisions, and a theoretical framework is developed to indicate the conditions under which brand development is likely to be successful. This model is used to test some basic hypotheses about the extent and nature of branding in the market for selected horticultural products.

The Branding Literature

The branding literature can be separated into normative and positive streams. The normative stream of literature concentrates on the processes involved with developing a successful brand. More specifically the normative approach develops definitions of brands, investigates the elements or components of brands, suggests how to successfully name a brand, and categorises different types of brands. Examples of this type of literature are articles by Crimmins, and Aaker. The basic objective of this literature is to provide firms with the steps or directions for implementation of branding strategies. This literature has little relevance to gaining an understanding of the validity of branding agricultural and horticultural food products, and consequently it is not investigated any further because it does not help identify the conditions under which we might expect to see branding.

The positive stream of literature has two components, one of which provides descriptions of the purpose of branding products the second component creates a linkage between consumer behaviour and branding literature. The latter more explicitly examines the value of a brand in the consumers' decision making process.

There has been little consideration of agricultural and horticultural products in the branding literature. However, one author who has attempted to bridge the gap between agricultural products and main stream marketing theory is Bowbrick. Within agricultural and horticultural products branding seems to include identifying a product with various types of labels (e.g. region of origin, variety to differentiate products. Bowbrick acknowledges this characteristic and suggests that a brand is a *label* attached to products from a specific manufacturer, distributor, country of origin, or retailer with the aim being to "convey information on, or persuade the consumer about; the quality, reliability, social status, value for money or safety of a purchase".

In this study the wider definition of branding is used to describe how products are differentiated. Some common examples of labels and brands found within the marketplace are: consumer brands, retailer brands, supplier labels, region of origin labelling, and varietal labelling. These types of labels and the situations in which producers or sellers use them will be discussed later. In the next section a framework will be developed to show the situations in which consumers require a label to assist their purchase decision.

The Role and Importance of Labelling in Decision Making

A product provides an array of cues that a consumer uses as

the basis for making judgements about which product they will purchase. Consumers form a composite judgement about which product to purchase by going through a process in which the consumer identifies, evaluates, and integrates some or all of the various items of information associated with the product. The cues that consumers use when making purchase decisions have been classified as intrinsic or extrinsic cues. Intrinsic cues are those cues which if changed would change the physical product itself e.g. taste, nutrition content, size, shape, and colour of a product). Extrinsic cues refer not to the physical product itself, but to other cues provided e.g. price, store image, label, advertising. The important distinction to note is that cues of an extrinsic nature can be supplied by either the producer or the seller, whilst the intrinsic cues are determined by the product itself. In order to determine the importance of providing a label on an agricultural or horticultural product (i.e. providing an extrinsic cue), we need to focus upon those product cues of an intrinsic nature which are of more importance to consumers in their initial assessment of the desirability of a product. Intrinsic cues pose further problems for consumers as they can be classified as either hidden intrinsic cues or revealed intrinsic cues. Hidden intrinsic cues are those product attributes which cannot easily be physically identified by the consumer before purchase, (e.g. the flavour or taste of the product, or the durability and reliability of a product). Revealed intrinsic cues include those product attributes which the consumer can identify and assess visually or physically, e.g. the shape, size and colour of a product.

The discussion to this point has suggested that consumers form judgements about the desirability of products using a combination of extrinsic, revealed intrinsic and hidden intrinsic cues. The combination of cues used depends on which product attributes are important to a consumer in making a purchase decision. Howard and Sheth suggested that choice among product category alternatives can be viewed as a hierarchical process. Hierarchical processing describes how a consumer compares groups of alternatives and subsequently eliminates products in order to reduce the choice set. Before choice among product alternatives can take place, consumers search for potential products to include in their final choice set. During this search, a consumer is looking for specific attributes to use in forming a judgement about the desirability of a product. Whether these important attributes are hidden or revealed becomes important to the consumer during this search. If the important cue to a consumer is revealed (e.g. a consumer wants a large red apple for display purposes and is not concerned with the taste of the apple) then they can physically select products for their final choice set. The consumer will subsequently eliminate those products which do not meet their final selection criteria by physical assessment. However if the important cue for a product was hidden, then the consumer will have difficulty assessing product attributes which are consistent with their final selection criteria, and therefore may experience difficulty finding suitable candidates to include within the choice set. To aid consumers in their search for the desired bundle of attributes, the seller can make an extrinsic cue available to act as a proxy for the important hidden cues. Consequently, consumers can make judgements about important hidden cues, and successfully eliminate those undesirable products from their choice sets. For example, as an indicator of the different taste characteristics different varieties of apples possess, retailers provide an extrinsic cue in the form of a variety label. Consumers subsequently use this cue to select the variety of apple that has the taste characteristics which correspond to their preference. This discussion has suggested that a label (an extrinsic cue) becomes relevant during consumer search when the important attribute of the particular product is a hidden intrinsic cue, as the schematic below shows.

When the important attribute a consumer is looking for is revealed the consumer can physically assess the product and therefore little emphasis is placed on extrinsic cues in making a purchase decision. It has been suggested that the value to consumers of attaching a label to a product is reduced when the product attribute of interest is revealed. However, the label does provide significant value to consumers when the important product attribute is a hidden intrinsic cue. It is now appropriate to look at the ability of producers or sellers to label agricultural or horticultural products, and their ability to ensure that the label provides consistent cues.

Labelling of Agricultural and Horticultural Products

The existence of labelling within the market place can be described as an equilibrium between the consumer requiring it and the supplier being able to provide the appropriate product to be labelled and recoup any costs associated with the labelling. A label has the ability to act as a proxy for quality which can be interpreted to mean that any product labelled should be of a consistent quality. The product attributes which a label represents must be consistent within a particular product line, so consumers can link a label with a product's desirability. This 'consistency' factor poses some problems for labellers of agricultural and horticultural products. Agricultural and horticultural products are the result of a biological growing process and consequently usually exhibit an element of variability between product attributes within a product line. This is due to the climatic, environmental and management differences which each product may be subjected to throughout the growing process. Contrasting these products with the consistently standardised form of manufactured or processed products, it would seem appropriate to examine the ability of producers or sellers to create consistency of attributes desired by consumers within agricultural or horticultural products.

As can be seen from the above, agricultural and horticultural products are characterised by relatively high levels of biological variability within product attributes. Thus any attempt to label a product must involve consideration of how much control can be exerted over various product attributes either during production or post production to generate the consistency within certain product attributes. This is essential if consumers are to generate positive connotations for the attached label. Some attempts at gaining this product consistency have become standard for many agricultural and horticultural industries. For example, selecting or grading methods are common. Examples within industry are grading apples by size, grading meat by weight and fat content, and wool by average diameter of wool fibres. However the level of consistency gained through this type of selection must also be traded off with economic considerations of market returns for different types of product. Typically there are some more financially attractive grades than others. However just strictly grading product to fit the attractive market specifications often results in lower overall average prices, as the balance of the product only falls into the lowest value grades. Therefore, due to the economic viability of such grading, the distribution of variability is not minimised in many instances. The other way in which consistency of product attributes has been maintained within various product categories is by controlling genetic material so that biological attributes can be controlled through genetic selection, or by increasing control of the production process. The poultry and pork industry are examples of industries within which producers have reduced biological variability in the associated products by being able to closely control the feeding, living environment and genetic material of their animals. Such control by a producer is valuable when the producer can physically differentiate the product from others with respect to the key attributes consumers look for in that particular product.

Where the consistency of an important attribute can be controlled we would expect the product to be labelled accordingly. For example, when differences in genetic make up of products consistently affects the products attributes (e.g. taste) we would expect to see variety labelling present, or when the country of origin consistently affects the nature of a product's attributes, we would expect to see a country of origin label on the product. Where particular product attributes are consistently provided by the supplier, retailer or seller, one could expect to see supplier label or retail and consumer brands. At the other extreme where sellers or producers cannot economically control the variability of important attributes within products, it is expected that these products will be unlabelled.

Therefore , it can be suggested that labelling a product can be related to the amount of control a producer or seller has over the consistency of particular product attributes. There would seem to be a range of levels of control over biological variability. A high level of control exists where sellers or producers have control over the important attributes so the product can be differentiated from similar products consistently and economically, either through controlling the biological production process, or through product management practices such as washing or selection (i.e. variation between product attributes is low). A low level of control exists where producers or sellers cannot economically control the variability of important attributes within products (i.e. large variations between product attributes).

Furthermore, we would expect the labelled products within a product class to fetch higher returns to recoup the associated costs of standardising product attributes as well as the cost of physically labelling the product. It has been suggested that consumers would be prepared to pay a price premium for those products which are difficult to inspect and too expensive to sample. Although many agricultural and horticultural products cannot be considered too expensive to sample, many are difficult to inspect. Where inspection is difficult consumer search costs are high. Labelling can reduce these search costs. Where producers have extra costs of labelling to retrieve, and consumers have high search costs, it would seem likely that labelled products would attract price premiums. This framework can be illustrated with a simple model.

A Model of Brand Development

The model is a combination of the ability of consumers to assess these important product attributes given that the attributes can either be hidden or revealed and the producer's ability to manage biological variability within important product attributes. Depending whether the important cue is revealed or hidden, and to what extent producers can control variability within product attributes, the model can be used to predict the type of labelling observed on a particular product.

In cases where the important intrinsic cues are revealed and a single producer has little or no ability to control biological variability of the important product attributes, we would expect to see no labelling. For those products which have important hidden intrinsic cues and where producers have little ability to control biological variability, country of origin or variety labels may be used. Country of origin labels may be used for those products where the region of production consistently affects product attributes, or variety labels may be used for those products which consistently differ due to the genetic make up of the product.

CUES

In those cases where the important attributes are revealed and the important product characteristics are controllable by the producer, a label will not be offered to consumers. However, as the producer is able to control the biological variability of important product attributes, or can use management practices to consistently differentiate products, a supplier label may be provided which is important to buyers within trade channels. Given that remote trading through auctions is a characteristic of the exchange mechanism which many biological products initially pass through, a label identifying the products producer becomes important to remote buyers. The remote buyers involved with the trade will be able to link a supplier label with product quality judgements.

Finally, where the important attribute is a hidden intrinsic cue and producers have a high level of ability to control the biological variability within important product attributes or use management practices to consistently differentiate their product from others, it is expected that these products will be labelled with consumer brands. In the case where the important intrinsic cue is hidden, and the seller is providing the management practice to consistently differentiate a product, it is expected that these products will be labelled as retailer brands. We now have a basis for formulating three testable hypotheses.

Hypotheses

Using the model of brand development and from the previous discussions we can now state three simple testable hypotheses:

1. When a product has some hidden intrinsic cues which are of importance in consumer decision making, labelling

will be provided by producers or sellers.

2. When low control over the biological variability of important attributes exists, and the intrinsic cues are revealed, it is expected that no labelling will be provided by producers or sellers.

3. To recoup economic costs from the processes involved with labelling a product, we expect to see a premium price charged for those products labelled within their product category.

Methodology and Results

To test the model of brand development and the three related hypotheses, data were collected from Christchurch supermarkets. Twenty one commonly purchased fruit and vegetable products were chosen. For each of these products, the presence of various intrinsic and extrinsic cues were recorded. To determine what product attributes are important to consumers for each product, supermarket produce managers were consulted. Using these data, the important product attributes were classified as either hidden or revealed intrinsic cues. The ability of producers or sellers to consistently control biological variability within the important product attributes for each product was determined by an agricultural product specialist. The predominant type of labelling used for each product was also recorded.

Relationship Between Cues Present and Labelling

The position in the model where each product is placed according to the observed combination of revealed hidden intrinsic cues and the level of control producers have over the biological variability of the product. For those products which are in capital print the model correctly predicted the type of labelling used. It can be seen that the model was most successful for predicting the level of labelling for products with low levels of producer control over biological variability. Where control is low it is difficult to ensure product consistency. In this situation no label will be used, or where some attribute of a product can be consistently differentiated from others on the basis of the product's genetic make up or region of origin, a variety or region of origin label will be used.

As suggested in development of the theoretical framework, where a producer has a low level of control over biological variability and the intrinsic cue is revealed, no label will be used.

This was the case for eight of the nine products falling in this category. Also of note is that all of these eight correctly predicted products are vegetables. Given that consumers can inspect these products for themselves to search for freshness, colour and size attributes of the products, then it is unlikely that a label will provide the consumer with any extra information which will be of value to them in their search activities.

Kiwifruit were predicted to have no label based on low control over the revealed intrinsic cue of ripeness. The predominant type of labelling used was actually the "New Zealand Kiwifruit" place of origin label. This is a reflection of the marketing activities of the NZKMB and was observed only because the majority of kiwifruit observed were fruit prepared for export that didn't make it to overseas markets. Our model would suggest that this labelling is an unnecessary addition to costs for produce sold on the domestic market. As consumers are only interested in the level of ripeness they are able to assess the product characteristics for themselves. In overseas markets the competition from kiwifruit from other countries may contribute to the desire to label the product with New Zealand origin. However, in the domestic market where there is no competition from overseas products the label would appear to be a waste of resources.

Where there is low control over the biological variability of a product, and the important intrinsic cues are hidden, the model correctly predicted the level of labelling for five of the seven products in that category. Products in this category are mostly fruits. For these products taste was the most important product attribute. Given that taste is most easily controlled between rather than within varieties, it appears logical to use a variety label so as to reduce consumer search costs. For grapes and mandarins a variety or place of origin label was predicted, but in our observations these products predominantly had no label. This seems unusual as the attribute of importance to consumers is taste. It appears that the use of variety or place of origin labels would be logical for these products, as this would indicate taste differences between products. This may be a missed opportunity on the part of retailers to reduce consumer search costs. Alternatively, it may be the case that consumers don't recognise differences in the taste attributes of different varieties and sources of grapes and mandarins, and therefore producers or sellers cannot benefit.

Where the products had revealed intrinsic cues and there was high control over the biological variability of the product, the model did not correctly predict the level of branding for any of the products. For this category of products the use of a supplier label was predicted. However, avocado had no label, bananas were labelled with consumer brands, and lettuce and potatoes had predominantly variety labels. This suggests that avocado suppliers are potentially missing an opportunity to label their product, given that they have the ability to control the variability in the ripeness of the product, and hence have the ability to deliver a consistent product. With this being the case, the potential for selling a supplier labelled product in an effort to gain greater market share exists. Bananas are labelled with brand names. These multinational brands could also be considered as supplier labels. There is a weakness in the model here, given that there is some ambiguity in distinguishing between supplier labels and brand names. Another problem is that the data was collected at the retail level, so there was little chance of observing supplier labels used at the trade level.

Lettuce and potatoes had variety labels, rather than the supplier labels predicted by the model. It should be noted that for potatoes there was some supplier labelling used, but variety labels predominated. This is most likely a result of the differences in product characteristics between varieties that consumers are aware of. Hence, the variety label is of most value in reducing search costs, so as to get the desired product attributes, and the supplier label is of secondary importance in providing a cue with regard to the consistency of the product attributes. Lettuce had equal proportions of variety labels and brand names. This appears to be a reflection of the greater range of lettuce varieties which have become available recently, as well as the sale of convenience oriented consumer packs of lettuce which present opportunities to label the product with a consumer brand.

Where there are hidden intrinsic cues and the producer has high control over biological variability, the model predicts that a brand name will be used. The only observation to fall into this category was sprouts. For this product consumer branding was the predominant form of labelling used. This reflects the producer's ability to deliver a consistent tasting product by controlling the growing conditions, and the fact that the majority of sprouts are sold in packages. This seems to be consistent with our theory as an extrinsic cue (i.e. consumer label) has been provided where the important attribute (i.e. taste) is hidden.

In summary, the model is most capable of correctly predicting the level of labelling used when there is low producer control over biological variability of the product. The observations indicate that for most vegetables where freshness, colour and size are the important attributes for consumers, and which the consumer can physically assess, no label will be used. For most fruits where taste is the important attribute and it can't be assessed pre-purchase, a variety label is used. Prediction by the model for products where control over biological variability is high has proven more difficult.

Price Effects of Labelling

Other data were collected on the presence of various cues and price. These data were used to test hypothesis three, that a premium price would be charged for those products labelled within their product category. To test this, a regression was carried out with price as the dependent variable. The price variable was calculated as the percentage deviation from the mean price for each product. The independent variables used were those variables for which data were collected from the supermarkets. The variables used in the regression were dummy variables, representing the presence of the particular variable being considered. The independent variables included, and their regression coefficients.

The regression results for all products indicate that there is a significant correlation between the store and the price of the product. This would seem logical, given that stores differentiate themselves on the basis of price and quality. The only other significant results for all products were for the display methods. All of the types of labels were found to have highly insignificant influences on the price of products. This does not support hypothesis three. Better results were found by categorising the products into fruit and vegetables. The regression results for these categories. For fruit, variety and place of origin labels were found to have statistically significant influences on the product price. This intuitively appealing given the earlier discussion in relation to important attributes to consumers. Where taste is the important attribute for fruit products (e.g. oranges, grapefruit) the variety or place of origin provides a means to classify products which taste different. For example, it is commonly believed that Australian oranges are juicier and have better flavour because they get more sunshine than New Zealand oranges. For this reason, identification of the variety or region of origin of the product assists the consumer in their search and so they are possibly willing to pay more for a product that more closely satisfies their desires.

For vegetables, the store has a significant influence on the price. The only other significant variable is the visibility of the product within packaging. This would seem reasonable, given that the majority of vegetables have important attributes that are revealed intrinsic cues. Where the product is packaged, the consumer is likely to buy those products which they have been able to inspect for themselves. For example, where potatoes are packaged in sealed paper bags the consumer is unable to assess the greenness and dirtiness of the potatoes. However, where they are in plastic bags the consumer is able to assess these attributes for themselves. Because of this they may be willing to pay more for a product that meets their personal quality standards than for a product which they cannot assess. For vegetables the types of labels all have insignificant influences on price. This is likely to be due to that fact that the important attributes of vegetable products are revealed intrinsic cues. As such, a brand provides no extra information to the consumer, and consequently they are unwilling to pay more for a branded product than for one that is the same but unbranded.

Overall, the regression results provide little support for hypothesis 3. Labelling does not appear to result in a premium price for fruit and vegetable products. While it was expected that the additional costs involved in labelling products (especially for brand names), would necessitate the charging of a price premium to cover the extra expense, the data collected does not provide support. Producers and suppliers may use brands to gain market share, rather than simply a price premium. The value of the brand to the consumer may be in the reduced search costs arising from the ability to identify a known label and purchase a consistent product each time they go to the supermarket. As such, the seller does not gain higher revenue through a price premium, but possibly gains an increase in market share resulting in greater revenue in the long run.

Conclusions

The aim of this study was to assess the validity of branding and labelling from the perspective's of producers and consumers. From the consumer's perspective, in their search activities a label is not required for attributes which have revealed intrinsic cues. Where the important attribute is a hidden intrinsic cue, a label provides the consumer with information to reduce their search costs. From the perspective of producers, the value of labelling is in reducing the search costs of consumers, so as to increase market share and in some situations to obtain a price premium. For products where labelling does not assist consumer search, then the producer will only increase costs, without a corresponding increase in revenue, by labelling such products.

Therefore the low observed level of labelling and branding

of agricultural and horticultural products appears to be justifiable where the important product attributes have revealed intrinsic cues and where producers have a low degree of control over biological variability. This was the case for most vegetables, where freshness, size and colour were the important attributes. For products where the important attributes are hidden intrinsic cues, use of variety and place of origin labels enables consumers to find the product with the attributes they prefer. For a number of fruits, where taste is the most important attribute, country of origin and variety labelling is predominantly used. For producers this is an easy, low cost means to reduce consumer search costs and was found to have a significant positive price effect for fruit.

Where high control of biological variability and hidden intrinsic cues are present the use of a consumer brand is expected. This was observed for sprouts, but for most products producers do not have high control over the biological variability of hidden intrinsic cues. As such, the relatively low level of use of brands in agricultural and horticultural marketing is explained by the biologically variable nature of production, and the consequent inability of producers to deliver a product which is consistent with respect to the attributes of importance to consumers. Future research in this area would be improved through the development of a measure of biological variability based on objective measurements of product characteristics. Also, greater insight into the role and importance of branding in agricultural marketing may be gained by including observations on a wider range of products, such as meat, eggs and dairy products.

Chapter 6

Agricultural Commodity Markets in India: Policy issues for Growth

Strengthening institutions in spot and derivative markets for commodities is a necessary ingredient of the liberalisation process in agriculture, and can impact upon the lives of millions. In this paper, we describe the existing market design prevalent on both the spot and the futures markets. We show some evidence on the role played by the nascent futures markets in price discovery. We document the problems of both the spot and the futures markets. We offer three policy proposals: using reference rates for strengthening transparency, exploring a greater role for cash settlement, and treating warehouse receipts as securities.

The importance of the commodity markets

As has been typical of the growth process in all countries, the importance of agriculture in the Indian economy has dropped steadily over the last two decades. Agriculture now accounts for 23% of GDP, as compared with the level of 50% in 1947. At the same time, 23% is a large fraction of GDP, by world standards. The overall average of 23% masks important inter-state differences. Roughly 60% of India's households depend on agriculture. This suggests that institutional development, which improves the liquidity and efficiency of commodity markets, would impact upon a large fraction of India's population. Agricultural markets have been in existence in India for centuries, and perhaps for millenia. At the simplest, each neighbourhood had its own 'designated' location, where producers and buyers met in order to engage in trade, in an institutional vacuum. The wholesale spot market for agricultural commodities, as seen today, very much reflects this history. From a financial sector perspective, the weak institutions of the commodity markets are sharply reminiscent of the state of securities markets in India prior to 1993.

After independence, many major policy decisions adversely affected agricultural commodities markets. The first was the government's policy of defining "primary commodities" for which the government would set a "minimum support price". The farmer had the choice of selling to the government at a price higher than the market price if the market price dropped below the MSP for that commodity. Over the years, MSPs have risen dramatically, so that the 'minimum support price' is no longer an exigency to be invoked by farmers under events when market prices have collapsed. Instead, the MSP is often higher than the market price, and the MSP has become a highly inefficient subsidy. Large scale public sector procurement and storage has led to a shriveling of the private sector in the trade, storage and transportation of commodities.

The second key event was the banning of futures markets, which took place in the sixties. The formal agricultural commodities markets have been restricted to localised wholesale markets, while the derivatives markets largely went underground. The ban on fowards trading in agricultural commodities was removed in the seventies, but the new futures markets never regained the levels of liquidity that they had enjoyed earlier.

These restrictive policies were accompanied by many other aspects of intervention, which included barriers upon movement of agricultural goods, an extensive system of state intervention for agricultural inputs, etc. These add up to a situation where the agricultural sector is now perhaps the most repressed sector of the Indian economy. There is a considerable consensus amongst economists that this policy framework has many weaknesses. It imposes considerable direct costs upon the government, and has led to a suboptimal resource allocation.

In a more market-driven agricultural sector, the spot and derivatives markets would be central, both in terms of direct transactions and in terms of the use of prices for information processing and making production decisions. The questions that naturally arise in debates about agricultural liberalisation concern 'who' in the country will maintain the buffer stocks which are currently maintained by government, how price fluctuations will be smoothed, how will farmers not be vulnerable to sharp falls in prices, how farmers will make sowing decisions with highly uncertain future prices, etc. Commodity futures markets could play a major role in addressing each of these questions.

In recent years, there has been heightened interest amongst policy makers about the importance of commodity futures markets, in the process of liberalisation of agriculture. For example, in 2000, there was a World Bank project on starting an exchange to trade futures on cotton, an economically significant commodity. More significantly, in early 2002, the government of India announced that it would step away from the rigid price and production controls it exercised on the sugar industry with the caveat that it would be done "once there were futures markets available to economic agents for hedging market price risk." Now that this political consensus in favour of active commodity futures markets has been established, there is an urgent need for skills and institutional capacity in building and operating modern financial markets infrastructure in these areas.

The spot and derivative markets for agricultural commodities have yet to develop a sophisticated institutional capacity. Over the last decade, the securities markets have experienced revolutionary changes, with the creation of new institutions Shah and Thomas the utilisation of cutting edge technology to give transparency and low costs, opening up to nationwide participation, etc.

In this paper, we argue that the securities markets are highly relevant in thinking about reforms to the commodity market.

There may be many opportunities to utilise the knowledge, technology and institutional capacity that is present on the securities markets, to help obtain a comparable transformation on the commodity markets. If this comes about, it constitutes a channel through which the securities markets could have an impact upon the lives of a very large number of people in India.

This paper seeks to shed some light upon the functioning of spot and derivative markets for commodities in India today. We seek to describe the institutional mechanisms in use today, to summarise some recent research about the nature of price discovery, and to offer some new ideas for public policy. The remainder of this paper is organised as follows describes the existing market design of the spot market, as it prevails across many products in the country addresses the futures market. In particular shows some recent research about price discovery in one market (the castorseed market), which is a useful illustration about the dual role of the spot and futures market under Indian conditions today gives a detailed description of one market the jaggery futures market, as a case study of the existing market design. Finally, Section 4 offers some ideas on current policy issues.

Spot market design

All agricultural commodities in India trade in wholesale markets or mandis where the price of the commodity is set. If it is a principal commodity and the market determined price is below a threshold the trader has to take delivery at the MSP. In return, the trader is compensated by the mandi which is in turn, compensated by the government. Some of the principal crops are rice, wheat, pulses, oilseeds, cotton and sugarcane. Today, there are approximately 25 agricultural commodities for which the government of India still sets a "minimum support price".

Agricultural commodity markets in India started as areas specific to limited geographical locations where producers and buyers collected to trade their goods. Today's markets are basically unchanged in comparison. Their structure is very reminiscent of the structure of the Indian equity markets before

1995 they are largely restricted to local fluctuations in demand and supply, which is also reflected in the local price of the commodity. Different regions in the country have different prices for the same commodities: the apparent presence of arbitrage could be the results of either a lack of good and cheap transportation infrastructure or of problems with the structure and design of the the market.

Mandis are set up only with the permission of state governments. Each state has a state agriculture marketing boards. These, in turn, set up mandi boards at the level of a district. It is the mandi board that evaluates proposals to set up new mandis and permits the creation of a mandi. Initially, mandis were set up only at the level of a specific district. But their numbers have been rapidly increasing to allow trading at a more micro-level.

Today there are several mandis to a district, with around 750 mandis that facilitate the trade of 140 crops and their different varieties, all across India. Most mandis in the same district trade a very similar set of commodities in the same district. This makes for a very fragmented market for any single agricultural commodities across the vast geographical reach of India. At the proposal stage, the mandi starts with the goal of trading a principal commodity. After it is commissioned and built, every mandiis physically a yard or a set of yards with platforms where licensed traders buy from the farmers and sell to wholesale dealers. Since almost all order flow goes through the mandis, they become a source of daily information about the quantity of commodities and the prices at which they trade. The market design of a mandi is as follows:

Products Every mandi trades in at least one primary commodity specific to the region. Typically, trading is done in a set of primary and non primary commodities at any one mandi. As the seller brings the produce to the market, it is first weighed and both the type and quantity recorded at the entrance by a mandi inspector. The seller is given a certificate of the type and quantity. Some mandis charge a fee at the entrance. Once the produce is recorded at one mandi, it has "free" access to other mandis in the district; ie, the produce does not get double-counted at other mandis, nor is the farmer double-charged. The probability that the farmer will access more than one mandi to find the best price in the region then rests on the cost of transportation, and the lack of good packaging and storage during transport.

Participants Other than the buyers and the sellers, the market has traders who intermediate between the farmers and the wholesale dealers or mill owners. These traders are licensed by the mandi to trade at the market. Once licensed, they are premitted to intermediate between buyer and seller orders. Traders may use brokers to expand their business.

Traders have to pay mandi fees, which are of two types:

- A basic transaction fee which is a fraction of the value of the trader's volumes.
- Other fees in the form of taxes, that are also typically a fraction of the value of the traders volumes. This is charged by the state and can vary widely across states.

These fees are usually passed back to the farmers sellers. However, in the case of the primary commodities, the farmer has to be paid the MSP. In such cases, the central government technically paid up the fees and the taxes which were owed by the traders to the mandi. Sometimes, these charges would add up to 12% of the transaction volume. Recently, the fees and taxes that the mandi charges traders has been fixed to a flat rate of 4%.

Trading Trading in the mandi has two stages: one is a dealer market where sellers typically approach the traders for a price quote. Once they find a favourable quote, it is considered sold to the trader. The second is an "open-outcry auction", where the commodity is sold. The auction process has a fixed time at every mandi. The auction is run sequentially, typically going from one lot of the commodity with a fixed grade to the next.

There is no central dissemination of information of prices. As every lot is auctioned, a new price is set. The collection of prices takes place when the clearing is in process. Once again, this is very like the situation of price dissemination at India's equity markets before the reforms.

Clearing Traders have to clear deals with buyers and sellers immediately. At the time the trade is cleared with the seller, the produce gets inspected for quality. Typically this is done by the traders themselves. If there is a dispute about the quality of the produce, the conflict is resolved by the mandi inspector who can certify the quality of the produce. At the close of the trading day, traders have to report both prices and volumes to the mandi. Since traders pay fees to the mandi based on reported traded value, it is incentive compatible for the trader to under-report traded values. This means a possibility that volumes are under-reported, since under-reporting prices could have the undesireable effect of keeping the farmers away.

A cross-check available to the mandi is to tally the total volume brought into the mandi with the volumes reported by the traders. However, this is not fully reliable if sellers choose to exercise their option of moving to another mandi in search of a better price. Settlement Farmers bring the goods to the mandi which they deliver to the trader to whom they sell. Traders, in turn, have this produce picked up by buyers. There are typically no facilities at the mandi for long-term storage. If there is excess produce than could be sold on the same day, the mandi permits the traders to keep the goods at the mandi yards overnight. There are either private or state-owned warehouses that provide storage close to the mandis at a cost. Once settlement takes place, any dispute that arises about the quality of the good delivered is between either the buyer seller and the trader. Since one counterparty is always the mandi trader, it is settled by a mandi inspector. Inspectors are the final arbitrators of dispute: they have the onus of checking and certifying the quality of the good, and they have the power to close the trade at a price that they deem correct. Both parties who trade at the mandi have to abide by the inspector's decision.

Governance The mandis are set up and monitored by the mandi board, which is a committee that has representations both by the farmer and the trader communities. There is also a presentative from the state government on the mandi boards. The chairman of the mandi board however, is typically from the farmer community. It is the farmer community that usually originates discussions with the SAMB to organise a mandi in a new locality, and this community typically has a large voice in the governance of the mandi.

The operations of the mandi are handled by a staff consisting of a secretary, clerks for record keeping, and at least one inspector who is qualifed to certify the quality of the produce. The staff are paid out of the fees collected from farmers and or market intermediaries. Oversight and regulation At the spot market, where settlement takes place on a T + 0 or T + 1 basis, there is very little scope for problems of regulation. The disputes that arise are about prices and quality of the produce, which are typically handled by the mandi inspector. The most important regulatory requirement is the reporting of prices and volumes to the SAMB. Every district mandi board takes the responsibility of collecting and dispatching this information to the SAMB. The SAMB, in turn, dispatches it to the Ministry of Agriculture, where the prices are available on the internet at the end of every trading day.

The presence of the state government representative on the mandi board appears to be the main link for the oversight role of the SAMB.

Problems of the spot market

Price dissemination Every mandi becomes a monopoly to the local producers, especially once they come to the market. Farmers typically face a short period between the time that they harvest and the time that they can sell the crop. In addition, the cost of transportation of commodities is typically significant, given the lack of good transportation alternatives. If they do not have access to reliable sources of price information, they become hostage to the closest source, ie the local mandi. Farmers should have access to prices not just at the local, but also the national level. In each case, when prices across the country are available, they will be better able to evaluate their ability to incur transportation cost to access the better price. This will help to reduce arbitrage opportunities and wide price differentials across geographical locations, and help farmers earn more for their produce.

The same rationale applies to buyers who need to take delivery of the commodity within a short time frame. Whole-sale traders who have the option of waiting for a better price, face a smaller problem of monopoly capture. Since they do not incur a cost of transportation of the commodity, they can readily move to markets with a better price. Today, with access to cheap telecommunication services that has spread to practically all corners of the country, whole-sale dealers have a better idea of prices in a larger area than before.

The lack of standards and certification Prices can be quoted and compared across the country once there is a good standardisation of commodities. Once commodities can be clearly categorised as one standard as opposed to the other, then prices become more meaningful for comparison at one mandi versus another. These standards should be applicable equally across all states.

If standards are in place, then there should be facilities that allow for reliable and easily accessible certification of these commodities all over the country. This need not be a huge bottleneck at every mandi, there are already inspectors who can form the base of a nation-wide certification network. The role of the mandi can be mutated to shift from trading, clearing, settlement to certification and warehousing. Once commodities are certified standards and if this can be accompanied by warehousing and warehouse receipts, then trading on the commodity can be done on an electronic exchange, pooling orderflow and liquidity from a much larger area than any one single mandi. Thus, certification and standardisation of commodities can facilitate important reforms in the agricultural commodities markets.

Futures markets

Derivatives markets for agricultural commodities have

undergone a more turbulent history than the wholesale spot markets. The first of the derivatives markets were the cotton forwards markets which started as far back as 1857 followed by markets in a wide variety of commodities. There is evidence to support the notion that it was used by farmers as well as wholesale dealers, traders and end-user enterprises and firms. The growth and development of these markets were halted when forwards on all underlying were banned by the central government, en masse, in the 1960's. Options, which was traded on cash crops like cotton, was banned even earlier in the 1930's. When the government finally brought back forwards trading on agricultural commoditiess in the early 1980's they did so with commodities that did not have a very significant role in the economy: castorseed and castor oil, jaggery, jute, pepper, potato and turmeric. During the liberalisation of 1990, there were recommendations that forwards trading start in a larger universe of commodities Kabra committee.

Since their revival, forwards markets have developed along the same lines as the spot markets. There are several exchanges to trade the same commodity, each of them with a local broker wholesale-merchandiser constituency. For example, by the late nineties, there were three exchanges - Ahmedabad, Bombay, Rajkot - which traded castor seeds and castor oil as the main commodity for forwards contracts. This was (and is) very different from commodity markets all over the world, where there is a single exchange that typically pools the demand and supply for one-commodity in one exchange; price discovery for the commodity is clearly centralised in one market. In India, volumes were fragmented across the local exchanges. Every exchange individually conducted a relatively small fraction of business. In addition, the business itself has been relatively small in the last two decades. For instance, at the peak of forwards trading in castor seeds and castor oil at the official exchanges, the annual volumes at the Ahmedabad Commodity Exchange Ltd. was of the order of Rs.70 million. Almost all other exchanges have trading volumes lower than this.

Price discovery in castorseed futures

Sometimes, in debates about commodity futures markets, grave concerns are expressed about the role of commodity futures. Are these merely gambling dens? Are they sources of price volatility which hurt the interests of farmers? In this section, we show some evidence about the role of the futures market in price discovery in one case (castorseed). We ask the following question: even with highly underdeveloped institutional capacity, what role does a futures market play in price discovery?

Thomas and Karande examined the question of where price discovery in the castor seed and castor oil commodity markets takes place. The castor seeds futures markets, like all agricultural commodities futures markets, have multiple trading venues. Both the Ahmedabad and the Bombay markets for castor seeds futures have existed from the 1980's. Each was important for very distinct reasons: most of the castor production in India takes place in Gujarat around Ahmedabad, where as most of the export of castor seeds and oils took place from the port of Bombay. Both futures markets also had associated spot markets.

This paper asked the following questions:

1. Do futures market prices lead spot market prices?
2. Does the Ahmedabad futures market lead the Bombay market, or vice versa?

If the futures do play a price discovery role, we would expect that futures prices should lead spot prices in both markets. In the case of Ahmedabad futures markets versus the Bombay market, since Ahmedabad is where the production of the underlying happens, it should have an advantage over the Bombay market. We should expect that if there are no barriers to information flowing freely between the two markets, there should not be any significant lead-lag relationship between the two locations. The definition of the contracts on both these markets are exactly the same: there are four contracts that trade with physical settlement on the same amount of the underlying and maturing in the same months.

The analysis is done for the period from 1980 to 1995. This period started with high costs of telecommunications which then dropped to much smaller levels towards the end of the period. In such a setting, we would expect to find that prices in these markets should be contemporaneous. If there is a lead-lag relationship, then Ahmedabad prices would lead Bombay prices.

The paper finds the following:

1. Futures markets lead spot prices in all but one contract, ie, the contract that matures in March. The "March" contract is the "harvest" contract - the production cycle for castor begins with the seeds being sown in September and the crop being harvested in March. Thus, we find that when the crop comes to market, the spot market dominates the spot market in price discovery; for all the other contracts, the futures markets do play a price discovery role.

2. The Bombay futures markets leads the Ahmedabad market in all but one contract, ie the March contract. This finding is counter-intuitive to our hypothesis of Ahmedabad being the market where information shocks first enters the market prices.

However, if prices in the castor markets were largely driven by demand (export demand) rather than supply (crop produced), then Bombay would be the market where information first enters prices. Our hypothesis does hold for the March contract where the product market of Ahmedabad is the dominant source of information.

The paper does show that futures markets do play a role in price discovery. Their development would have a positive impact on the development of the agricultural commodities markets. However, it is puzzling as to why the volumes in these markets are so low. Sahadevan documents annual volumes in the period from 1995 to 2000. The largest market in this period in terms of annual volumes was the Muzaffarnagar market for Jaggery with average annual volumes of 4.5 million tonnes. The spot market for jaggery had a size between 9 to 10 million tonnes. These volumes have remained reasonably constant since then.

In comparison, the equity futures market that started with index futures in 1999, reached an annual volume of Rs.3.3 trillion at the end of March 2003 at the National Stock Exchange. During this period, the underlying spot equity market saw an annual volume of Rs.6.2 trillion. Volumes on the equity futures markets quadrupled over volumes in the previous year, while the spot market volumes grew at 20%.

The economic role of both these markets is to provide efficient prices and liquidity to their constituencies. However, the reach and efficiency of the equity market far outstrips that of even the most liquid of the commodity markets in India. This difference might be explained in terms of the different structure of the two markets: starting from the mandate to the issues of operations, risk management, technology and governance. In the following section, we examine the structure of the futures market for Jaggery at Muzaffarnagar, U.P.

The Muzaffarnagar jaggery futures market

When we seek to understand commodity futures markets in India, there is a need to know more about the market design which is presently in use. In this subsection, we seek to closely describe one commodity futures market as a case study: The jaggery futures market, which is located at Muzzafarnagar. 6The structure and performance of the equity market have been discussed in Shah and Thomas and equity derivatives markets in Thomas and Shah.

There are five jaggery futures markets in India, which are all located in the U.P.-Haryana 'sugar belt'. They are located at Bhatinda, Delhi, Hapur, Meerut, Muzaffarnagar. All these have jaggery spot markets as well. The futures markets at Muzaffarnagar is operated by a private firm, Vijai Beopar Chamber Ltd. In India, jaggery has only been used mainly as a sugar proxy and the consumption of jaggery has been on the decline. This decline is reflected in the volumes that are traded on the jaggery futures market. Nonetheless, the Muzaffarnagar jaggery futures exchange remains one of the more active and profitable exchanges while others trading futures on commodities that have much larger spot volumes and economic importance languish. Contract design There are different types in the jaggery produced, depending up on the region where the cane is grown. Some of the different types of jaggery are chapu, khura, pansera. Khandsari is a crude sugar-jaggery mixture. However, VBCL trades only one grade of jaggery for its futures contract, pansera.

If the trader delivers any other kind of jaggery instead of Pansera, the exchange specifies the premium which the seller will have to pay to the buyer to compensate for the difference in the delivery quality. Typically, only one contract trades at a given time on the exchange. The maturity is tightly linked with the harvest cycle of jaggery (just as was the case with castor seeds futures). There are four maturities: a six month contract expiring in mid July, a two month contract expiring mid January, a three month contract with expiry in mid March, and a five month contract expiring in mid July. The exchange has to obtain permission from FMC for every new contract it trades, irrespective of whether it has been traded before in the market, or a new contract design.

All contracts are written with physical settlement at maturity. The settlement price are decided by an exchange committee at the end of every trading day, based on intra-day traded prices at the exchange. Trading system Trading at VBCL takes place on an open outcry market. Trading opens at 10am and closes at 3pm. There are no designated market makers in the market, with all members offering two-way quotes.

Price limits are imposed uniformly on all contracts, irrespective of their maturity. The price band is 15% up or down on a weekly price for a quintal, set by the FMC, and are said to be rarely binding. The price at every half hour is collected by polling eight large brokers for bid and ask quotes by an employee of the exchange, and posted on the doors of the exchange.

The exchange charges Rs.2.5 per contract traded, out of which Rs.1.5 is brokerage that has to be paid to the trading member at the end of the month. The dominant cost in carrying out spot-futures arbitrage are the costs of trading on the spot market, rather than those on the futures market. The impact cost on the spot can work out to around 8%, and 12% if the position is held to maturity.

Clearing system The exchange has a clearing house that records transactions by members and calculates and implements risk management at the exchange. Clearing of trades is done both by the clearing house as well as the Trading Member's back office. Every trade is recorded twice: one record that is retained by the broker and the other that is stored at the clearing house.

Counterparty risk management is done through a system of Initial margin Rs.5000 when the member joins the exchange and Daily Mark-to-market margins. Any daily MTM loss has to be paid to the clearing house between 11am and 1:30pm the next day. All members clear through a designated clearing bank. There are approximately five clearing banks, none of which do nation-wide funds transfer. These banks are: SBI, Punjab Bank, Syndicate Bank, All India Bank of Commerce.

Any disputes between the accounts of the clearing house and the member is brought to the exchange board for arbitration. Settlement Even though all contracts on the exchange are based on physically settlement, for all practical purpose, there is no delivery in these contracts. The exchange actively discourages physical settlement. In the case of a dispute, the exchange provides certification of the delivery, which is cumbersome and leaves the exchange vulnerable to the high costs of resolving arbitration cases.

A second problem is a deep seated fear of short squeezes. This inhibits members from taking large open positions that carry over from day to day, and is indicative of a lack of transparent and frequent spot market prices.

Participants Trading on the exchange is done by Trading members or TMs Brokers. Brokers can clear their trades only through trading members. They can take either proprietary or client positions. Members can only join the exchange based on recommendations from existing brokers. This implies an entry barrier with potential social biases, rather than the credit worthiness of the individual. There are typically around 120 members who trade when jaggery is in season, and approximately 40-60 in the off-season period.

Governance The exchange is governed by a board of directors comprised of: four members from the spot market community, six from the futures community, two "shareholders", four nominated by FMC, two "nominated by the board". The board is in charge of taking important decisions like how a bankruptcy is to be "dealt with". The day to day management of the exchange operations is carried out by the 18 member exchange staff. None of the management staff can take positions or trade themselves.

There are several trading member committees to deal with specific problems at the exchange, such as:

1. Clearing house committee: decisions on disputes at the clearing house.
2. Daily rates committee: decides the daily opening, high, low and close of the day.
3. Survey committee: certify the quality of the goods transfered from buyers to sellers.
4. Arbitrators: Every dispute is handled by two designated arbitrators, one appointed by each of the two conflicting parties.
5. Vigilance committee: investigates any violation of the exchange bye-laws, rules, regulations and the FCRA, 1952.

Regulation The Forwards Markets Commission (FMC) is the regulatory body for commodity futures markets. It is an offshoot of the Department of Civil Supplies. Daily reports of the prices, positions and margins of each of the trading members are passed onto the FMC at the end of every trading day. Position limits, margin rules, fees and charges have also to be approved by the FMC. The FMC plays a much stronger regulatory role in the running of the futures markets compared with the SAMB and the mandis.

Problems of the futures markets

Lack of price transparency The commodity futures markets also suffer from problems of lack of price transparency. There is no common interface or communications infrastructure using which prices from one market become accessible at another. The collection of price information is done at the initiative of individual traders and dealers. This works in situations where the cost of collecting information is low for example, using cellphones to get real-time updates on prices from nearby markets but becomes a bottleneck when the cost is high. The human and telecommunications cost of getting real-time price updates from far-flung markets is prohibitive. This implies markets with relatively high price efficiency among local markets, but poor efficiency across national markets.

Lack of contract and product standardisation The cost that traders are willing to pay to access price and orderflow information from distant market is exacerbated by the lack of product standardisation and differences in contract design from one futures market to the next.

Fragmented order flow and the lack of economies of scale There are several similarities between the equity markets of the nineties and the commodities futures markets today. But, commodities exchanges suffer from a much higher degree of fragmentation than the equity markets in the late nineties. In the case of the equities markets, the typical structure of markets was to have one exchange per state: this meant that the economic order flow was fragmented at most at the level of the state. In the case of commodities markets in India, there are typically multiple exchanges to a single district for commodities!

This implies that the volumes get split between a large number of exchanges, making the viability of running an exchange a tenuous proposition. When this is compounded by the fact that the commodities that futures markets trade on today, tend to be the smaller of the agricultural commodities, the probability of reaching economies of scale in setting up exchange infrastructure become smaller. Economically, this implies that today most of these exchanges are too small, and their profit margins too weak, to support the investments in technology and human capital that are required to be credible players in the modern financial sector.

The equity markets offer a sobering lessons for the commodities markets in this regard. When the NSE was setup in 1994, and became the largest exchange by volume by the end of 1995, almost all the regional exchanges sought to emulate the NSE and put in place infrastructure to support electronic trading that had proved to help the NSE gain liquidity. However, it is very difficult to take away liquidity from an 7For example, jaggery futures trades in a set of seven to eight exchanges in the U.P. Delhi region within 100km of each other. entrenched market, especially when the entrenched market offered the most transparent and the safest platform for trading, clearing and settlement.

The NSE was competition for the local exchanges, who had to incur costs to match the facilities of the NSE without having access to the revenues of their order flow. Of the 23 local exchanges that India had in the mid nineties, today there are two national exchanges that can be said to be economically viable presently. All indicators point to the probability of this reducing to one national exchange in the future.

Today, the cost of setting up similar infrastructure and technology that helped the NSE become the market leader has dropped by orders of magnitude. In the face of the small-sized revenues that the commodities futures markets currently access, it is not clear that they can be profitable if the systems are put into place, even at such low costs of technology. Thus, any policy directive that seeks to improve the liquidity, access and usage of commodity futures markets much aim at building these markets at low costs.

A case in point is the Bombay Oils and Oilseeds Exchange which was the Bombay exchange for castor seeds and castor oil futures studied in Section 3.2. In the 1997, the FMC mandated that the BOOE upgrade their facilities to make the exchange a more transparent and safe market along the lines of the NSE. At the time, Bombay was losing volumes to the Ahmedabad exchange, and the exchange members were willing to invest in alternative mechanisms to get back or increase the orderflow. In order to do this, the exchange:

Partially set up an electronic floor

They retained the open-outcry floor, but purchased computers that would allow the brokers to put in limit orders on the market if they wanted to.

Set up a clearing house

This was accompanied by a system of initial and daily margin collection, but the exchange did not offer novation, which is still a service offered only by the National Securities Clearing Corporation, Ltd. for the equity and equity derivatives markets.

Set up a warehouse to store commodities

For the rest, the membership, governance and the ownership of the exchange remained the same unlike at the NSE where the membership spanned the entire country, and the exchange was governed by a professional team rather than the broker community. None of the changes instituted helped the BOOE increase the liquidity of the exchange. "Illegal" derivatives markets" The most robust competitor for orderflow in the commodity futures markets is not other futures markets, but the black market in future trading in India. In addition to a visible local exchange, every commodity has got a local shadow market where futures trading takes place. For example, the largest castor seeds and oils futures market is said to be located in the small town of Bhabhar in Gujarat, 100kms north of Ahmedabad. The trading community categorically assert that the price discovery is driven out of this town. Similarly, there is said to be a large black market for jaggery futures based in Delhi. These markets started with the ban on futures in the sixties and have flourished since then. Policy directives to improve and increase the liquidity of commodity futures markets will have to create a market to compete with these shadow markets if they are to be successful.

Policy proposals

With this backdrop, where we have described the existing spot and derivatives markets, and summarised some of their problems, we now turn to some specific policy proposals, which could possibly play a positive role in strengthening the functioning of these important markets.

Price transparency

A key weakness of the existing framework of commodity markets in India is the lack of price transparency. It is difficult for each farmer to know the correct price that is prevailing in surrounding spot and futures markets. This problem is deeply related to the lack of modern institutions on the spot and futures markets. If the spot market operated using electronic trading, then there would be full price transparency in realtime. However, at present, the spot market and the futures markets are both characterised by weak institutions, bilateral transactions, and an absence of transparency.

The spread of modern telecom has had a substantial impact upon sheer price access. Farmers in remote areas are now able to use cellular phones or STD booths in order to place a few phone calls and glean some information about prices. However, even if a farmer had plentiful access to telephones, there is a genuine problem with obtaining price information.

Access to prices that can be trusted is also extremely important to the financial sector. For example, if a bank gives out loans against collateral, then it is crucial to have daily official prices which can be used for marking to market. These official prices should be such that when a risk management system within the bank triggers a decision, collateral can be sold at the official prices.

These problem is not without precedent in the financial sector. In India, the fixed income and currency markets are similarly characterised by weak institutions, bilateral transactions, and a complete absence of price transparency. In this case, one important success story of obtaining a trusted price series even from a primitive underlying market is that of the NSE MIBOR which stands for Mumbai Interbank Offer Rate. The basic principle of NSE MIBOR is that in the non-transparent inter-bank market, dealers operating in the market have information about current market conditions, but nobody else has that information. A set of dealers is asked the question: If you had to buy or sell in the market right now, what are the best prices available in the market?. Each dealer reports one value for the best buy price available in the market, and the best sell price available in the market. These are put through a robust estimator in order to obtain two values, MIBID and MIBOR. The methodology uses bootstrap techniques to adaptively drops extreme values reported by dealers, so as to reduce the extent to which dealers can manipulate the official prices. This basic approach appears to be quite relevant for the commodity spot markets. It should be possible to put together groups of dealers in the country for each grade of each commodity, poll them every day, obtain official prices, and disseminate these through a wide variety of mechanisms. The proliferation of telecom and cybercafes implies that it is now increasingly possible to communicate these prices to the remotest farmers and other users of markets.

As with MIBOR, at some point in the future, when strong institutions develop on the market, such polling would become irrelevant. When trading takes place using advanced concepts like the electronic call auction, or anonymous order matching, the trading process innately lends itself to price transparency. However, until this transformation of the spot market comes about, such polling-based creation of "official rates" can play an important role.

Cash settled derivatives

If trusted official spot prices are known, then the problem of designing a derivatives market simplifies dramatically, since cash settlement can be employed.

In a futures market with physical settlement, a buyer of gold at a future date at Rs.5,000 tola is obligated to bring Rs.5,000 to the clearing corporation in exchange for a tola of gold on expiration date. If the price prevailing on the spot market proves to be Rs.6,000 on the expiration date, then settlement could equally be achieved (for all practical purposes) through a payment of Rs.1,000 by the clearing corporation to the futures buyer. This design is termed 'cash settlement'.

Broadly speaking, whenever the spot market is trusted and can yield sound prices, cash settlement is generally superior to physical settlement, for two reasons. First, cash settlement avoids the costs of settlement in physical goods. Second, the possibility of a 'short squeeze' is eliminated with cash settlement.

It may be possible to have cash-settled derivatives on commodity underlyings on the mainstream derivatives exchanges of the country. The spot price time-series would be treated as an economic index, and the futures settlement would be construed as a "contract for differences". In this fashion, cash settlement can be a useful tool for breaking down the regulatory barriers which separate the commodity markets from the mainstream financial sector.

Warehouse receipts as securities

One mechanism through which major change can be obtained relatively easily consists of exploiting warehouse receipts. In a modern agricultural sector, a key element is a modern 'warehousing industry', which would accept goods, verify the grade, and issue a receipt to the customer. This receipt is then tradeable. In a world with warehouse receipts, farmers would take their output to a suitable warehouse, and convert it into a receipt. This is comparable to the step of 'immobilisation' in an old fashioned securities depository. Once this is done, the receipt becomes the tradeable instrument, and can change hands many times until it reaches the end-consumer of the commodity.

We can conceive of a legal framework where these warehouse receipts are maintained as dematerialised securities in the existing securities depositories, NSDL and CDSL. Once this is done, everything about the market design for spot and derivatives markets on the securities markets would become applicable to commodity markets. The spot market would operate using nationwide, electronic trading. Netting would take place intra-day using novation at the clearing corporation. On T+2, settlement would take place at the depository, and the buyer would be the owner of a warehouse receipt.

Similarly, it would be easy to create futures and options on the warehouse receipts, using physical settlement whereby the short delivers these securities at the depository.

This proposal is a remarkably powerful one, in that if we can make warehouse receipts to be dematerialised securities, at one fell swoop, the entire complexity and sophistication of India's securities industry can be brought to bear upon the commodity sector.

The hurdles faced in making progress in this direction:

1. Establishing a sound system of warehouse receipts is not easy. This system has been discussed in various fora and projects over the last decade, but has not yet seen any progress.

2. The horizontal extension of the securities industry could encounter turf problems. In particular, once warehouse receipts are securities,

the regulation and supervision of the spot and derivatives markets for commodities would vest with SEBI and not with FMC.

Conclusions

India differs from most other countries in the world, in having a substantial agricultural sector. Looking forward, there is a clear opportunity for India to greatly increase value added from agriculture, through a much more liberal policy regime. To the extent that such a policy program makes progress, it could positively impact upon the lives of hundreds of millions. The repressed policy regime has stifled market development, and given weak institutions. Strengthening institutions for spot and derivatives markets is a key aspect of a reforms effort.

The first financial market which enjoyed the benefits of liberalisation was the equity market. Over the last decade, we have seen a flowering of a considerable institutional capacity on the equity market, giving nationwide trading, the elimination of entry barriers into intermediation, anonymous electronic trading by price-time priority, risk management at the clearing corporation, dematerialised settlement at the depository, and derivatives trading. The new institutions thrown up on the equity market have considerable strengths, by world standards.

This institutional capacity is an important potential asset for solving the problems of the commodity markets, since there is a great commonality between all kinds of trading, ranging from crude oil to wheat to government bonds to equities.

Chapter 8

Problems Encountered by Agricultural Marketing Firms in Food and Agricultural Product Exporting

---

Agricultural marketing firms encounter many problems in their exporting efforts. Unfortunately, many of these problems deter value-added firms in particular from exporting, and their potential contribution to reducing the United States' trade deficit could be substantial. This paper evaluates potential problems common to agricultural exporting firms to determine major deficiencies in trade support services. A three-page survey was mailed to 219 Texas agricultural firms, 55 of whom responded. Survey responses were elicited for three problem areas Knowledge Gaps, Marketing and Market Access, and Export Finance along three time frames Start-up, Ongoing, and Expansion) An analysis of the means of the survey items showed start-up and financial problems to be the areas of greatest concern to agricultural exporters. Furthermore, export finance problems were found to be especially troubling for smaller firms and firms with fewer years of export experience. A revised, comprehensive export policy with an emphasis on financial assistance targeted to smaller firms or designed to encourage new exporters could serve to increase total United States' agricultural exports while helping those who are not able to compete effectively in existing world market structures.

The Texas Agricultural Market Research and Development Center celebrated its 20th anniversary of providing timely and unique research on issues affecting agricultural markets and commodities important to Texas and the nation this year. T AMRDC is a market research service of the Texas Agricultural Experiment Station and the Texas Agricultural Extension Service. The main objective of T AMRDC is to conduct research leading to more efficient marketing of Texas And U.S. agricultural products in domestic and intemational markets. Research areas include domestic and foreign market opp01tunities for Texas and U.S. produced agricultural products; marketing of tTaditional bulk and high value value-added products in a global setting; the impact ofnew technologies on markets and price,' efficiency of market infonnation systems; market structure and perfonnance; consumer attitudes and preferences.

Problems Encountered By Agricultural Marketing Firms In Food And Agricultural Product Exporting: Analysis of Survey Results One of the major problems facing the United States economy is its massive trade deficit. The positive overall trade surpluses of the 1950's and 1960's ended in thee 1970's, primarily due to the OPEC oil embargo. The trade deficit increased from $52 billion in 1981 to $150 billion in 1989, with little evidence of a significant reversal in the future. The trade balance consists of a non-agricultural trade deficit, which has increased throughout the 1980's, and an agricultural trade surplus, which has declined in the past eight years from $26 billion in 1981 to $15 billion in 1989. Thus, the ability of the agricultural trade surplus to counteract the non-agricultural deficit has been diminished. Further investigation of agricultural exports reveals the contribution which has been made by the value-added sector. Approximately 50% of the United States' agricultural export revenue in 1987 was generated by processed foods (Ruppel). In the future, the demand for value-added exports is likely to grow more rapidly than the demand for bulk commodities as countries become more developed, their incomes rise, and value-added foods become a more affordable option. The importance and success of these value-added agricultural firms depends on their ability to penetrate foreign markets. The collective contribution of an increase in the number of agricultural exporting firms could have a substantial effect on the mounting United States' trade deficit. In addition to the contributions that agricultural exports make to the trade balance, there are many other benefits. For every $1 billion of United States exports, there are 25,000 jobs created (University of Houston Small Business Development Center). Since the world population is increasing at a faster rate than that of the United States, export markets represent a vast potential growth market (de Silva). There are also direct benefits to the exporting firm. The additional sales volume translates into lower unit costs through economies of scale, and thus greater profits. A stabilization of total sales patterns often results from exporting, as overseas sales tend to moderate seasonal or cyclical conditions in the domestic market. Various federal, state, and local programs have been enacted with the specific goal of enhancing United States agricultural exports. The Agricultural Trade Development and Assistance Act of 1954 was one of the first. This Act created the Foreign Agricultural Service's Cooperator Program and Export Enhancement Program, which together with PL-480's concessional programs wasdesigned to rid the government of its massive accumulation of CCC stocks. There was very little export legislation in the 60's or 70's. Recently, however, the Targeted Export Assistance program was created in the Food Security Act of 1985, and the Agricultural Trade and Competitiveness Act of 1988 called for the development of International Agricultural Trade Development Centers to assist in the export of agricultural commodities and products.

At the state level, the Texas World Trade Development Act in May of 1985 etablished the Texas World Trade Council and the Texas World Trade Development Authority to facilitate the activity of Texas businesses involved in international commerce. Other major exporting states have similar programs. Statewide services targeted towards agriculture include the Texoort Food and Fiber Directory, published by the Texas Department of Agriculture, and designed to match Texas agricultural suppliers with buyers abroad. The University of Houston Small Business Development Center provides educational services, counseling, business development services, and network activities. Texas is ranked fourth in the nation among states that benefit from federally-supported trade and foreign economic assistance disbursements. Although these federal and state policies are well-intended, they do not address problems unique to small and mid-sized agricultural firms, as many of these policies are targeted towards non-agricultural firms or to large agricultural firms dealing in bulk commodities. They also reflect a very uncoordinated approach to export expansion, as evidenced by the scattered nature of the programs. Finally, current policies do not adequately address start-up or financial problems, areas that are in particular need of attention.

Problems facing agricultural exporters can be categorized into three arr as: knowledge gaps, marketing and market access, and export financing. Knowledge gaps include inadequate price, economic, and social information needed by an exporting firm. Examples of knowledge gap problems include inadequate country-specific information, lack of information sources for assistance with export questions, a lack of coordinated trade services, and ignorance concerning import restrictions. The marketing and market access problem area is associated with problems in the flow of goods from the production point to the final consumer. Examples of problems in this area include poor knowledge of emerging markets, foreign market entry problems, product adaptation and promotion,and international transportation logistics. Financial problems are those encountered in the financing of export activities domestically and internationally, such as credit availability for export expansion, banking assistance, exchange rate and interest rate variability, and export tax treatment. Collectively these problems may cause a "fear" of exporting, especially among agricultural firms with little or no experience in international trade. Thus too few firms enter what could be potentially lucrative markets.

Research Objectives

The objective of this paper is to assess the problems confronting Texas agricultural exporters. This objective will be accomplished through the analysis of a survey of 219 Texas agricultural exporting firms in April, 1989. This assessment will proceed along two fronts, the first concerning the three problem areas mentioned above (knowledge gaps, marketing aspects, and export financing), and the other related to the time dimension of these problems. The time dimensions are categorized into start-up, ongoing, and expansion phases, where start-up problems are those associated with the initial export experience, ongoing problems are reflected in day-to-day operations, and expansion problems are those associated with a firm's movement into additional product lines or new countries. An implicit null hypothesis throughout this study is that all export problems are equal. In other words, firms on average would view knowledge, marketing, and financial barriers to be of equal difficulty, as would be problems associated with the start-up, ongoing, and expansion phases of exporting. The results and conclusions from this analysis will be relevant to state and federal agencies in identifying the areas of trade support services in greatest need of improvement.

Methods

A survey entitled "Problems Encountered in Food and Agricultural Product Marketing" was mailed to 219 agricultural exporting firms listed in the Texas Department of Agriculture's 1989-1990 TexDort Food and Fiber Directory. The three-page survey covered three major topical areas: Knowledge Gaps and General Issues, Marketing Agricultural Products Internationally, and Financial Aspects of Exporting. Each area had 12 or 13 items to which the appropriate firm decision-maker was asked to respond. These items are listed in Figure 1. Also, as mentioned above, there were Figure I. Problems encountered in food and agricultural product exporting

Knowledge Gaps and General Issues

1. Language barriers and or inadequate overseas telecommunications facilities
2. Lack of knowledge of cultural heritage in importing countries
3. Poor guidance concerning assistance with export questions
4. Need to hire international personnel

5. Inadequate public marketing strategy for Texas export products
6. Small number of private trading companies and export marketing firms serving agribusiness
7. Absence of a coordinated firm-oriented trade services network
8. Poor access to foreign markets due to import restrictions
9. Firm awareness and firm-specific implications of foreign safety and health regulations
10. Knowledge of trade legislation and or political considerations
11. Export competition from foreign and domestic suppliers
12. Negotiating with foreign buyers

Marketing Agricultural Products Internationally

1. Assessment of a firm's "readiness" to export agricultural products
2. Willingness to engage in long-term export planning and to make a long-term committment to exporting
3. Awareness of export profits potential; need for an export-oriented benefit cost analysis
4. Poor knowledge of emerging markets or of country-specific information on potentially profitable markets
5. Foreign market entry problems, overseas product promotion and or selling through foreign distributors
6. Product diversification, modification, or adaptation necessary for international markets
7. Lack of a statewide computerized trade lead service
8. Absence of worldwide product-specific information on market conditions

9. Domestic transportation and handling
10. International transport logistics, including freight coordination and insurance availability
11. Package design for international transport or foreign market regulations
12. Licensing regulations and or labeling requirements
13. Complexity of the export transaction, including documentation and "red tape"

Financial Aspects of Exporting

1. Enormous initial capital investment associated with exporting, including possible facilities expansion
2. Limited access to government-guaranteed export loans
3. Limited availability of commercial funds for export expansion
4. Unwillingness of banks to serve small and medium-sized businesses
5. Inabilities of local banks in international business finance
6. Inventory carrying and lack of working capital financing
7. Lack of familiarity in legal matters and export terms of payment
8. Length of time for payment receipt for export transactions
9. Variation in the exchange value of the dollar
10. Risk of default on payment
11. Availability of risk insurance for international transactions
12. Confusion surrounding domestic and foreign tax treatment and or investment incentives
13. High and or unpredictable interest rates three time frames for each item: Start-up, Ongoing, and Expansion.

> The respondents were asked to indicate their degree of concern on a scale of 1 to 7, depending on the nature of the problem. A severe problem was indicated by a 7, while a minor problem was indicated by a I. Additionally, "no problem" elicited a zero response.

Results of the survey were analyzed by comparing the means of the item responses. Two types of analysis were utilized. The first compared the means of different variables over the same population. In this analysis the means of the responses were compared within problem area and time frame, resulting in 9 sets of pairwise comparisons. That is, pairwise comparisons were generated for the means of each of the variables within each problem area and time frame. The second type of analysis was a comparison of means of different classes of respondents with respect to the same variable. For example, the means between firms with many years of exporting experience and firms having only a few years of exporting experience were compared for significant differences. The null hypothesis in both cases stated there was no sigificant difference between each pair of means.

Results

Of the 219 firms surveyed, 55 usable responses were received approximately 25 percent. Means from survey responses were generated for each item in the three problem areas and are presented. Three observations are immediately apparent. The first is the noticeable difference between the start-up means and their magnitudes, as compared to the ongoing and expansion phases. A total of 37 out of 38 means were higher in the start-up phase than in either the ongoing or expansion phases. Differences between the ongoing and expansion means are mixed.

Chapter 9

Agricultural Price Policy, Farm Profitability and Food Security

Agricultural price policy has come under serious attack recently for recommending support prices higher than what the costs of production warrant, supposedly leading to a distortion of the market, and, therefore, to food deprivation. With an in-depth analysis of costs and returns in rice and wheat, which are the most state-protected crops and underlie the livelihoods of millions of farmers, this paper examines the effectiveness of agricultural price policy in enabling farmers to obtain sufficient profits to promote investment, technology and productivity and thereby to food security. The rising cost of production due to the overemphasis on getting input prices right is a major factor that has led to higher support prices. Another factor is the percolation of volatility in global prices through trade liberalisation. Because of this, wheat support prices had to be hiked steeply in recent years so that sufficient quantities are procured. This has distorted parity between the prices of rice and wheat.

Agricultural price policy plays an important role in achieving growth and equity in the Indian economy in general, and the agriculture sector in particular. The major underlying objective of the Indian government's price policy is to protect both producers and consumers. Achieving food security at both the national and household levels is one of the major challenges in

India today. Currently, the food security system and price policy basically consist of three instruments: procurement prices minimum support prices, buffer stocks and public distribution system Agricultural price policy is one of the important instruments in achieving food security by improving production, employment and incomes of the farmers. There is a need to provide remunerative prices for farmers in order to maintain food security and increase the incomes of farmers. There has been a debate on price versus non-price factors in the literature. However, a review of literature shows that they are complements rather than substitutes.

In the post-reform period, it was viewed that reforms in non-agriculture would shift the terms of trade in favour of agriculture and lead to enhancement of private sector investment, which, in turn, would raise growth in agriculture. The favourable ToT in agriculture have had some impact on agriculture in the post-reform period as the periods of improving ToT like in the early 1990s and more recently after 2004 onwards, witnessed a robust growth in agricultural production in general, and in foodgrains in particular. However, the slackening of the efforts in non-price factors has affected the growth of production in the recent period.

Food inflation of around 18%-19% in 2009 is a concern for the poor and vulnerable. Several factors such as shortages in domestic supplies due to a poor monsoon in 2009, the rise in international prices, shortages in global supplies mainly due to diversion of significant foodgrains to biofuels, increase in demand due to higher growth, implementation of the National Rural Employment Guarantee Act and the loan waiver scheme, inefficiencies in the marketing system, speculation, etc, have been responsible for the price rise in cereals, pulses, sugar, fruits and vegetables, milk, etc. An increase in domestic supplies of agricultural production is important to provide food to the poor and others at reasonable prices. An increase in supplies is also necessary for the success of the PDS, which is supposed to be an important instrument for food security at the household level. Prices and supply-side non-price factors can enhance yields and provide higher incomes for the farmers apart from providing food security for the poor.

Agricultural price policy has come under serious attack in recent years for recommending higher support prices than warranted by the costs of production (CoP) and supposed distortion of the market, leading to food deprivation. It is also blamed frequently for the spikes in prices of food items that reached their peaks in 2009. Rice and wheat are the most state-protected crops and the millions of farmers are dependent on incomes from these crops, grown in an area of nearly 75 million hectares or more than 40% of the gross sown area. An analysis of costs and returns in these crops gives some idea about the profitability of Indian agriculture and provides insights into the working of price policy.

Against this background, the overall objective of this paper is to examine the effectiveness of price policy in helping farmers get sufficient profits to promote investment, technology and productivity, thereby to the food security of the country. The specific objectives are to find out the trends in the movements of costs, prices and returns in rice1 and wheat farming to throw light on the impact of price policy on the profitability of farming in two of the most cultivated and consumed food crops in the country. It also tries to bring out the causes that necessitated the recent increases in support prices and their relation to food security of the country.

The data generated under the cost of cultivation scheme of the Directorate of Economics and Statistics, ministry of agriculture, is used for the analysis in this paper. The data, collected annually under this scheme, covers all the major crops. This mine of data is largely unexplored for policy relevant research and encompasses 9,000 farmers every year. This data helps in analysing the economics of cultivation of different crops as well as to see the effectiveness of macro policies like price policy. The costs and returns are calculated for all-India using this data to see the emerging trends in profitability. The weights based on area and productions of respective crops are developed to combine the data from states. We have used the area-based weights for all the variables except the CoP. The growth rates used are based on semi-log trend and deflation is done using consumer price indices for agricultural labourers of individual states. The study analyses the data for rice and wheat for a period of more than 25 years from 1981 to 2007-08 for all major growing states. However, 2006-07 is the last year for which the data for different states are available for rice and 2007-08 for wheat. The study is divided into two periods, roughly synchronising with the pre- liberalisation and post-liberalisation eras. The first period starts with 1981 and ends with 1992-93 and the second period covers the years from 1994-95 to 2007-08.2 The costs and other data under the CS data are comparable over time except for a minor change in the valuation of family labour. Since 1991, family labour is now valued at casual labour wages and not those of attached labour. Nevertheless, this does not alter the overall conclusions of the paper.

The rest of the paper is structured into six sections. Section 1 presents the costs in cultivation and production of rice and wheat, while Section 2 gives the movements of MSPs and prices realised. Section 3 examines the relationship among the CoP, support prices, prices realised and wholesale prices examines the trends in returns at all-India and across different states and Section 5 brings together all these threads to identify the causes for higher support prices in recent years. Section 6 provides concluding observations.

Trends in Costs and Yields

The trends in C2 cost of cultivation per hectare and C2 CoP per quintal and A2 CoC for the period 1981-82 to 2007-08 for rice and wheat crops are examined here. The A2 paid out costs include the value of hired labour human, animal, machinery, value of seed both farm produced and purchased, value of insecticides and pesticides, value of manure owned and purchased, value of fertiliser, depreciation on implements and farm buildings, irrigation charges, land revenue, cesses and other taxes, interest on working capital and also miscellaneous expenses (artisans, etc) and rent for leased-in land. The C2 costs include paid out costs plus imputed value of family labour, rental value of owned land and interest on value of owned fixed capital assets. There have been debates that rice should be given an MSP as similar to wheat as the costs of both the crops are similar. We examine this issue here by looking at the trends in ratio of rice costs to wheat costs. The total CoP per unit of rice and wheat, which include imputed values of land, labour and capital, shown in Table 1, reveal that the unit costs of the former are somewhat lower than those of the latter. However, the situation seems to have changed after 1994-95 and there are several years in which the paddy CoP per unit exceeded that of wheat. This was particularly noticeable after 1999-2000.

The ratio of paddy CoP to that of wheat is lower than the ratio of their CoC because of the higher yields in paddy. The ratio of A2 CoC of rice to wheat was higher than the corresponding ratio of C2 CoC as shown in Table 1. This may be because of the lower imputed values of land, labour and capital in case of paddy compared to wheat. The conclusion is that the costs of rice have been similar to those of wheat since the mid-1990s. The ratio came down to 0.90 and 0.91 in the case of CoP in the years 2005-06 and 2006-07. On the whole, the demand that the MSP of rice should be closer or slightly below than wheat, based on the cost data, may need a sympathetic hearing. However, it may be noted that although the cost is a major one, it is not the only one factor in determining MSP.

The growth rates in the real CoP declined in the background of a robust gain in per hectare yields in the first period, while these costs went up in real terms in the second period (Table 2). As can be seen from the table, the growth rate in yields (per annum) came down from 2.67% to 0.86% in rice and from 2.54% to 0.52% in wheat in the first and second periods, respectively. The growth in yield outstripped the growth in CoC during the 1980s enabling the cost per quintal to go down. The reverse can be noticed for the later period. Another important point to be noted is that the CoC has grown at a lower rate in the recent period indicating that the lower profitability might have discouraged farmers to invest in higher use of inputs and technology.

Which states are relatively efficient in CoP relative to all-India average? The states of HP, AP and Punjab are the efficient producers of rice in the triennium ending 2007 (Table 3). The farmers of AP and Punjab could produce a quintal of rice at 27% and 23% lower cost than that of the all-India average and they have improved the efficiency of production by reducing the CoP relative to all-India average during the study period. The obverse is true in case of Assam and Madhya Pradesh produces rice at 30% higher costs. Also, farmers from Assam and Tamil Nadu are expensive in rice production, which may be impinging seriously on their profitability. Rajasthan, Punjab and Haryana are the efficient producers compared to all-India average for wheat. Here, Jharkhand, West Bengal and Chhattisgarh produce wheat at whopping 87%, 57% and 49% higher cost than all-India.

Trends in MSPs and Prices Realised by Farmers

In this section, we examine the trends in MSPs and the prices realised by farmers. The CACP reports provide implicit prices which are derived from the CS data for different states. Implicit price is the ratio of value of the output of main product per hectare to the yield per hectare. It is known the CoP given by the CS are the reported data by the farmers. In other words, the implicit prices reflect the prices realised by the farmers.

Changes in MSP

The changes in MSP show that the increase in rice and wheat prices are the highest during the period 2000-01 to 2009-10 as compared to those of earlier decades. The rice prices for the common variety increased

from Rs 510 to Rs 1,000 (while the wheat prices rose from Rs 580 to Rs 1,080 during this period. In the 1990s, the rate of increase in MSP of rice was lower than that of wheat. The annual changes reveal that the MSP increased significantly in the first few years after the reforms were introduced. Again it rose substantially during 2006-07 to 2009-10. Rice and wheat prices have risen respectively by 62% and 54% during this period.

The intercrop price parity between rice and wheat shows that the ratio of paddy to wheat increased from 0.89 in 1981-82 to around 1.0 in 1989-90. It ranged between 0.94 and 1.04 during 1989-90 to 1996-97. The ratio declined significantly in 1997-98 because of a sharp rise in MSP for wheat. The MSP of wheat increased by 25% compared to 12.7% rise for rice in that year. This increase in the form of bonus for wheat distorted the intercrop price parity. It was below 0.90 from 1997-98 to 2007-08. Only in the last two years had the ratio reached 0.90 and beyond. Similar trends can be seen for the ratio of grade A paddy to wheat.

Trends in Prices Realised by Farmers

Farmers are more concerned with the prices they realise rather than the MSP per se. The ratio of price realised to MSP was higher than 1.0 for rice and wheat almost during the entire period. Only in the case of rice, it was lower than 1.0 during 2000-01 to 2003-04. In the subsequent years, the ratio was closer to one. On the other hand, the prices realised by farmers were more than MSP for wheat in all the years during the period 1981-82 to 2007-08. Growth rates of prices realised in real terms show that rice prices had a declining trend in both periods while wheat prices showed a positive growth rate and increased in the second period. In other words, prices realised by wheat farmers have been higher and increasing as compared to that of rice farmers.

Regional Disparities in Price Realisation

There are significant regional disparities when we consider the ratio of price realised to MSP. There was a decline in the ratio in the triennium ending 2006-07 at the all-India level and in several states excluding Punjab, HP and Haryana for rice. It was much lower in states like Orissa, Bihar, Assam, West Bengal and UP (Table 8). In the case of Haryana, the ratio was higher by 32% in the same triennium, which means that the realised price is 32% higher than respective support price. The ratio for wheat was much higher than for rice. For example, the realised price for wheat was 22% higher as compared to MSP at all-India level in the TE 2007-08. The higher ratio for wheat is true for all the reported states.

Relationship between Costs, Prices Realised and MSP

In this section, we compare the trends in costs, realised prices, MSP and wholesale prices. The trends in CoP and price realised for rice show that the latter moved faster than the former till around 2000-01. Later the prices realised were almost similar to the CoP without any margin except in 2006-07. On the other hand, the prices realised by farmers for wheat have always been higher than the CoP. Particularly, the margins have been higher since the mid-1990s and more so in the last three years of the study, i e, 2005-06 to 2007-08.

Another issue is growth in CoP relative to the respective wholesale price indices . The WPI for rice increased from 100 in 1981-82 to 478.5 in 2006-07. The index of CoP shows that it was moving almost on par with the WPI till 2001-02. In the last five years of the study, i e, 2002-03 to 2006-07, the CoP has risen faster than WP. Here rice farmers were in difficult situation in terms of CoP compared to WPI. The index of MSP of rice increased from 100 in 1981-82 to 539.1 in 2006-07. The growth in MSP is almost similar to that in CoP till 2001-02 after which spikes in CoP are much higher relative to the MSP. As shown later, the increase in MSP in 2007-08 and 2008-09 was much higher than costs and WPI.

The index of CoP rose from 100 to 505.8 only during the same period for wheat (Figure 4). The WPI, MSP and CoP changes were similar till the early 1990s. Thereafter, the MSP and WPI were always higher than CoP for wheat, especially after 1997-98. In other words, input costs including imputed costs were lower than output prices for wheat crop and the margins were higher for wheat as compared to rice.

Returns to Farming

Ultimately, one has to look at the trends in profitability in order to examine the viability of farming. For this purpose, we have examined the trends in net income gross value of output and farm business income. We also looked at trends in the ratio of gross value of output to C2 cost, the ratio of GVO to A2 cost, which gives the level of margin over total costs and variable costs, respectively. The ratios of GVO to costs show that the value of output has been more than all the costs throughout the period for both rice and wheat. The averages given in Table 10 show that the ratio of GVO to C2 cost for rice has been maintained around 1.25 till 1995 but declined to 1.17 in 1996-2000 and to 1.07 in 2001-07. If we take the ratio of GVO to A2 cost for rice, gross value of output has been twice to variable costs, viz, A2-cost in most of the years except in the last seven years. The profitability of rice seems to have been going down, while wheat farmers improved their profitability during 1981 to 2007. If we consider C2 costs, the rice farmers could get only 9% returns over their total CoP in the TE 2006-07, when the wheat farmers got 26% net returns over costs. Significantly, the wheat farmers reaped more than 50% margin over total costs in 2007-08. Though their counterparts in rice cultivation could get 13% margin in 2006-07 and probably slightly higher in the later years, it still is nowhere near that for wheat farmers.

In contrast to rice, the ratio of GVO to C2 cost for wheat increased over time. The ratio increased from 1.21 in 1981-85 to 1.33 in 1996-2000. The ratio of GVO to A2 cost has also risen as compared to the early 1980s. This profitability ratio was around 2.6 in the triennium ending in 2007-08 (Table 10). It may be noted that this ratio for wheat was 2.41 and much higher than that of rice at around 1.9 in the TE in 2006-07.

Profitability across States

The returns over C2 costs show that the states like Assam, Bihar, Karnataka, MP, Orissa, Tamil Nadu, UP, and West Bengal witnessed negative returns for rice in the latest triennium. On the other hand, all states covered all costs for wheat except for Jharkhand and West Bengal. The profitability improved for rice in AP, HP, Haryana and Punjab during the study period, while it declined for other states. On the other hand, returns for wheat rose for all the states considered in the study.

However, all the states cover variable costs in rice and wheat with the exceptions being Uttarakhand for wheat (Table 12).

The situation in Jharkhand is also not remunerative enough to the farming community of wheat. The returns over variable costs for rice are much higher for HP, Punjab, Haryana, Chhattisgarh than other states. The returns for wheat are more than twice over A2 costs for the major wheat producing states. Figures 5 and 6 show that the ratio of returns over total costs (C2) and variable costs were higher for wheat as compared to rice since the mid-1990s. The higher profitability for wheat as compared to rice can also be seen in the growth rates of returns in constant prices. Rice recorded positive and high growth rates in net income, farm business income and farm investment income in the first period. However, it showed a negative growth rate in all these returns in the second period.

The growth rates of rice in farm business income were similar to those of wheat in the first period. However, the major point of distress for paddy farmers is that the returns over paid-out costs

On the other hand, the growth rates in profitability for wheat recorded positive growth rates of more than 2% in both net income and farm business income in the second period also. In spite of similar growth rates for yields, the profitability for wheat is much higher than that of rice. This could be partly due to better realisation of prices for wheat. At the state level, the growth rates in returns for rice in Punjab rose in the second period, while MP showed negative returns in the same period. The growth in rice for Punjab has risen in spite of the decline in yields for the second period, and this may be because of the high level of yields even with some decline and higher price realisation relative to the support prices. In the case of wheat, the growth rates for MP increased, while those of Haryana declined in the second period. Although the growth rates in returns declined for wheat in Punjab, they were nearly 3% per annum in farm business income and above 2% for net income in the second period. The data on costs and returns of crops from the cost of CS are available with a lag, and therefore, actual cost data for the years 2008-09 and 2009-10 are not available to compare with MSP data. Therefore, we have used the projected cost data which is used by CACP for recommending MSPs. As can be seen from the table, the margin over cost declined over time for rice from 30% in 1999-2000 to 7.6% in 2005-06. But, the margin of MSP over cost for rice rose significantly from 14% in 2006-07 to nearly 60% in 2009-10. As compared to rice, the margins of MSP over C2 cost have been much higher for wheat except in 2009-10. The margin for wheat over cost was around 67% in 2008-09. Therefore, it can be said that the recent increases in support prices have the effect of ameliorating the distress of rice farmers.

Increased Role of Price Policy

Agricultural price policy was earlier meant to mitigate the impact of any undue rises in prices on the vulnerable sections of the population. After the formation of the Agricultural Price Commission, it has always tried to maintain a balance between the interests of consumers and producers. Nevertheless, the limits of price policy in achieving these goals are recognised by the government and other non-price interventions are used primarily for the purpose. While a large network of the PDS ensures cheap food to the needy with appropriate levels of subsidy from time to time, many policy initiatives have been put in place to make farming profitable enough for farmers to invest sufficiently in technology for improving productivity per unit of land so that food security is not threatened. The policy aimed at encouraging higher production and that the resultant food produce should be available at lower prices. Both higher production and cheap food are considered necessary for food security. Thus, price policy remained subservient to the overall societal goal of poverty reduction on the whole until the new economic policies were introduced. The higher emphasis and reliance on price policy in the 1990s altered the situation drastically, as price interventions to the relative exclusion of non-price interventions marked the new regime as pointed out by Sen. As a consequence, the earlier policy of "low-input and low-output" prices shifted to "high-input and high-output" prices. On the other hand, public investments on irrigation, research, extension and other related infrastructure went down from 3.4% of agricultural gross domestic product in the early 1980s to 1.9% in 2001-03. Though private investments increased initially, it later stopped flowing due to the operation of complementarity between public and private investments, by the late 1990s. Technology development, dissemination and adoption received a major setback due to this.

As a result of this policy shift, growth rates in yields have gone down and eventually the CoP started rising. These rising costs necessitated higher support prices to sustain the long-run margin of 20% over total costs. The analysis in the paper brings out this phenomenon clearly. The MSPs in real terms declined in the 1980s and still returns to farming did continue to be sufficient for the farming community. This is because the CoP of both rice and wheat fell during that period as productivity improved at more than 2.5% per annum and outstripped growth in CoC. On the other hand, the CoP rose at the rate of nearly 1.5% per annum in both the crops during the 1990s and beyond, making rising MSPs necessary to help the farmers maintain the same incomes. It is important to note here that these higher support prices are meant to compensate the slowdown in yield growth and the consequent increase in CoP that is the result of dwindling non-price interventions through public investments. In this situation, if the MSPs are not hiked sufficiently as in case of rice in the late 1990s and early years of the new millennium, margins would have gone down and distress would have spread. The analysis in the paper shows that farm business income in real terms declined by 1.15% per annum for rice farmers. To sum up, the farming community is not necessarily better off as a result of higher support prices, as these prices are meant to compensate for the rising CoP in the absence of yield increasing public investments. The second major factor driving higher support prices is the operation of market forces in a liberal and open trade regime. Price policy faces different challenges in such a scenario. For example, low production can coincide with low prices with liberalised imports and exports. When the international market prices are higher and rising as a result of a supply shock, domestic prices of the respective commodity shoot up and procurement of sufficient quantities to the required levels to ensure food security becomes difficult. Therefore, the government will have to offer higher prices4 as happened in 1997 and 2007 and 2008 in the case of wheat, making the gross margin more than 50%. The pulls and pressures of democracy and farmer lobbies make it impossible to roll back these prices without very high political costs, even if global prices recede considerably. The forced unidirectional movement of support prices also has an advantage in that assured prices and continuity in price structure can only stimulate supply response for agricultural commodities. The result of these higher support prices is that it hurts the consumers and has an adverse impact on poverty reduction.5 It was estimated by Parikh et al that a 10% increase in MSPs of wheat and rice leads to a decline in overall GDP by 0.33%, increase in aggregate price index by 1.5%, reduction in investments by 1.9% and has a minuscule impact on agricultural GDP. They also conclude that the bottom 80% of the rural and all of urban population is worse off. The experience of the past few years clearly reveals that the option of trade for food security has limited scope in view of the huge demands of a large population of the country. This means that the balance between price and non-price interventions has to be struck as in earlier decades. Therefore, non-price interventions through public investments have to be accelerated to reduce the CoP, and thereby, the need for higher support prices. Also, a system of variable tariffs has to be implemented to insulate domestic prices from the impact of higher volatility in international food market.

Concluding Observations

Agricultural price policy has been largely successful in playing a major role in regard to providing reasonable level of margins of around 20% over total costs to the farmers of both rice and wheat. In turn, it seems to have encouraged farmers' investments in yield increasing technology and in increasing production and enabling sufficient procurement for buffer stocks and providing physical access to food by achieving and maintaining self-sufficiency. The need to supply food to the PDS and various poverty alleviation programmes has also been increasing at a faster rate. The price policy could help in procuring 43 mt in TE 2008-09 compared to a mere 13 mt in TE 1982, providing buffer stocks for an offtake of 38 mt in TE 2008-09, which is a steep increase over just 14 mt in TE 1982. These huge tasks of production, procurement and distribution would not have been possible without the efficient working of the country's price policy. The country is, by and large, insulated from supply shocks because of its operation. For example, the prices of cereals increased by only 20% while they spiked by 150% in the international market during 2005-08. This does not mean that there are shortcomings in its working, but only to highlight the fact its utility far outweighs any such problems to be rectified. Nevertheless, agricultural price policy does face some new challenges in the current period with reduced non-price interventions in the form of public investments and also the percolation of some of the global price volatility through open trade. In fact, the analysis in this paper shows that these two are mainly responsible for higher support prices. The trend of declining CoP with higher growth in yields got reversed in the 1990s and beyond and they went up to nearly 1.5% per annum for rice and wheat. The returns over paid-out costs for rice farmers also declined at 1.15% per annum in real terms leading to distress. This declining profitability seems to have discouraged them from increasing spending on yield augmenting technology as shown by the relatively declining growth rate of CoC. The price intervention in enhancing MSPs for wheat in 1997-98, 2006-07 and 2007-08, keeping in view the fact that the market prices were higher, has distorted the intercrop price parity between rice and wheat. Though the CoP is similar for these two crops since the mid-1990s, the wheat MSP has been 14% higher than that of paddy since then. Since 2000-01, rice farmers have also suffered from lower price realisation than the respective MSPs, lower (7%) returns over total costs compared to 27% in wheat and a higher growth in CoP compared to the wholesale price indices between 2002-03 and 2006-07. On the whole, the analysis presented in the paper shows that there is some merit in the argument that the MSP of rice should be closer or slightly below that of wheat. The recent hikes in support prices for rice are therefore justified against this background. The averages tend to mask regional variations and the impacts of price policy in a vast country like ours with divergent climatic conditions. The CoP is higher than the all-India average in some of the poorer states due to low productivity and prices realised do not cover all costs. But the price realisation does cover variable costs and leaves a reasonable margin over that in all the states. At the same time, the prices realised cover all costs in states producing efficiently at low cost. To sum up, a higher emphasis has to be given to non-price interventions through public investments to supplement price policy measures.6 They can help in increasing yields, reduce the exclusive reliance on prices for farm profitability and food security, and also hasten poverty reduction, as the history of poverty reduction in the country shows that the proportion of the poor declined at faster rates when food prices are low. Decentralising the procurement operations by building necessary infrastructure in states like UP, Bihar, MP and Orissa is critical in achieving

Chapter 10

Macro-level Analysis of Food Supply Chain Dynamics and Diversity

Definition of sustainability for food products

A term "sustainable food products" is seldom used in Latvia. The terms "biological products" or organic products (both terms are used as synonymous) are used more broadly. A number of recently adopted laws form a legal basis for Latvian organic farming policy. The Law on Agriculture defines: "organic farming – an agricultural method which is based on enhancement of the self-regulating processes of nature and an increase of biological activity of the soil and precludes the utilisation of mineral fertilisers and pesticides obtained industrially by chemical synthesis, as well as the use of genetically modified organisms and products thereof." Those farms, which produce organic products, can receive a certificate issued by an accredited institution. The circulation of organic farming products is supervised by the Food and Veterinary Service. The institution also supervises and controls the certification procedures for organic farming products and registers persons involved in the circulation of such products. After Latvia's accession into the EU, the Law on Agriculture and regulations relevant to organic agriculture adopted by the Cabinet of Ministers will not be in force. Instead, the new Law on Agriculture and Rural Development will be enforced. The law will replace the Law on Agriculture and will define the procedures for circulation and supervision of production of organic farming products. In Latvia, two organisations are entitled to issue certificates to those farms, which operate in compliance with standards of organic farming, namely, a public organisation "Environment Quality" and "Centre for Certification and Testing of Agricultural Equipment Ltd.".

Only 0.4% of all farms operate in the organic farming sector. Organic farmers cultivate only 0.7% of agricultural land in Latvia (Kalnins, 2003). There are now approximately 300 members in Latvian Association of Biological Agriculture Organisations.

A label "Latvian eco-product" is used to mark organic foodstuff in Latvia. Latvian Association of Biological Agriculture Organisations is the owner of the label. To be entitled to use the label, producers should obtain a certificate issued by a public organisation "Environment Quality". To get 1 The Law on Agriculture, "Regulations Nr. 514 on the circulation of organic farming products and the procedures for their certification" and "Regulations Nr. 232 on the procedures for the registration of persons involved in the circulation of organic farming products and on the procedures for State supervision and control of the circulation of organic farming products" issued by the Cabinet of Ministers, respectively on November 26, 2002 and April 29. 2003 the certificate, producers should observe the regulations of Latvian Organic Farming. These regulations are in compliance with the EU directive No. 2092.91.

There are a number of labelling marks in Latvia that may confuse customers to choose and understand the meaning of the label "Latvian eco-product". A labelling mark "Qualitative Latvian Product" in a form of a spoon is the most recognised label in Latvia. Products containing at least 75% of ingredients of Latvian origin and complying with quality standards can be marked with the label (Source: http: www.marketingapad.lv precu_zime.html). A public organisation "Marketing Board" is the owner of the labelling mark. The purpose of the label is to help Latvian customers to find a qualitative product, which is produced using local ingredients. Besides, Marketing Board issues a label "Growing Green in Latvia" aimed to mark Latvian products for export. In addition, there is a label "VP - healthy product" recommended by Latvian Diet Doctor Association having evaluated the biological and chemical content and value of a given product. Also a labelling mark "Latvian Quality" can be often seen in Latvian shops. Latvian Quality Board is the owner of the labelling mark. The label is aimed to mark Latvian products. Those products produced in compliance with security and quality standards can be marked with a LATSERT label issued by Latvian Certification Centre. The standards are set according to a respective European standard No. 45011. Health Promotion Centre has developed a labelling mark "Healthy diet". The label can be put on products containing less fat and salt.

Turnover and consumption

Statistics indicate that the trade turnover of food and other goods has increased during these recent years. Between the years 1997-2002, the average annual growth rate of trade was 12.8% per year, and, in 2002, the sector accounted for 17.7% of the gross domestic product. At the same time, the retail trade structure has essentially changed in the last decade. In 1995, the retail trade of food products constituted 63% of total retail trade turnover. Such a retail trade structure was created in the conditions of dynamic decline of the real disposable income of residents in the beginning of 1990s. After 1995, the share of food products in total retail trade turnover rapidly decreased, and, in 2002, it was by 26 percentage points smaller than in 1995. These changes were partly determined by the changes in the consumption structure triggered by the growth of income of people3. The majority of changes in the retail trade structure were determined by the difference in the dynamics of consumer prices in various groups of products. In the last years, the volume of trade of non-food products has increased faster than the trade of food products. It indicates improvement of the well-being of people. Retail trade of food products in the first 9 months of 2003 in comparison with respective period of 2002 went up by 8.9%.

Retail Trade Turnover by Commodity Group at there have been quite significant changes concerning food consumption in these recent years. For analytical purposes, one can discern three different groups of food products. The products whose level of consumption approximates that of 1990 i.e. right before the liberalization of the market) form the first group. In 2000, the consumption of bread and cereal products nearly reached the level of 1990 (96%. It should be bear in mind that prices for such products considerably increased in the beginning of 1990's. Fish products were also consumed in 2000 as much as in 1990. It holds true also for cheese (95% of the level of 1990) although it was consumed on average 2.3 times less than in EU 15 and considerably less than in other candidate countries (the only exception is Lithuania with the same level of consumption).

Those products whose consumption has decreased during these last ten years form the second group. The consumption of dairy products has stabilized although the level of consumption approximates only 61% of that in 1990. In Latvia, milk is consumed 1.4 times less than in EU 15 and less than in other candidate countries, for example, in Estonian and Lithuania where milk is consumed 1.4 times more than in Latvia. Butter is also consumed less in Latvia, i.e. 2.3 times less than in EU 15 although it is consumed more than in other candidate countries such as Hungary and Slovenia. Perhaps, the exception could be cream. In Latvia, it is consumed more than in EU 15 and other candidate countries. It should be noted, however, that the level of consumption of cream has decreased 1.8 times in comparison with that of 1992.

The consumption of eggs and sugar has also fallen. The consumption of meat and meat products considerably decreased in the beginning of 1990's. Although the consumption of meat increased after 1994, nevertheless, the level of consumption still fluctuates around 78% of that in 1990. At the moment, pork is consumed 2.7 times less than in EU 15 and considerably less than in other candidate countries like Estonia and Lithuania where pork is consumed 1.6 times more than in Latvia. The similar pattern can be discerned concerning the consumption of poultry. It is consumed 2.6 times less than in EU 15 and considerably less than in other candidate countries. It should be noted that, for example in Hungary and Slovenia, poultry is consumed respectively 1.7 and 1.6 times more than in EU 15. In Latvia, beef is consumed as much as in other candidate countries although less that in EU 15. People in EU 15 consume beef 2 times more. It should be noted that the consumption of beef has decrease 3 times since the beginning of 1990's.

Those products whose consumption increased during these recent years form the third group. In 2000, vegetable oil was consumed 3.9 times more than in 1990. However, the figure 9 litters per capita within year is considerably smaller than in EU 15 and the US. The consumption of margarine also increased during the last ten years (183%). In 2000, it appeared that people in Latvia consumed potatoes 1.5 times more than in 1990 the level of consumption of potatoes is one of the highest in the world. In comparison with 1990, the consumption of fruits and vegetables has considerably increased respectively 142% and 133%. However, the authors of the report are of the opinion that one should look at these figures with some reservations. It should be noted that the share of the so-called "grey economy" is still substantial in Latvia. Some experts believe it generates approximately 1 3 of GDP.

Experts are of the opinion that such expensive food products as meat and fish will be consumed more in the future and their share in the so-called food basket will increase although the proportion of those expenditures allocated for food products will decrease. Experts also believe that the consumption of almost all dairy products will increase except cream and butter because of the expected increase in real income per capita, integration into the Single Market, increasing level of variety and increasing share of out-of-home food consumption. The consumption of meat products will be influenced by the increase of health consciousness.

Prices

Consumer price inflation in Latvia in the recent years is close to the level of inflation in the

developed countries and is among the lowest in the countries of Central and Eastern Europe. Also in the future, Latvian government has declared a goal to keep inflation within the limits of 2-4%. Inflation in Latvia in 2002 was lower than established by the Maastricht criteria. Price changes are different in different groups of goods and services.

Prices for non-food products in the same period of time went up by 5% and prices of services -- by 3.6%. Prices of pharmaceuticals, clothes and footwear from the group of non-food services went up by 4.7%. In the group of services, prices for hairdressers' services, waste collection and medical and public catering services went up most dynamically.

Experts are of the opinion that prices for food products may increase by 30-50% in the coming years. At the same time, representatives of food industry expect that the increase will not be rapid. It may come after the increase in real income. Prices for dairy products may increase more rapidly because these products cost about 50% more in EU 15 than in Latvia.

Trade channels

Riga's inhabitants do shopping on average 4.7 times a week, i.e. almost every day. During workdays, purchases are made in the vicinity of one's dwelling place. On weekends, people go for shopping to more distant places. Total trade area of stores has substantially increased during these recent years. In 1995, trade area was 1192 thousand square meters but, in 2001, 1711 thousand square meters. The structure of retail business has substantially changed. There are more and more supermarkets. In the time period from 1999 till 2001, the number of small shops has decrease almost twice but the number of huge retail stores has increased four times. According to a journal Food International, the following foreign companies operate in retail business in Latvia: ICA Ahold Axfood Rietan Narvessen, SOK, Rauakirja Kesko Coop AS Smarten Vilniaus Prekyba. According to the survey data, the market share of supermarkets in Riga was 48%. The share of open marketplaces was 28% of total retail turnover. As experts suggests, customers chose supermarkets because there are sufficient numbers of supermarkets in all neighbourhoods and they can be easily reached by all means of transportation. Supermarkets have now become principal delivers of foodstuff to Riga's residents. Researchers from TNS Baltic Data House arrived at similar conclusions. According to the data of a research carried out by the aforementioned organisation, a number of shoppers in supermarkets increased by 20% in 2003 alone. 73% of residents of Riga and its vicinity do shopping in a supermarket at least once a week. More than 50% of those shoppers are regular customers. People in their 60's and older or with low incomes seldom do shopping in the supermarkets. Experts are of the opinion that the number of shoppers in supermarkets will increase with the growth of income.

However, the development of retail business in Latvia lags behind that of in Lithuania and Estonia. The share of marketplace in retail business is larger in Latvia. According to the information provided by Latvian Marketplace Association, there are 87 marketplaces in Latvia. There were 58 in 1995. It should be admitted that a number of them are open only a couple of days a week. Marketplaces are open daily only in major cities. According to the data of a research carried out by TNS Baltic Data House, 24% of Riga's residents do their shopping in marketplaces several times a week.

There are only few farmers selling their products in marketplaces because they do not have any time to carry on trade. Most farmers sell their products to dealers although they loose their profits. As a survey's data indicated, there were only 12 farmers selling their products in the mid of a workweek in one of the biggest marketplaces in Riga. There are more sellers in marketplaces in summers, fewer in autumns and winters. Marketplaces are busier on Fridays and Saturdays. However, marketplace looses its share and attractiveness.

More and more supermarkets and other retailers take over marketplaces, which are often situated in the vicinity of one's dwelling place, are more convenient and are providing better services. For example, a total turnover of trade generated by farmers and individual sellers in a marketplace in Agenskalns (a neighbourhood in Riga) decreased twice as it was before when a supermarket "Rimi" started its business here.

Views of experts are quite contradictory on the issue of the demand for organic farming products. The price for such products is similar to that of products produced using traditional methods. A group of customers for such products is still forming. According to some rough estimates, only 2% of customers in the Baltic States are ready to pay 30% more of the price of products produced using conventional means. In addition, only 3% of customers are willing to pay 21-30% more. In sum, approximately 5% of people could form a customer group for organic farming products. A number of experts are of the opinion that the supply of organic farming products does not meet the demands of potential customers. In a seminar organised within an exhibition "Riga Food 2003", Daiga Kreismane, a chairperson of the Council of the Association, stressed that the demand for chemical-free products are much greater than the supply.

Most experts are of the opinion that there are good prospects for such products both at home and abroad. There are no export quotas imposed on producers of organic farming products. When the purchasing power of Latvian customers is greater and when more and more people become aware of the implications for health, there will be more demand for healthy organic farming products and foodstuffs.

These experts believe that one of the preconditions for the development of organic farming in Latvia is the increasing awareness of more and more people that organic farming products are of crucial significance for their state of health. They know that well-thought-out diet is one of the ways to stay healthy.

Consumer behaviour towards sustainable food products

There have not been any academic studies carried out to find out consumers' values, needs and motivation to buy organic farm products. Moreover, there are studies on organic farming where, though indirectly, analysis of existing and potential demand for such products was carried out. They are some marketing and case studies surveys, which allow to evaluate farmers, retailers, producers, consumers, experts opinions and attitudes. The largest part of marketing research data is not available for academic researchers. The samples of all these surveys have been rather small, and the main task of the research was to study particular groups of products. Therefore, the research results may give only some insights and understanding of consumers' values. The data obtained by K.Peipina indicates that most consumers first pay attention to the price of a given product. There are fewer respondents who pay attention to so-called health criteria. The third criterion is whether a given product contains preservatives. Only 28% respondents pay attention to the name of producer and 24% - to expire dates. According to the data, people prefer well-known products (35%) as well as those that can be purchased in the nearest shop (27.5%).

A.Runce, a chairperson of Latvian Association of Organic Agricultural Organisations, thinks that the low purchasing power of Latvian consumers is the main cause for the low and insufficient incomes of green farmers. Other experts argue that organic farmers cannot sell their products for a higher price most consumers look for cheaper, not better products. The view is also shared by one Internet discussant: "People buy cheaper, but not more expensive. It is utopia that most consumers will be willing to pay more for such products. Quality of products produced using biological methods does not differ at all in comparison with that of conventional products."

However, many experts believe that Latvian consumers will be willing to pay more for such products in the future. Thus the income level of organic farmers will reach that of other farmers. Latvian Food Centre in co-operation with Association of Latvian Diet Doctors and Federation of Latvian Food Producers organised a survey of consumers to find out the healthiest cereal and dairy products. According to the survey data, 52% consumers choose a given product for its taste, 34% for its value, 10% looking at its price, 4% - out of habit, 3% for its package. A.Bremanis, a chairman of Association of Latvian Diet Doctors believes that "There are more and more people in Latvia that want to lead healthy life and use healthy food products in their diet"

b. Information, knowledge, and uncertainty

Most experts are of the opinion that consumers are not sufficiently well informed about organic agricultural products. It also holds true for retailers and distributors of such products. In one of surveys, it was found out that distributors do not know all characteristics of food products, they are not sufficiently well informed about ingredients used in their production, impact of products on human health. Store personnel are less competent on these issues. Consumers are the least competent persons because they do not receive full information about producers and distributors. M.Zelmenis thinks that fines and punishment for inadequate labelling are inconsiderable. It does not stimulate retailers to pay more attention to elaborate precise and fully informative labels. He argues that problems are caused by the fact that a labelling mark "bio" is also used to mark two other product categories: traditional products containing bifido and acidophil bacteria.

Similar concerns are also expressed by other experts. They think that there are too many labels marking the quality, healthiness, ecological purity and other characteristics of products. Margers Rava, a chairman of the Board of Latvian Dairy Committee, thinks that "two labels are enough "Latvian eco-product" and "Spoon" also known as "Qualitative Latvian Product". All others labels only confuse people's minds. As one journalist jokes: "the very product could not be seen under jungles of labels. There are more and more labels year by year and it cause confusion among consumers and chaos in the market. It does not mean that a given food product is produced by Latvian farmers even it is labelled with a title and name in Latvian. To inform consumers about the issues, a number of Internet sites are created where every Latvian consumer can get necessary information about products, their purchase and use. Both producers and distributors lately take measures to inform and increase the competence of consumers. However, these measures are taken irregularly and they cover only small target groups of a given product. The activities in the organic sector are rarely represented in the mass media. There have been a couple of articles in the national media. Organic farmers themselves use local press to put some announcements, as well as the association's leaflet and webpage. Also the information about coming seminars is published in the local media. Thus, everybody who is interested may attend them. Since the beginning of 2003, LAOAO disseminates its monthly leaflet to organic farmers.

Altogether, around 380 farmers receive it at their farms. It is available also on the association's website, as well as it is distributed through the offices of Agriculture Advisory and Education Centre. "The leaflet is a step forward. The leaflet does not contain yet a lot of information, but at least the main questions are presented there." The leaflet does not appear only as top-down information. It serves as well to be a communication tool among the farmers themselves they use the leaflet rather actively to express their needs, experience, advice, supply and demands etc. The themes covered in the leaflet gives a list of urgent 'keywords' in the organic community legislation and subsidies; market, opportunities, co-operative projects, trademark certification, training, etc.. This information helps in farmer's communication with consumers and sellers. Casual vis-à-vis interactions with consumers have had positive outcomes, tool.

LAOAO has created a deeply green organic farmers' Internet site www.ekoprodukti.lv . It offers comprehensive information about organic agriculture in Latvia legislation, organisations, market, organic farming, current events, and advertisements. General information about organic agriculture in Latvia is accessible also on some other strategic internet sites that of the Ministry of Agriculture, the Council of Collaboration of Agricultural Organisations, Agricultural Advisory and Education Centre. Informative leaflets about organic agriculture were prepared by local organic farmers group, too. Farmers take part in various public activities and events. Various exhibitions on food, gardening, health, etc are a popular mean of communication among organic farmers. Exhibitions are both a market place and a way to advertise and popularise organic agriculture, organic products. Several organic farmers from Cesis district have taken part in a competition organised by the Ministry of Agriculture and the Ministry of Environment Protection and Regional Development "Sower". On March 21.2003, there was organised the first conference "Organic Agriculture and Health". The event brought together farmers, representatives from universities, health care institutions, organic agriculture advisors, food technology and domestic animal specialists, certification inspectors, etc. The organisation of the conference was financed by the Mortgage bank.

Cesis district organic farmers have engaged in the association's initiative to develop a network of health farms. However, these farmers' activities not always reach their goals and only partly help to elaborate communication between market agents.

Even if the demand for organic products is still low, there have been some cases when uncertified farms have offered their products as organic, thus misleading consumers and potentially shaking their faith in organic food.

c. Availability of products and behavioural control

At the moment, organic food products are distributed in a number of ways:

1. Supermarkets. As a survey carried out by a newspaper "Lauku Avize" indicates, retailers are willing to buy organic food products but they need a regular supply in large quantities. Some supermarkets already co-operates both with farmers and local producers. For example, one of the largest retailers Rimi Ltd. has 240 suppliers in total including 98 local producers and 12 farmers.

Supermarkets are one of the few retailers who control that consumers really buy organic farm products not adulteration. Therefore, a lot of customers trust in this distribution channel. It cannot be said about other distribution channels. In Latvia, a number of supermarkets develop conceptions how to market organic food products. They also try to set a particular section for organic food products. A retailer "T-Market" is one of the largest sellers of organic food products. Experts are of the opinion that more and more Lithuanian organic farm products will be brought to the Latvian market in the immediate future. Experts also think that smaller suppliers incur losses in the competition among supermarkets because they have to choose with whom they will cooperate. It is not always good and profitable for the suppliers.

2. Specialised marketplaces. There are a number of counters allocated for producers of organic food products in Riga Central Marketplace. On several occasions, organic farm products are sold in the Alberta Square in Riga.

3. Hotels, restaurants. At the moment, these distribution channels were only partly used for selling organic products. The Radisson SAS Daugava Hotel is one of the few organisations that has actually launched co-operation with organic farmers. The hotel was opened in Riga in 1995 - a time when biological agriculture had not yet received much publicity, and hotel managers lacked information about abilities to purchase organic products locally instead, they were imported from Denmark. Since 1998, however, the hotel has been concluding agreements on the supply of produce from local organic farmers. The hotel pays top prices for certain types of organic produce. At the same time, the hotel is also forced to buy conventional products, because organic farmers cannot entirely meet the demand. Cafes and restaurants often become partners when individual farmers seek marketing outlets. During a case study, a restaurant director affirmed that their restaurants chain purchase ecologically clean products when possible, but once the foodstuffs are processed, organic products are not differentiated from the conventional ones. He said that they sometimes have some doubts about food compliance with standards of organic farming. He spoke cautiously about company's readiness to purchase these products on an ongoing basis.

4. Direct sale. The so-called direct sale as a method hasn't been sufficiently and broadly used in Latvia except green markets, which have been established recently. In the meantime, the agricultural market in Latvia is characterized by the presence of

broad networks of informal direct supplies and sales from farms to local shops, schools, kindergartens, hospitals etc. These direct sales intensify during the harvest season, e.g. sales of strawberries and apples during the season.

There isn't any specialised shop in Latvia that is selling only organic food products. There have been several attempts to set up such shops, however, difficulties with supplies and a lack of coherent marketing strategies lead to the bankruptcies of these enterprises. The Association of Biological Farmers Organization organised two shop stands in Riga for organic produce.

d. Decision process

Decision process of customers hasn't been studied in Latvia so far. An academician Arnis Kalnins is of the opinion that customers keep asking and saying that they are ready to pay more but, when in a shop, the final decision is determined by amount of money in their pockets. This is indirectly proven by the expanding initiatives and practices of food supplies from organic farms to urban families.

There are customer surveys and marketing research polls, which occasionally includes questions about organic food or healthy food products. In a survey carried out in the March of 2003 a polling company SKDS asked Latvia's people: "On the whole, are foodstuffs you use daily healthy or unhealthy?" The survey indicated that approximately a half of respondents believed that, on the whole, they use healthy foodstuffs 3% indicated "very healthy" and 47% - "rather healthy". However, 40% indicated that the foodstuffs they consume are unhealthy. 10% could not give a definite answer or could not assess the quality of products they use. It should be bear in mind that respondents were likely to think of the foodstuffs with calories and salt, not properly prepared meal, the foodstuffs containing preservatives. The latter is considered unhealthy by most consumers.

e. Socio-demographic profile

In her study, Anita Villerusa arrived at a conclusion that those better educated and better off as well as city dwellers can change their habits and turn to healthier diet quicker than others. Women think of changing diet more frequently than men. Therefore, it is much easier for organic farmers to win the hearts of those women that live in cities and are better educated and better off.

Data of polling company SKDS (the survey carried out in the March of 2003) shows that respondents from different socio-demographic groups quite differently assess their consumption of healthy food. In a group with no more than 42 Ls per a member of family a month, 45 % respondents considered that they use healthy foodstuffs. But in a group with income more than 127 Ls per a member of family a month, considerably more respondents expressed such a view. The data of the survey also reveals that respondents in an age group from 25 until 34 as well as respondents with higher education and those employed in the public sector more frequently consider the foodstuffs they use healthy. Experts argue that groups with high incomes are potentials consumers of organic food products too. Mothers form a particular group. They are more concerned about the diet and health of their own children. The youth does not seem to care much about healthy diet at the moment.

f. Social embeddedness

There is a widespread belief in Latvia that we have a natural, uncontaminated land, diversified fauna and flora as well as experience in "natural" management of all this. Producers of organic food products think that people are tired of stress and products containing chemical substances. They want to enjoy life consuming healthy products. Inguna Gulbe, head of the Centre for Enhancement of Agricultural Market, is of the opinion that a growing interest of consumers about such products can be explained by the successful efforts of producers to tell society what are these products and why they are to be chosen. There is a wide-spread recognition among policy makers and farmers organisations that currently there are no serious environmental problems in Latvian agriculture. Nevertheless, agroenvironment policy is given an increasing attention by the politicians and decision-makers. There are several reasons behind this:

awareness that environment is a priority in EU countries and that Latvia has to enforce agroenvironmental regulations as a part EU integration; growing awareness that economic recovery and growth of agricultural production may involve negative impact on the nature; growing awareness that rural development should be considered in broader that agricultural terms and that agro-environment is part of integrated rural development.

High prioritising of environmental regulations in agriculture is stipulated by the necessity to fulfil EU accession requirements and to adopt the Communities agro-environmental legislation. Environmental concerns are also enhanced by the values and attitudes of emerging urban middleclass towards landscape, food security. Environmental and organic farming initiatives are explicit in rural and regional development programmes of local communities and government.

The representatives of state administration accept environmental goals in agriculture in official discourse. Decision makers are also aware that approximation of EU agro-environmental regulations is a part of EU accession strategy which is a national priority. Major political parties have included proposals for environmental protection in their programmes. These signals demonstrate rising public awareness of rural and regional development and environmental issues.

The new life-styles and consumer patterns of the urban middle-class are being somewhat constructed around ideas of rurality, green consumerism and nature and could be looked as driving force for rural tourism, ecological food, improvement of rural infrastructure and landscape. The urban consumers start to play increasing role in advocating organic farming and integrated rural development like elsewhere in the developed countries.

To facilitate public awareness about organic products and to facilitate the consumption of organic food products, a number of seminars and exhibitions have been organised5. Promotion campaigns of a labelling mark "Qualitative Latvian Product" or "Green Spoon" is one of the ways to facilitate this. It should be added that the President of the Republic of Latvia Vaira Vike-

Freiberga has agreed to become a patroness of the Program for Enhancement of Latvian Agricultural Market. She thinks that the labelling mark "spoon" symbolises a good co-operation among and between Latvian farmers and producers. The "green" agriculture becomes popular: on the one hand, there is increasing demand for healthy foodstuffs, on the other hand, state provides substantial subsidies to support "green" agriculture and attract more and more small and medium size farms to such a production.

Barriers for consumption of sustainable food products

As indicated above, the purchasing power of Latvian consumers keeps down the consumption of sustainable products. There is no stable middle class in Latvia that might be a target group for organic farmers. Products costs for organic food production are approximately 30-40% higher than those in the conventional agriculture sector. Besides, state support in the organic agriculture sector is not that significant - 60-150 Euro per hectare. Thus, most people in Latvia cannot afford to buy such products because of their price. The following factors can be also mentioned as barriers for the consumption of sustainable food products:

- Organic farming sector is very fragmented. There are farms that produce more than 10 different products for the market.
- Major producers of meat and dairy products do not even intend to process products from organic farms because of small quantities and irregular supplies. There isn't any consensus among "green" farmers themselves whether to co-operate with major producers. There is a belief that organic food products loose their value in complex producing process.
- The consumption of organic products was impeded not only by the low purchasing capacity of population but also by the lack of common production and marketing activities of farmers. For the most part, producers, retailers and supermarkets have not distinct marketing

strategies for organic products. The marketing strategies have not been adapted to the local market, where consumers, due to their low purchasing capacity, usually choose the cheapest products, not that of high quality. Thus, also the demand for organic products still remains rather low. Organic food products are "invisible" and largely "inaccessible" to consumers.

- The main reasons for low and irregular supplies of organic products are a lack of knowledge about collective economic activities and a lack of trust in collective actions. Farmers do not know how to harmonise individual and collective interests. Most of them are already engaged in individual distribution chains, and it is difficult to change their orientation. Part of farmers is not much interested in working with less commercially successful colleagues.
- Unprocessed products are mainly supplied to the market There are only four companies entitled to process such products.
- Only small quantities of cereals, meat and dairy products reach consumers as an organic farm product. Milk, cereals and meat are for the most part processed together with conventional products from the rest of the farms in Latvia.
- The large part of supermarkets currently do not have a distinct approach towards marketing of organic agricultural products;
- There is no one single place or particular places for selling such products except the socalled "green" market on Fridays in Riga;
- A number of problems are caused by procedures for labelling foodstuffs;
- Products produced using conventional methods are often advertised as organic farm products. There is a real threat that, because of great demand for such products and

loose control, organic food products will be mixed up with products produced using conventional methods. In such a case, people's trust and anything achieved during these years will be lost.

- Consumers are sufficiently informed about the impact of products on human health as noted a shopkeeper: "As long as biological products are not known to the consumer, there cannot be any price difference.";
- There are also shortcomings in the quality evaluation of organic food products microbiological, physical, chemical indicators;
- Not all experts have positive attitudes towards organic food products. Organic farmers often face a lack of interest about their products from the side of other market agents.
- The relative weakness of consumer organisations.

In the future, sales of organic food products could be impeded if stricter regulations concerning public catering of guests in rural tourism business will adopted.

Possibilities to remove barriers

Both producers and retailers of organic food products cannot expect that most barriers will be removed in the immediate future, basically, for economic reasons. At the same time, those involved in market activities lack necessary marketing information. As a result, it is impossible to evaluate all opportunities and risks involved in producing and selling organic food products. During the exhibition "Riga Food 2003", experts representing the agriculture industry arrived at a conclusion that prospects for a organic food industry, science as well sales of such products would not change without a support to organic farmers. The growth of the middle class with a higher purchasing power and the accompanying shift in values more attention to the quality of life will stimulate the consumption of organic and safe food. Different agents supermarkets, restaurants, hotels, etc are interested in organic products. Certain dynamism in this sector could be foreseen, as supermarkets will seriously undertake sales and promotion of organic and other sustainable products. Collective market initiatives can increase interest and demand of organic food and will improve co-operation between farmers and sellers of organic products.

The larger part of farmers understands that it would be easier to sell products through collective organisation and not through individual efforts. There is support to collective economic project from the farming consultants and the leaders of LABAO, who are encouraging farmers to set up joint economic activities. Farming co-operatives can serve as intermediaries between farmers and their organisations on the one hand and retailers and consumers on the other hand.

Strategies to stimulate consumption of sustainable food products

Latvian scientists suggested that at least 3% of products should be produced in organic farms in the coming years. Unlike their counterparts in Lithuania and Estonia, Latvian politicians have not developed indicators for a preferable development of organic farming (Lithuanian politicians set a target that organic farmers will cultivate 15% of agricultural land by 2010, Estonians - 10%. The Ministry of Agriculture expects that organic farmers will cultivate 46 000 hectares or 2% of agriculture land by 2005. At the moment, the Ministry of Agriculture works out a program for the development of organic farming according to which 10% of agriculture land will be managed and cultivated by using organic farming methods.

The Minister of Finance Valdis Dombrovskis is more cautious. He believes that, initially, a marketing research should be carried out to find out whether there are enough opportunities for organic farmers and producers. And only then plans of development could be worked out.

A chairperson of Latvian Association of Organic Agriculture Organisations A.Runce is of the opinion that organisation of cooperatives is one of the priorities in the organic farming sector. It will allow to deliver organic farm products to shops, marketplaces and public catering sector better. Co-operation should be developed on two levels national and local. "Green" farmers should establish co-operatives whose tasks will be processing and storing of their products. There is also need for co-operatives dealing with buying up organic farm products. Thus retailers could buy all necessary products at one place. There should be co-operation to process and pack products in order to reach supermarkets. It is reasonable to concentrate organic farms around places where processors of products are situated. It will allow to attract more investments.

Chapter 11

Rethinking Tropical Agricultural Commodities

Production of agricultural commodities continues to play a major economic role in many developing countries, especially in the small and Least Developed ones. An estimated 75% of the world's poor live in rural areas, and a large part of them are engaged to some extent in commodity production. Over the past few decades, the market for agricultural commodities has shown a pattern of long-term price falls and short-term price instability. Agricultural production has increased due to improved technology and a general fall in border protection. Demand for primary agricultural commodities has fallen as population growth has slowed and the number of substitutes and higher value-added products has expanded. While declining and volatile prices are unfavourable conditions for any commodity producing country, they have particularly adverse affects on ACDDCs. ACDDCs are often dependent on revenue gained from exporting only one or two specific agricultural commodities, so declining and volatile prices are harmful to both individual producers and governments, both of which face shrinking returns and high risk. Volatile and falling agricultural commodity prices can also aggravate the ratio of debt to exports, undermining debt sustainability. Much of this problem lies in the failure of ACDDCs to diversify into other sectors. Efforts to diversify vertically into higher value-added processed agricultural products or horizontally into other non-agricultural and agricultural primary commodities have had only limited success, compared to efforts to diversify into new areas of economic activity such as manufacturing and services.

Beyond efforts to diversify, both the developed and developing world have considered and implemented various policies to reduce price declines and volatility. Over the last two decades, as government spending and the desire to intervene in markets has decreased, most of these traditional instruments have disappeared, in part due to the deregulatory and liberalising thrust of donor thinking and structural adjustment programmes.

First, there have been attempts, both nationally and internationally, at supply management. Nationally, supply of some agricultural commodities in developing countries has been managed by state marketing boards, which relied on national stockpiles to regulate and manage the supply of commodities for export. While state marketing boards proved beneficial in providing ancillary services to farmers, there were frequent problems with price setting, quality and efficiency of the board.

Internationally, the International Commodity Agreements of the 1970s and 1980s maintained physical buffer stocks to influence world prices. Although these managed to maintain price levels for a number of agricultural commodities (notably coffee), their eventual collapse reflects both the withdrawal of support by consuming countries and the difficulties involved in attempting to influence prices via output management in an environment of supply expansion brought about by productivity increases and limited financial resources.

Second, alongside supply management schemes were a number of broadly complementary international initiatives that made financial transfers to national governments in compensation for falls in agricultural export earnings: the IMF's Compensatory and Contingency Financing Facility and the EU's STABEX and later the FLEX. All these schemes had drawbacks associated with their operation on an ex-post rather than an ex-ante basis; their strict eligibility requirements; and, the conditions they imposed in return for receiving finance.

Third, as donors have given up on supply management, they have increasingly switched attention to the use of market-based risk management tools such as derivatives and insurance. However, the use of these instruments remains limited in ACDDCs because of the costs associated with their use. Moreover, they are only suitable for addressing short-term price and volume instability, rather than long-term price falls.

This combination of deregulation, liberalisation and the shift to market-based policies has yet to produce an improvement in the livelihoods of commodity producers, or the situation of ACDDCs. Prices have become more volatile and their long-term decline has continued.

Against this background a number of new measures for dealing with the 'commodity crisis' have been put forward as increasing attention has been paid to the problems of long-term price decline and volatility in particular sectors, most recently in the cases of coffee and cocoa.

First, questions have been raised over the role of donor interventions in agricultural commodities with respect to their net poverty impact in different sectors. The concern is that while donor support, e.g. for raising productivity, may make benefit producers in one country or area, the cumulative effect will be to increase supply and further reduce prices, outweighing the positive effective of increased sales volume and leading to a net loss in producer welfare.

Second, responding to the challenges of ACDDCs may require an enhanced role for the state, in contrast to the deregulatory and market-based approaches of the past. Here the challenge is to ensure that the state does not replicate past mistakes, but equips the poor to engage with the market on more beneficial terms through providing assistance to diversify assets and improving social and physical infrastructure. Third, more attention should be given in post-liberalisation countries to the need to deal with the fragmentation of the market which has disempowered producers relative to buyers. Strengthened producer organisations are essential if farmers are to establish a stronger bargaining position within the supply chain

Fourth, there has been increased interest in revisiting the feasibility of international supply management, given the relative success of the International Coffee Agreement compared to the events since its demise. The main obstacles to such strategies are likely to be opposition from consuming developed country members (who oppose higher prices) and resistance from other competitive developing country producers who oppose controls on their production.

Fifth, ACDDCs are capturing an ever-smaller proportion of the final retail value relative to processors, wholesalers and retailers. This can be increasing concentration of international trading and processing of commodities. Any oligopsony has market power that must be regulated in some way to produce an efficient outcome. An international competition agreement could, therefore, support the development of competitive markets in agricultural commodities.

Sixth, the development of niche markets (such as Fair Trade and organic products) or the establishment of voluntary commodity funds may be able to assist agricultural commodity producers in developing countries. In particular it has been proposed that Fair Trade principles be mainstreamed into government procurement policies and that targets are set for Fair Trade as a proportion of total trade in some agricultural commodities. There are however, limits to the potential of these approaches to assist large numbers of producers.

Seventh, more attention is required to improve the effectiveness of compensatory funds, and there is a need to examine other income-raising options such as voluntary levies, or commodity-specific taxes in consumer countries.

In designing and refining policy in such areas, researchers need to seek a more evidence-based approach to the social and environmental impacts of past, present and proposed policies. More weight needs to be given in policy design to the lessons to be derived from specific historical evidence, rather than to general assertions about the relative merits of markets and states.

What is the problem and why is it important

The 'commodity problem' is often described as a combination of declining terms of trade commodity prices rising less rapidly than those of manufactures and price volatility. Producers therefore face the dual problem of low returns and high risks.

This paper reviews the long history of thinking and literature on agricultural commodity dependence. It discusses the evidence and experiences of national and international efforts to reduce agricultural commodity price volatility and the adverse effects of this on poor people in poor countries. The focus is on 'soft' tropical agricultural commodities (such as coffee, cocoa and tea), which tend to be produced in developing countries and consumed in developed. These commodities display certain defining characteristics:

- They are often produced by a number of small producers in rural areas; and
- They are 'low-tech' primary products, as opposed to manufactures, and involve minimal levels of processing within the producer country.

For 'hard' agricultural commodities, notably sugar, cotton, wheat, beef, rice, and other commodities where market intervention is significant in developed countries, the trends in the levels and fluctuations in prices will be in part the result of such policies, which can lead to dumping at artificially low prices, driving developing country producers out of both their own and others' markets. In such cases, reform of developed country policies may offer the most pro-development outcomes. This paper, however, focuses on 'non-competing' commodities such as coffee, cocoa and tea.

Long-term decline in prices

Analytical work concluded that in the long run, the price of primary commodities declines relative to manufactures. This hypothesis has been repeatedly tested and found valid.

Theoretical analysis suggests that agricultural commodity prices fall relative to others because of relatively inelastic demand and because of the lack of differentiation among producers, which means that the markets are competitive. Moreover, the decline in agricultural commodity prices is likely to continue. On the supply side, technological improvements, increased competition, reduced protection of markets and devaluation of some national currencies of many agricultural commodity-producing countries following structural adjustment programmes have all contributed to significant increases in production. On the demand side, the development of synthetic substitutes, which further displace agricultura' commodities as intermediate inputs and consumption items, and slower population growth will act to depress demand growth.

Price volatility

In addition to their long-term decline, the prices of many agricultural commodities show a high degree of volatility, caused by time lags between production decisions and delivery to the market; delayed and inappropriate responses by producers to price signals; inelastic supply and natural shocks. The characteristic behaviour of commodity price cycles is one of 'flat bottoms punctuated by occasional sharp peaks' , i.e. periods of low prices endure for longer than price spikes.

There are two types of commodity price fluctuations short-term under tour years for half the shock's effects to dissipate and long-term where there are permanent effects. This distinction is important for informing policy responses: short-term shocks should be dealt with by saving or borrowing, whether by private or public sector, or through market-based risk management mechanisms such as insurance. Long-term shocks require permanent changes in the economy. Agricultural commodities found to have shock persistence of less than a year include bananas and tea while long-term shocks affect coffee, cotton, and cocoa.

The impact of agricultural commodity price decline and volatility

These problems face all countries that produce commodities,

but are more serious for agricultural commodity-dependent developing countries. ACDDCs are defined as being those countries which are more dependent on agricultural commodity exports and specialise in producing one or a few commodities. In many ACDDCs the producers and workers directly affected by agricultural commodity exports are among the poorest of the population. Cocoa, for example, provides livelihoods for 14 million rural workers on big plantations and for a further 2.5 million small producers. Coffee provides income for 25 million producers. Price falls or fluctuations put exceptional strains on efforts to reduce poverty. For many governments, uncertainty of foreign exchange earnings combined with lack of access to credit that could smooth fluctuations in income makes long-term planning of spending difficult. Debt sustainability then becomes a major issue. Sharp falls in prices can threaten the ability of Heavily Indebted Poor Countries to exit from unsustainable debt. If prices fall after the required level of debt relief has been pledged, this level will be insufficient by the time the country completes the process.

In some commodities such as bananas, palm oil and tea, NGOs claim that the downward pressure on prices has triggered a 'race to the bottom' in wages and working conditions on plantations, including casualisation of labour, the use of child labour, increased workloads, reduced benefits such as health provision, schooling and housing.

A number of authors also raise concerns about the environmental impact of some commodity sectors. Intensification in commodity production can lead to increased soil erosion and exhaustion, reduced biodiversity, increased pollution (e.g. through the excessive use of pesticides) and can divert scarce water supplies. At a global level, there are concerns over the use of fossil fuels (e.g. in fertilisers) and the impact on climate change of intensive soil use.

Trends in agricultural commodity prices

Markets for primary commodities are characterised by long periods of low prices and short periods of price rises (IMF, 2000).

This trend. The UN notes 'the two groups for which the developing countries account for the largest shares in world exports, namely tropical beverages and vegetable oilseeds and oils, show the highest rates of decline in prices'. However, whereas the relative growth of global demand for traditional agricultural commodities has weakened in recent years, that for some agricultural products has been on the increase. These new dynamic products include fruits, vegetables, fish, and dairy products. The different demand growth for different products reflects, in part, changing consumer habits. In addition, recent price increases for some agricultural commodities since mid-2002 reflect strong demand growth in China, poor harvests, and speculative buying owing to political developments surrounding the oil market.

The extent of agricultural commodity dependence

The effects of long-term declines and volatility in agricultural commodity prices are greater when a country remains particularly dependent on agricultural commodity exports. This is principally a problem of small developing countries which have found it difficult to diversify due to political, economic or entrepreneurial obstacles. Many of these countries are Least Developed and or among the EU's associated countries in Africa, the Caribbean and the Pacific. Almost all of the countries in sub-Saharan Africa rely on primary commodities (including non-agricultural) for over half of their exports, with some countries relying particularly on one, two or three commodities.

The current evidence: policies to help agricultural commodity dependent developing countries

Over the past two decades many of the classical instruments for public intervention in agricultural commodities have disappeared as the scope for national policies has been constrained by pressures to cut government spending and reduce intervention in markets. At the same time, the increased openness of all countries to trade and improvements in transport and communications have increased pressures on commodity prices.

Reducing dependence on agricultural commodities

In the long run, diversifying into other activities is the best way to reduce dependence on agricultural commodities and the associated vulnerability to negative price declines. There are three diversification routes available to ACDDCs: horizontal diversification into alternative crops; vertical diversification into agricultural products and processes that capture a higher proportion of the value chain; and, diversification into non-agricultural activities that exploit comparative advantage (such as manufactures and services). Of these, diversification into new areas of economic activity is the only solution in the long run and should, therefore, be a long-term objective of development strategies.

Horizontal diversification

Diversification into other internationally-traded agricultural commodities has a principal disadvantage: with few exceptions, the prices of all agricultural commodities appear to be in decline, so the problem of declining terms of trade will remain. In order to reduce exposure to risk, countries need to diversify into several different agricultural commodities. For a small country, even if agro-ecological constraints can be overcome (e.g. limited internal market, climate changes, vulnerability to natural disasters), this may imply quantities that are too small for efficient production, transport or marketing. Alternatively, for countries that are heavily dependent on one or two agricultural commodities for the bulk of their export earnings, but also produce and export several other commodities although in lesser quantities, 'diversification' could mean increasing production of these minor exports, rather than necessarily finding new commodities. For smallholders in developing countries, existing patterns of diversification for food crops are typically well-established and may be so entrenched that they constitute a barrier to further diversification into new cash crops. A further problem is that of 'adding-up'. Agricultural commodity prices could become further depressed if all countries diversify into the same products simultaneously prawns and pineapple became notorious examples in the 1980s.

A further possibility is to diversify into crops for the domestic market. The key issue here is that agricultural-based growth is perhaps the best way to reduce poverty, but a number of countries have achieved this kind of take-off by producing cereals for the domestic market, rather than by export-led growth . The potential for cereal-based import substitution strategies is not an argument for a shift to a more protectionist stance for all developing countries. Indeed the general strategy of openness and state withdrawal may well be appropriate for middle income developing countries, but for some least developed countries import substitution may be a better way forward.

Vertical diversification

Higher value-added agricultural exports offer good prospects for long-term growth due to their relatively high income elasticities. However, there are a number of problems and difficulties associated with this approach. High transaction costs (associated with storing and processing) are perhaps the most important impediment. Other major obstacles to the development of modern processing capabilities in developing countries are poor infrastructure; the lack of investment; and, the high marketing costs and constantly-rising product standards faced in penetrating retail outlets in developed countries.

Diversification into new activities

The main benefits of diversification away from agricultural commodities and primary commodities in general are reduced risk and more stable export revenues. A number of developing countries have succeeded in diversifying away from agricultural commodities into new areas such as manufacturing and services. For manufactures, this has mainly been the case in Asia and Latin America. For services, the Caribbean has shown some success in diversifying into tourism and financial services. This has occurred as a result of the promotion of long-term economic transformation, often involving an enhanced role for the state, for example in industrial policy. Export promotion and tariff preferences in export markets have been less important and, where these have existed, unhelpful. High investment and savings were significant in developing supply capacity, while public investment in infrastructure and education, as well as foreign direct investment, played key roles.

Nevertheless, diversification into manufactured products and services destined for the world market or to substitute for current imports presents its own challenges. The significant investment associated with tree crops e.g. cocoa and coffee makes producers reluctant to destroy these in order to move into other sectors. Already established players provide fierce competition. Banking systems and capital markets in many ACDDCs, particularly in sub-Saharan Africa, are underdeveloped, making it difficult for new producers to raise the necessary capital to move into new sectors.

Trade preferences and diversification

Commodity protocols for bananas, beef veal, rum, and sugar attached to the Cotonou Agreement and before it under the Lomé agreements extend quota access to the highly protected high price European market for those products from traditional exporting countries of the ACP group. For many ACP states, these generated substantial foreign exchange revenue and employment. In some cases preferences also encouraged export diversification by providing tariff exemption for most other ACP exports. Examples include Mauritius and Zimbabwe (from tobacco to textiles, clothing and horticulture). In general, however, preferences have stifled diversification, by making commodity-dependence profitable. Exporters of bananas in St. Vincent and St. Lucia remain vulnerable in this respect: exports of bananas account for over 90% of their exports to the EU and about 50% of their exports to the world.

Supply management

In some developed countries, a form of price stabilisation policy has been that of buffer stock intervention by a central authority that maintains commodity prices at a particular level by buying up excess supply and releasing stocks whenever the market tightens and prices rise. The most notorious example has been the EU's Common Agricultural Policy. Such interventions have helped prevent large temporary shocks from affecting producers. They have, however, faced a number of problems because they have relied on administratively set prices; they were not designed to address the issue of declining terms of trade; and, they were intended to shift risk away from individual producers to national governments. Efforts to support prices by controlling supply are difficult to enforce particularly for agricultural commodities where artificially high prices encourage new producers to enter the market and can be undermined by competition from substitutes.

The experience of developing countries, however, has been different. Often producing a narrow range of agricultural commodities on which they depend for foreign exchange and government revenues, and enjoying only limited shipping outlets for sale on to international markets, ACDDCs have relied on national stockpiles to regulate and manage the supply of the commodity for export. These were until recently run by state-owned market boards, or *caisses de stabilisation*, which served the additional purpose of collecting output from small and large producers across the country, notably in the cases of tree crops tropical beverages, e.g. West African cocoa and coffee. The national stockpile was therefore part of a much larger exercise (UNCTAD, 2003a). For marketing boards, the government would normally set an annual price at which it would purchase the commodity through intermediaries (cooperatives or licensed traders), who were given a fixed margin. *Caisse de stabilisation* systems differed in that although they controlled export contracts they did not handle, export or acquire physical ownership of the commodity in question: primary processing, marketing and exporting was done by cooperatives, private traders or state enterprises. Marketing boards and *caisse de stabilisation* had the advantage that farmers knew the price they would receive at harvest. By aggregating the output of a large number of small producers, they also strengthened their bargaining power relative to buyers. The records of marketing boards have been mixed. In the late 1970s and early 1980s, they struggled to determine the right level of support prices. In several instances, the value of administered prices was not sufficiently and regularly adjusted to reflect inflation in the domestic economy, exchange rate movements, or the medium-term trend in world prices. If administered prices were too low, farmers were cheated, while excessive prices created financial difficulties for the marketing board. In addition, they provided little incentive for quality improvements and suffered from inefficiency and rent-seeking behaviour.

Some argue that crop marketing boards did play a vital role in the development of the agricultural export sectors in several African countries and the policy of dismantling them as part of structural adjustment programmes has been widely criticised. Apart from their role in stabilising prices, they were important for providing ancillary services, such as extension and rural infrastructure, including input provision, product distribution services and credit.

State marketing boards also played a role in building globally-recognised national quality standards. These territorial reputations were built on local specificities of climate, soil etc., but state bodies ensured consistency in sorting, grading and description, and applied sanctions when these standards were violated. National reputations established in this way attracted premia for growers of higher quality products.

International: International Commodity Agreements

John Maynard Keynes included a commodity control organisation in his grand design for the Bretton Woods institutions. However, the US opposed any restriction of free trade. The General Agreement on Tariffs and Trade allowed commodity agreements in some circumstances, specifying in article XXXVIII that contracting parties shall where appropriate, take action, including action through international arrangements, to provide improved and acceptable conditions of access to world markets for primary products of particular interest to less-developed contracting parties and to devise measures designed to stabilize and improve conditions of world markets in these products including measures designed to attain stable, equitable and remunerative prices for exports of such products'.

The 1970s saw a brief period of 'commodity power' (1973-79), which put control of supply in the hands of developing country exporters. Collective action was taken first for phosphates and then, in 1973-74, for crude petroleum. In the case of these particular (non-agricultural) commodities, this strategy worked. Stocking costs for non-perishable standard products were relatively modest. These were supplied by developing countries and enjoyed strong international demand, concentrated in developed countries. The strategy also worked because the commodities themselves were not easily or cheaply substitutable. The formation of supplier cartels or quasi-cartels seemed to show that concerted producer supply-regulation could raise international prices.

International momentum built up in the 1970s for an international Integrated Programme for Commodities (IPC), which had managed buffer stocks as its key element. UNCTAD took the lead in promoting the IPC, which had as an explicit objective raising the price of commodities.

International Commodity Agreements (ICAs), by contrast with OPEC, played by GATT rules and incorporated both consumers and producers. Those that were negotiated under the auspices of UNCTAD in the 1970s were designed ostensibly to prevent unexpected price fluctuations through price controls and subsidies. However such international efforts to replicate OPEC for agricultural and other primary commodities met with less success and eventually collapsed, often after the withdrawal of consuming countries. The ICAs no longer maintain physical buffer stocks. Many of them have reduced their activities to those of mere study groups, some with new purposes, such as providing data and research and promoting sustainability.

The Common Fund for Commodities was initially envisaged as an instrument to fund buffer stocks of core commodities that were to form part of the IPC. The Agreement establishing the CFC was signed in 1980 but only became operational in 1989. By then, the world had changed. National, as well as international, markets had been liberalised. In response, the commodity agreements that were to serve as the foundation for the buffer stocks had dropped the objective of market stabilisation. Consequently, there was no longer a role for the main 'first account' of the Fund and it was left with other supporting activities to be financed through its 'second account' undertaking technical assistance pilot projects in developing countries focusing on individual commodities and multi-country projects examining market chain strategies.

A number of reasons have been advanced as to why this generation of commodity agreements failed. Some believe that the breakdown reflects the difficulties involved in attempting to influence prices via output management, in an environment of supply expansion brought about by productivity increases. Others propose that it is difficult, if not impossible, to agree on price ranges or to determine accurately the correct long-term price trend. Lack of enforcement mechanisms and the free-rider problem have also been suggested. The ICAs' failure to curb supply has also been cited, while in the case of competing commodities, such as sugar, the impact of developed country farm policies played an important role in undermining the agreement. On the other hand, it has been argued that many of these challenges would not have been insurmountable had there been sufficient political will and financial resources.

While some authors see ICAs as a policy dead end, doomed to fail, others feel that the obituaries are premature. Oxfam views the International Coffee Agreement, which lasted from 1975-89, as a 'golden era of good and stable prices.' (Oxfam, 2002). The International Coffee Agreement regulated exports and imports within price bands, but the economic clause in the agreement was abandoned in 1989. Until 1989, governments in both producing and consuming countries sought to agree to pre-determined supply levels by setting export quotas for producing countries. The aim was to keep the price of coffee relatively high and stable, within a price band ranging from US$1.20 - US$1.40 per pound. The agreement succeeded in stabilising prices and persistently raised them by 24-30% over what would otherwise have been market clearing levels.

Policies to alleviate the effects of volatility in agricultural commodity prices

The EU-ACP STABEX arrangement was established in 1975 under the first Lomé Agreement and continued through until the recent Cotonou Agreement. In the form in which it operated in the 1990s, the instrument had serious drawbacks. First, transfers had to be used by the recipient government to support the commodity sector that had suffered the price falls, even if this aggravated the commodity dependence problem. Secondly, the EU placed ever-greater restrictions on the use of transfers, which had to be spent according to provisions negotiated with each recipient country, so transfers frequently remained unspent for long periods of time. Thirdly, time delays built into the system for assessing and making transfers and approving expenditures, coupled with the cyclical nature of international prices for commodities, meant that support often arrived just as commodity prices were rebounding, exacerbating rather than mitigating the impact of price instability.

In the end, at least half of the EU member states wanted STABEX abolished because they deemed it inefficient, inequitable and counter-productive (Hewitt, 1996). The ACP maintained solidarity in demanding that STABEX continue, even though only a handful of countries (Senegal and Côte d'Ivoire in the early years but a broader range towards the end) obtained most of the transfers. Some small countries like the Solomon Islands and Comoros became highly dependent on regular STABEX payments.

In total, STABEX transfers totalled €4.4 billion and were by far the fastest disbursing instrument in the EU's aid portfolio. The leading commodities triggering STABEX payments were coffee, cocoa, groundnuts, cotton and copra (representing four-fifths of total transfers. With the entry into force of the EU-ACP Cotonou Agreement, a new instrument was established to compensate countries for sudden falls in export earnings: the FLEX. FLEX allows ACP governments to use the finance for a wider range of purposes, e.g. in order to safeguard macroeconomic and sectoral reforms. It provides support to countries that have registered a 10% loss in exports earnings 2% in the case of LDCs *and* a 10% worsening of the programmed public deficit. Initial experiences with the FLEX have shown that several countries that experienced significant losses in export earnings were not eligible for compensation, due to the stringent eligibility criteria. It has therefore been proposed to extend to landlocked countries and island states the special clause applied to LDCs, lowering the eligibility threshold to a 2% loss in export earnings, and to also reduce to 2% the benchmark on the worsening in the programmed public deficit. Had the proposed criteria been applied from 2000–02, ACP countries would have received €255 million through the FLEX system, six times more than the amount actually disbursed.

UNCTAD (2003b) supports the continued use of compensatory finance to insulate developing countries from international price volatility. It has made a number of proposals to make existing schemes, such as the FLEX, more effective, including: operation on the basis of ex-ante rather than ex-post mechanisms; easing eligibility requirements, and ending conditionalities for receiving finance.

Market-based risk management

As donors have given up on supply management for agricultural commodities, they have increasingly switched their attention to the use of market-based risk management instruments such as futures, options and swaps. These are intended to enable producers, whether farmers' organisations or governments, to limit the risks arising from price volatility by transferring some of the risk to financial providers, in exchange for a fee. In 1999, the World Bank, with the assistance of UNCTAD, convened an International Task Force to assist developing countries in piloting these approaches. The ITF consists of international institutions, producers' and consumers' groups, commodity exchanges, commodity trading firms and private sector entities from the commodities sectors. Although the use of derivative instruments is not widespread in ACDDCs some African countries, such as Côte d'Ivoire and Ghana, have sold forward their cocoa exports, and some West African countries their cotton exports. Several reasons have been put forward for the narrow use of these instruments in developing countries: limited know-how and awareness of the alternative instruments available; regulatory and institutional barriers; and creditworthiness problems that make it difficult for developing countries to access financial markets. In addition, the coffee market is rather atypical of most commodity markets, in that it is traded on major futures markets, whereas many commodities are traded only by private contracts between buyers and producers, greatly complicating the use of derivatives. Finally, derivatives are unsuitable for addressing long-term instability for agricultural commodities, coverage is generally restricted to a few months and they cannot maintain higher prices for sellers.

Five years on, the ITF has carried out an active and innovative series of pilot projects, but has yet to produce significant breakthroughs on price risk management. According to delegates at the Annual Meeting of the ITF in Rome in May 2004, pilots and research continue to show bottlenecks and constraints rather than workable solutions: the minimum size of commercially viable transactions is proving extremely hard to generate. Finally, security concerns are placing increasing legislative demands on financial houses to 'know your client', which is both time-consuming and requires levels of data that are sometimes unavailable in ACDDCs. Microinsurance, along the lines of microcredit, seems to offer little hope, given its much higher demands in terms of data, proof of loss and danger of moral hazard.

An alternative, but potentially more realistic, approach might be to encourage the use of longer-term contracts between producers and buyers. This would not only solve the problem of declining prices, but would provide a measure of stability that would allow producers to plan several years ahead, thus avoiding some of the negative consequences of price volatility (DTI, 2004). Although long-term contracts are frequently used in Latin America, this approach, for Africa, suffers from the perception of traders that African producers cannot supply consistent qualities and quantities of some key agricultural commodities such as coffee.

Market concentration and the value chain

Agricultural products are linked to final consumers through so-called global value chains. A value chain describes the full range of activities that are required to bring about a final product from the growth of a primary commodity, through the intermediary phases of production transformation and producer service inputs, delivery to final consumers and final disposal after use.

As with all raw agricultural producers, ACDDCs are capturing less and less of the value of their markets relative to processors, wholesalers and retailers. This can be explained in part by a loss of market share and market power in agricultural commodity exports.

In addition, two closely related changes have occurred in the market structure for most agricultural commodities. First, in producer countries, farming is highly fragmented, and the destruction of marketing boards has further reduced the capacity of farmers to raise their share in value chain rents by removing a useful intermediary that could improve farmers' bargaining power with large corporate buyers. Secondly, the international markets for agricultural commodities have become much more concentrated. Perhaps in response to declining profit margins, large trading companies dealing in many commodities have replaced smaller and specialised companies, while the total share of all trading companies has fallen relative to direct purchases by processors or final sellers. In coffee and cocoa, 4-5 branded processing companies jointly control 60-70% of world production. The concentration and the removal of the buffer layer of traders tend to weaken producers' market power, although the removal of the middle level may increase the share of the price going to producers. The growing role of integrated companies also leads to more direct control of what is produced technical and quality standards. The interaction of these two trends has meant that some of the services formerly provided by governments, e.g.

finance and stockholding, are now provided by foreign companies, decreasing the share of commodity income remaining in the producing country.

The stage in the value chain where concentration is largest tends to acquire a large share of the profits, with a smaller share of the final price going to other stages. African producers have incurred income losses while traders and firms in higher stages of the value chain have received significant benefits. In the early 1990s earnings by coffee producing countries (exports f.o.b) were some US$10-12 billion and the value of retail sales of coffee, largely in industrialised countries, about US$30 billion. Now the value of retail sales exceeds US$70 billion but coffee producing countries only receive US$5.5 billion. The asymmetrical character of power in the coffee value chain helps explain the increasingly unequal distribution of total incomes. At the importing end of the chain, importers, roasters and retailers compete with each other for a share of the rents but combine to ensure that few of these accrue to producer countries. Real profits in the agricultural commodity chain are made by those who control critical points along the chain, own established brands, or have access to shelf space in supermarkets. A major implication of this for developing country producers is that they must enter into networks if they want access to developed country markets. These networks disseminate information about markets to producers and enable buyers to obtain information about and develop confidence in the suppliers.

The concentration of agricultural markets is unquestionable. Although there is no substantive evidence of deliberate abuse of market power, it is a commonplace of theory on oligopoly that no formal collusion is necessary for monopolistic pricing to occur: oligopolistic companies can tacitly understand that it is in none of their interests to challenge each other's prices. Any oligopsony has market power that must be regulated in some way to produce an efficient outcome. Some have advocated an international competition agreement to strengthen the framework to support competitive markets.

What we don't know new and revised initiatives to assist agricultural commodity dependent developing countries

Most donors have invested heavily in projects aimed at diversification of agricultural commodities, as well as increasing productivity via credit-based input supply measures. Advocates of such programmes highlight that if agricultural commodities can be produced more efficiently in new locations, or with new technologies, then they can be of benefit nationally and improve the total efficiency of world production. Opponents criticise such approaches citing the 'adding-up problem': they may reduce world prices for the commodities concerned and may be damaging to producing countries *as a whole*.

The role of the state

Responding to the challenges of small or Least Developed ACDDCs may require an enhanced role for the state, in contrast to the generally deregulatory and market-based approaches of the 1980s and 90s. Here, the challenge is how to ensure that the state does not replicate past mistakes, but equips poor producers to engage with the market on more beneficial terms. Rather than get involved too directly in production, successful Latin American initiatives in the 1980s 90s focused on providing services such as acting as an information point for new entrants and new buyers. Governments in Asia and Mauritius were more active, ensuring a broad level of cooperation between the state and the private sector.

General state support to enhance and diversify assets, and to increase productivity and value-added through the development of agro-processing, includes: access to finance, rural credit facilities to non-farm activities, provision of extension services, and training. Improving social infrastructure, health and education, or physical infrastructure that can enable new economic sectors to emerge transport and communications - will also enhance productivity.

In conjunction with international schemes, national supply management approaches have also been encouraged. UNCTAD cites the example of Malaysia's levy on palm oil production, imposed in times of high prices and then used in periods of low prices to subsidise the use of palm oil in a non-traditional way, namely, for electricity generation. In West Africa studies by the French Government have concluded that the remaining *caisses de stabilisation* offer a more effective means to protect small cotton producers from price volatility than new market-based risk management approaches. The researchers propose the creation of national 'stabilisation fund mechanisms', building on embryonic mechanisms in Cameroun and Burkina Faso. The stabilisation funds, which could be either private or publicly run, but in either case require a single nation-wide purchasing organisation to be viable, would be akin to collective self-insurance, taking a share of any surplus in good years and redistributing it to farmers and ginners in bad years. A regional fund, capitalised by donors, would underwrite national stabilisation funds against exhaustion.

If donors are to revisit the issue of state marketing boards, they need to consider the increasing pressures on state trading enterprises within the WTO. Although these are largely targeted at developed country state trading enterprises, such as the Canadian Wheat Board, any move towards rules that prevent a new generation of more effective state interventions in ACDDCs may have unintended negative consequences for the poor.

Producer organisations

A closer examination of the role of producer organisations in improving the outcomes for small farmers and poor farm labourers could also produce new policy ideas, especially in post-liberalisation situations where the role of the state remains constrained. At least five types of producer organisation can be identified large estates, small estates, large modern cooperatives, small cooperatives and contract farming and outgrower schemes. Scale and organisational model affect the benefits that accrue to farmers. For example the FNC, the Colombian national coffee growers' federation, claims 500,000 members with an average of 2 ha of coffee each. FNC operates an extension service with over 800 staff, as well as its own agricultural colleges and a research and development centre. It runs a price stabilisation scheme and has diversified downstream into freeze-drying and own label sales. Cooperatives in Africa on the other hand, have often failed to grapple successfully with the market and high demands on quality and reliability.

In cotton, post liberalisation structures fall into three groups: geographical monopolies (Ghana, Mozambique), systems with numerous players concludes that the last category produces the best outcomes, by combining the positive benefits of competition with a scale that can deliver price stabilisation and other benefits and that 'rebuilding local-level economies of scale is becoming a strategic issue in the wake of increasing buyer-drivenness on a global plane on the one hand, and the fragmentation of that has frequently followed market liberalisation on the other.'

Revisiting supply management

There has recently been increased interest among the academic community, NGOs and some developing country governments in revisiting the feasibility of international supply management, not least because effective schemes would help secure higher incomes for commodity producers, potentially providing investment for long-term diversification efforts (Robbins, 2003). International commodity arrangements are specifically allowed under the GATT.

Advocates of this approach cite the qualified success of the International Coffee Agreement, compared to events since its demise (see above), as well as examples such as diamonds. In the case of the latter the monopoly producer De Beers has traditionally maintained a large stockpile and acted as supplier of last resort in order to keep prices high, although it now claims to be moving more toward demand management under pressure from the US, where it has been barred from operating since the early 1990s for alleged antitrust activities. Arrangements to manage the gold market in the same way have prevented price falls over the last decade. Gold and diamonds, however, are not agricultural commodities and are not included in the CFC or under the IPC. Each of these examples works quite differently from each of the others. This is no accident, since each commodity market is different. This may be one of the reasons for the ICAs' failure: they followed a one-size-fits-all policy. Successful attempts at international supply management have often depended on a dedicated core of producer countries, with a common sense of solidarity Examples include the Middle Eastern countries in OPEC and Indonesia, Malaysia and Thailand in the tin agreement. Coffee offers a counter-example, where international supply management has proved difficult because of the free rider and coordination problems that arise when a large number of countries export the commodity.

Oxfam has proposed a high-level review of the issue, involving UNCTAD, the WTO and the CFC. Citing coffee as an example, Oxfam proposes that a large proportion of export supply be removed from the market. However, given the difficulties with previous efforts at international supply management, a weakness of the proposal is that it fails to elaborate on the 18 mechanisms that should be employed to do this, other than offering broad support for a renewed effort by producing and consuming countries to bring supply in line with demand on a more systematic basis across a range of agricultural commodities, and noting that limiting supply by means of quality criteria could be an option.

Several agencies have looked at the issue of quality. UNCTAD has proposed the introduction of 'a rigid system of quality assurance' to reverse the decline in quality which in many cases has followed deregulation, adding that quality improvement should be complemented by programmes that 'fund the withdrawal of productive capacity in high-cost producing countries and of low-quality stocks.' The International Coffee Organisation has proposed a similar instrument, the Coffee Quality Improvement Mechanism, setting target standards for exportable coffee. The ICO argues that poor quality is a more important factor than price in slowing demand growth. In a paper for ICO, Kaplinsky argues that major roasting companies should work together to reposition coffee as a consumer product comparable to wine, greatly increasing the possibilities for developing regional and speciality coffees. However, measures to remove the production of low-value coffee from the market can be criticised for raising prices for poor consumers.

Contributors to DFID's 2004 International E-forum on New Directions for Agriculture in Reducing Poverty argued that production cuts are the only way forward on supply management, perhaps involving export taxes and production quotas - other approaches such as buffer stocks and export quotas merely lead to the problems of oversupply and circumvention that brought down previous ICAs.

A new generation of supply management agreements would also have to involve farmers associations to a far higher degree than the previous generation of ICAs. One participant believed the present climate is actually more conducive to ICAs than the 1970s, when they were set up low prices should galvanize support in developing countries, while improved information technology makes it easier to administer production controls presumably this could involve satellite photography, as has been done in coca eradication programmes.

The main obstacles to such strategies are likely to be political. Without the assent of the consuming developed country members, international supply management is extremely difficult. Winning that assent may involve demonstrating that inadequate farm income can be linked to pressure to increase narcotic drug production, political and economic instability, and a shrinking market for goods and services from developed countries - all of which are of significant concern to the main consuming countries of agricultural commodities. In addition, there is likely to be resistance to such schemes from other competitive developing country producers, who would oppose controls on their production e.g. Vietnam in the case of coffee. Any supply management scheme will at some point come under unpredictable financial strain, and provisions to accommodate that strain should be in-built. Finally, effective international supply management schemes would need to demonstrate determination and credibility in bringing supplies more in balance with demand. If sentiment can be changed in this way, market traders will purchase the commodity in the expectation of selling it at some future date at a higher price, thus pushing up prices and completing a virtuous circle.

Incorporating price and volume risk into debt sustainability calculations

Volatile and falling agricultural commodity prices can aggravate the ratio of debt to exports, yet commodity price risks have so far not been sufficiently considered in design of debt relief schemes such as the HIPC initiative. A substantial drop in the prices of key export commodities explains the deterioration in the net present value of debt-to-export ratios relative to ratios projected at decision point for 2001 of 15 HIPCs, of which 13 were African. Uganda found itself in an unsustainable debt situation at completion point, due to steep declines in the price of coffee and completion point debt relief for Burkina Faso had to be topped up by US$129 million because of the decline in the price of its main export, cotton.

In addition, there remains concern about the low priority being accorded to the agricultural sector in PRSPs, and the consequent impact on levels of investment, e.g. in rural infrastructure. The failure to tackle the link between agricultural commodity dependence and extreme poverty has been dubbed as a 'conspiracy of silence' by President Chirac, and described as the 'major sin of omission' in current international efforts to reduce poverty. Although implementing such strategies may not require large financial resources from governments, they would require sufficient technical capacity and political will, something that has been an impediment in the past. UNCTAD (2003b) has called for increased donor support to build such capacity.

Proposals to reduce the adverse impact of market concentration

A number of recent studies point to the high concentration of both international trading and processing in agricultural commodities among a few countries. These studies assert that high rents are being extracted by enterprises in developed countries although they often do not provide any supporting evidence. Consequently, a number of measures have been proposed that would contribute to reducing market concentration and thereby would increase competition in these segments of the marketing chain. The main proposal is that developed countries assist in the creation of domestic trading companies in producing countries that would process products in the latter countries in association with developed country processors.

Within WTO negotiations a separate debate is under way on the issue of developing multilateral rules for competition policy. In their communication to the WTO, Tanzania, Uganda and Kenya requested that the WTO examine steps to deal with anti-competitive behaviour of large foreign firms and to improve the bargaining position of small producers *vis-à-vis* these firms. If core principles on competition such as non-discrimination and transparency and an undertaking to outlaw hard-core cartels can be established then this could be relevant to agricultural commodity markets.

Unfortunately, the controversy surrounding this makes the likelihood of a multilateral agreement difficult to achieve. Many developing countries see the WTO as an inappropriate forum for such a competition agreement, arguing that the agenda there is more likely to be driven by transnational corporations' desire for improved market access than by a concern to improve development outcomes. Some authors and NGOs believe a pro-development competition agreement is more likely to be achieved elsewhere in the UN system. They do, however see other roles for the WTO. Current WTO rules require governments to complete questionnaires about any state trading enterprises operating in their country. That approach could be expanded to include any company, public or private, with more than a given percentage of the import or export market. Such improved transparency would help in checking restrictive business practices at an international level. In June 2004, for example, delegates from 70 countries attending a 'World Farmers' Congress' organised by the International Federation of Agricultural Producers adopted resolutions to collect and publicise concentration information and demand that government anti-trust agencies provide economic impact statements of proposed mergers and joint ventures. IFAP supports introducing a pre-established level of concentration that triggers a presumption of a violation of anti-trust law.

Niche markets – Fair Trade and organic agricultural commodities

Fair Trade organisations have created a parallel marketing chain that allows consumers to pay a premium that directly supports agricultural producers. This constitutes a different approach to marketing, in that buyers are informed and concerned about the nature of production, not only about the quality and other characteristics of the product. Proponents of Fair Trade argue that paying producers a 'living' price, above the cost of production, is the only sustainable long-term strategy for consuming countries. They also point to the positive impact of the community projects funded by such schemes.

Fair Trade commodities represent a small share of world trade in commodities. Westlak for example, estimates that Fair Trade coffee only accounts for 1.0–1.5% of total global trade in coffee. However, year on year growth far exceeds that of trade as a whole, with UK fair-trade produce sales rising 46% in the year 2002-03. While it remains to be seen whether Fair Trade agricultural products can secure a significant share of the conventional market for any particular commodity, there are questions in any case about the long-term effectiveness of such a solution on a large scale. Sceptics argue that Fair Trade arrangements are analogous to a voluntary tax or charitable contribution paid by developed country consumers. They question the potential for helping a large number of poor producers in this way because of the correspondingly large number of consumers required to contribute.

Some organisations have proposed that Fair Trade principles be mainstreamed into government procurement policies and that targets are set for Fair Trade as a proportion of total trade in some commodities as part of the Millennium Development Goals. There are two main problems with these approaches. First, EU and UK government rules on value for money place severe limits on governments, although there may be waysthat procurement contracts be drawn up (and audited) from developed country governments specifying that a certain percentage of the retail price go to the farmer. Second, for example in the case of coffee, if large roasters agreed to cooperate in purchasing Fair Trade coffee this might well violate strict US antitrust laws.

The emergence of organic commodities, which also compete with Fair Trade products, has allowed some production to be marketed at a price premium. The emergence of organic coffees, in particular, is frequently cited as a major reason for the consumption of coffee in the US not falling, despite health concerns.3 An increase in organically produced commodities represents a potentially attractive means of assisting poor producers, since the poorest farmers are the least able to acquire chemical fertilisers and sprays. However, in practice the processing and marketing of these commodities is more difficult and complex than for those traditionally produced. In particular, the system requires that the commodity be traceable from its source through the value chain. This requires comprehensive inspection and certification, which is much easier for large farms in developed countries than for scattered smallholders in developing countries. The price premiums obtainable from producing organic commodities may therefore not cover the additional marketing, certification and inspection costs and would yield lower returns than investing similar resources in efficiency or quality-enhancing measures at the national level.

Voluntary commodity funds

A number of proposals have been made (often for the coffee sector for introducing voluntary commodity levies to fund demand, efficiency and livelihoods-enhancing measures in the agricultural sector. UNCTAD and Oxfam have both proposed an 'international diversification fund'. The Walter Zwald proposal for the International Coffee Organisation was for importers to pay a voluntary levy of US$20 tonne into a coffee fund which would raise an estimated US$84 million per year (Zwald, 2001). The fund would be used for promotional activities aimed at expanding demand and for a range of production-related activities, including support for sustainable livelihoods.4 In return for their contribution, roasters would be permitted to use the fund's logo on their packaging, which would yield publicity benefits in terms of increased sales.

There are a number of problems with these proposals as they currently stand. In particular, there is no guarantee that participating enterprises will not pass the cost of the levy on to consumers in the form of higher prices reducing demand and therefore lowering producer prices or that the levy will not be passed back directly in the form of lower producer prices. A further idea that has arisen in the context of the reform of the EU sugar regime is that a compensation fund for the impact of European sugar policies on developing countries could be financed by a small tax on European sugar consumption. This would also ease health concerns over the impact of a sudden fall in sugar prices, following a shift to a more liberalised regime.

Poverty and environmental impact

Much of the discussion on commodities takes place in something approaching an evidential vacuum, concerning the actual social and environmental impact of particular commodity booms and busts. In many cases, evidence exists, but policy makers are unaware of it, or find the generalisations of economic modelling simpler to use, despite its mixed predictive track record. There is a clear case for a greater degree of case study-based research into the poverty, gender and environmental impact of processes such as export-promotion, liberalisation and market concentration, as a means of informing future policy choices.

Closing the policy gap

Several avenues of possible research arise out of this discussion of agricultural commodity dependence that would help promote understanding of the impact of different commodity experiences on poverty.

Global value chains

While much work has been done in analysing international

commodity markets in terms of global value chains, it has so far generated little in the way of public policy ideas. Two areas of work which merit further research, and dialogue with both producers and buyers, are:

- Poverty Impact: which global value chains are more less poverty reducing and why? For example, are those that have a higher level of smallholder involvement more desirable than those that rely on large farm production, and what are the features that determine the nature of the supply base?
- What public policy interventions at national or international level might improve the poverty outcome of the trend towards buyer-driven global value chains?

Supply management

There is clearly a demand for DFID to revisit this issue of supply management, if only to satisfy itself that its current pessimism is justified. Areas that should be covered include:

- A review of past international and national supply management efforts to establish the success and failure factors behind the varied experiences.
- A comparison of price stability and poverty impact under ICAs with that of the post-ICA regime.
- Some initial thinking on the design of possible international supply management schemes based on production cuts, taking a crop-by-crop approach and looking at the political economy of implementation; the strengths and weaknesses of producer-only and joint producer-consumer agreements; the threat of crop substitution in response to price rises; the technical feasibility of production control and surveillance and

Chapter 12

Rural Poverty, Agricultural Production, and Prices: A Reexamination

In his insightful but unfinished work, Dharm Narain drew attention to the behavior of prices as one of the important factors determining the extent of poverty in rural India. His empirical investigations, summarized in Gunvant Detail contribution 10 this volume, provide strong prima facie evidence of such influence. Dhram Narain found that rural poverty is not only inversely related to the level of output per head of the rural population, as established in Ahluwalia, but also positively related to the level of prices. What is equally interesting is that he found that when account is taken of the effect of variations in both output per head and prices, the underlying time trend in rural poverty, is negative, a very different conclusion from mine I reported no underlying trends and the very opposite of that of Griffin and Ghose and Saith who assert a rising underlying trend.

This chapter pursues the issue raised by Dharm Narain using an expanded data base. His results are based on all-India data comprising 12 observations for 1956-57 to 1970-71. An additional estimate is available for the year 1936 99, and the period can he extended by including data for 1971-72, 1972-73, 1973-74, and 1977-78.

Rural Poverty in India, 1956-57 to 1977-78

A complete assessment of trends in rural poverty should take account of several dimensions of poverty, of which income or consumption levels per head is only one. Equally relevant are factors such as longevity, access to health and education facilities, and perhaps also security of consumption levels from extreme shocks. However, time-series data on all of these dimensions are not available. Data from a series of consumption surveys conducted by the National Sample Survey Organisation are available, and these data have been used in most of the studies of rural poverty in India. In this paper, I use NSS data on the distribution of consumption expenditure in nominal terms, combined with poverty lines in current prices, to compute two indices of poverty, the percentage of the rural population in poverty the traditional head-count measure and the Sen Index, which takes account of extent of poverty within the population below the poverty line. The poverty line for each year corresponds to a constant-price poverty line of 15 rupees per capita in 1960 61 prices adjusted using the consumer price index for agricultural laborers. The numerous deficiencies in these estimates have been well documented. Nevertheless, they present a unique picture of changes in rural poverty over more than 20 years No comparable time series for such a long period are available for any other developing country.

The expanded data set bears out my conclusion that there is no underlying time trend in poverty for the period as a whole. The percentage of the population in poverty declined through the fifties, rose to a peak in 1967 68, and then declined substantially, though unevenly, through the seventies. The Sen Index shows an almost identical pattern. The absence of any time trend is confirmed by the following results.

Both indices show great variation in the extent of poverty. This could have been expected with the head-count measure, which lakes no account of the intensity of poverty. When there is a substantial concentration of the population at the poverty line, as in India, small changes in the level of consumption can shift large numbers of people above or below it. This would show up as large changes in the measured incidence of poverty even though the changes in real consumption levels were marginal. This problem does not arise with the Sen Index, which gives due weight to the extent to which the consumption of individuals falls below the poverty line. It is therefore significant that the Sen Index also shows a coefficient of variation of 0.18 compared with that of only 0.12 for the head-count measure. Clearly, the variations in the measured degree of poverty over time reflect substantial variation in the measured levels of real consumption. It is important to explain these changes and to study their implications for policy. The addition of data for the seventies materially affects some assessments of the underlying trends in rural poverty in India. For example, Griffin and Ghose , in their critique of Ahluwalia argued against the use of data from the fifties. They argued that the impact of the green revolution on rural poverty could be assessed only by focusing on the period after 1960 61. Using data for 1960 61 to 1973 74, they concluded that there was a significant trend increase in rural poverty in the period despite the downtrend from the 1967 68 peak. However, as shown in figure 7.1, the trend completely reversed in the 10 years following 1967 68. There is no basis whatsoever for asserting that the incidence of rural poverty in India has been rising from the sixties onwards.

My own assessment that there were movements in both directions, with no underlying trend, needs to be qualified in the light of two observations by Tyagi . The first relates to Tyagi's argument that CPIAL, which is used to compute the poverty line in various years, exaggerates the extent of the rise in prices because it is based on 1956 57 weights. Tyagi points out that prices of wheat, production of which has increased rapidly, rose somewhat less than prices of items such as barley and gram (chickpeas), whose production growth has been more modest. Consumption patterns have changed in favor of items whose prices rose less. Tyagi does not present an alternative price series for rural consumption, but he shows that a composite index of cereal prices for 1973 74 using CPIAL weights is 2.6 percent higher than one using weights derived from the 1973 74 consumption pattern. However, cereals account for only about 50 percent of total consumption expenditure in the rural expenditure classes, and unless there is a similar weighting problem for other food items, the overstatement of the rise in overall prices would be less than for cereals. Thus, this particular bias may well be small. However, any upward bias in the price index would lead to some overstatement in the extent of poverty in the seventies.

Tyagi also questions the accuracy of the NSS consumption estimates for 1960-61 and 1961-62. He shows that NSS estimates for these years show much higher levels of foodgrain consumption by households than do the official estimates of total foodgrain availability, a discrepancy that narrows considerably in the seventies. Tyagi argues that the most plausible explanation is that the NSS overestimated foodgrain consumption in 1960-61 and 1961 62. If this is indeed the case, the NSS consumption estimates for 1960-61 and 1961-62 may need to be revised downwards, which would raise the estimates of poverty in these years. An upward adjustment in the estimates of rural poverty in 1960- 61 and 1961-62, combined with a downward adjustment in the seventies to correct for the exaggeration of the rise in prices by the base weighted price index, would have the effect of showing a modest trend improvement in rural poverty. It is not possible to resolve these questions satisfactorily with the data available. We can only note that even when there is a prolusion of apparently comparable data, our assessment of trends can only be tentative. This also qualifies any attempt to explain observed trends.

The Narain Equation and Some Alternatives

Dharm Narain s analysis of the determinants of rural poverty was based on an equation that both expands and restricts the equation used in Ahluwalia in which rural poverty is shown as a fun agricultural income per head of the rural population y and time t. Dharm Narain expanded this specification to include p, the consumer price index for agricultural laborers, as an explanatory variable reflecting the prices faced by the rural poor as consumers He restricted the Ahluwalia formulation by using current agricultural income per head, while the Ahluwalia equation used income not only in the current year but also with a one-year lag.3 A further difference is that in Dharm Narain's formulation all variables (including time) are entered in logarithmic form. The effect of extending the period under study on the estimated coefficients of the Narain equation can be seen by comparing equations (3) and (4) in the table, which relate to the full period, with equations (1) and (2), which relate to the shorter period covered by Dharm Narain.4 The explanatory power of the equation is considerably less for the full period than for the shorter period, but the results are qualitatively similar and statistically impressive. The coefficient on the agricultural income variable is negative, and on price positive, and both are highly significant. The Coefficient on time is also negative and significant. These conclusions hold whether we use the head-count measure of poverty or the Sen Index as the dependent variable.

An interesting aspect of the comparison is that the coefficient on prices for the shorter period is reduced by half in the full period On the other hand, the income coefficient doubles in the full period. Clearly, in the Narain equation the role of prices is substantially reduced when data for the seventies are included, while variations in income per head become much more important. One possible reason for this could be that the vulnerability of the poor to sharp increases in prices declined in the seventies owing to the expansion and extension of public distribution into rural areas, which helped the poor protect their consumption in periods of rising prices.

The explanatory power of the Narain and Ahluwalia equations is broadly comparable. The explanatory power of the Narain equation is lower when the head-count measure is the dependent variable but higher when the Sen Index is used. These comparisons suggest that the effect of lagged agricultural income on rural poverty is at least as important as prices if we are concerned with explaining variation in poverty. What is more, this is not, as might be supposed, a case where lagged income per head acts as a proxy for prices. The correlation between y-1 and p is only 0.17, and the correlation between the logarithms of these variables is only 0.20. The low correlation may appear counter intuitive, but it is not surprising when one considers that p is heavily time-trended, whereas y-1, is not. The significance of y-1, as an explanatory variable is therefore clearly independent of prices and is much more plausibly explained in terms of the cushioning effect through borrowing or sale of assets mentioned in note 3. The effect on consumption, and therefore poverty, of a fall in income in one year can be cushioned by borrowing or sale of assets, a cushion that is exhausted if there are two successive bad years. For this reason, a decline in income in one year does not lead to as large an increase in poverty as when there arc two bad years in succession Equally, a rise in income levels immediately following a bad year docs not reduce poverty as much as might be expected, since consumption loans undertaken in the previous year would have to be repaid, and assets sold replaced, before consumption levels could recover fully. Lagged agricultural income is therefore an important explanatory variable in its own right.

The composite includes both y-1, and p as explanatory variables The composite equations and have a higher explanatory power than either the Ahluwalia or the Narain equation. They explain three fourths or more of the variation in rural poverty, depending upon the measure used. The coefficient on p is positive, but the significance level declines. It is below acceptable levels when the dependent variable is the head-count measure of poverty but remains highly significant when the Sen Index is used.

In summarize the expanded data base for 1956-57 to 1977-78 confirms that rural poverty agricultural income, prices and time are related broadly as indicated in Dharm Narain's results, but with important differences. Rural poverty appears inversely related to income per head in the rural areas, and the relation is considerably strengthened it agricultural income is also lagged. The addition of lagged agricultural income somewhat weakens the significance of the coefficient on prices but does not negate entirely. However, the absolute size of the coefficient on prices is considerably reduced in the extended period and is further reduced if lagged agricultural income is included.

Problems of Interpretation

Interpretation of the estimated equations reported above is not as it may seem at first. Aggregate relationship of this type are often consistent with more than one underlying causal mechanism, and it is important to subject them to close scrutiny before accepting them as evidence for one or another point of view. This applies to both the observed positive relationship with prices and also the inverse relationship with agricultural income.

The Role of Prices

The positive coefficient on the price variable in the Narain equation has been interpreted as confirming the hypothesis that inflation tends to accentuate rural poverty independent of the level of agricultural output per head. The hypothesis is entirely plausible on a priori grounds, but this does not mean that the equation as specified is appropriate to test it.

The a priori case is easily established. Sen's model of a rural economy illustrates the plight of wage earners when there is a sharp rise in food prices. Such a rise could take place without any change in production per head in the rural economy because of a general inflation in which food prices move up with other commodity prices. Food prices also could rise owing to developments outside the rural economy, such as a rise in export demand cr reduced imports of food. In either case, if rural money wages do not rise sufficiently to offset the increase in prices, the real incomes of the poor decline.7 Such real wage effects are not the only mechanism through which price changes may affect rural poverty. Even if the rural poor are self-employed peasant producers who produce goods other than those they consume, arise in food prices could accentuate rural poverty if it is not matched by a rise in the prices they receive.

This misspecification also introduces a bias m the estimated equation. Since the excluded variable p is bound to be highly correlated with time because of the inevitable trend element in prices, its exclusion from the estimated equation biases the estimated coefficient on t. In effect, the expected negative coefficient on p will be reflected in the estimated coefficient on t, which is biased downwards. It is because of this bias that in spite of the high t ratio, we cannot take the estimated negative coefficient on t at face value. This brings into question Gunvant Desai's interpretation, in chapter 1 of this volume, of the negative coefficient on time in the Narain equation as indicative of the operation of other processes conduct a separate analysis for the incidence of poverty in each group.

A crude alternative, though perhaps the only feasible one, is to treat pd. the national accounts deflator for agricultural gross domestic product as a proxy for prices received by the rural poor and then use the relative price variable p pd as an explanatory variable. The coefficient on the relative price variable p pd is positive but not significant in the logarithmic form, especially when t is included. However, it is positive and significant in the linear form. When p and pd are separately entered in the logarithmic equations we obtain the expected positive coefficient on p and the negative coefficient on pd, but the significance levels are low. Removing the time term improves the significance level of these coefficients, but they still remain below the conventional limits.

A second way around the specification problem is to test for the impact of prices by using the rate of inflation, rather than the level of prices, as the explanatory variable. There is considerable a priori justification for this. If the problem arises because of the stickiness of money wages, then we can expect poverty to increase in periods when prices rise, but once prices stabilize, money wages can be expected to catch up, so that in time the initial adverse effect of inflation would be corrected, even though the level of prices remained high. Thus it is not the level of prices but the fact of rising prices that is important.

Agricultural Production and Poverty

The rationale for using agricultural income per head of the rural population as an explanatory variable affecting rural poverty is self-evident. If the distribution of income remained constant and there were no adverse terms-of-trade effects, then an increase in agricultural production should raise income levels for all sections of the rural population, thus pushing some individuals above the poverty line. We cannot, of course, assume that the distribution of income would remain constant or that terms-of-trade effects would not occur. Nevertheless, a significant negative coefficient on the agricultural income variable tests whether the net effect of rising income per head after allowing for these other considerations is a reduction in poverty to some extent. This is the so called trickle-down mechanism, about which much has been written. The existence and strength of such mechanisms is clearly important for policy. They hold out the hope that strategies for raising agricultural production would tend to reduce poverty even if they were not accompanied by radical institutional changes such as land reforms, which, desirable though they are, have proved extremely difficult to implement in practice.

To begin with, we must recognize the difference between saying that trickle-down mechanisms exist and saying that trickle-down has worked. To assert that trickle-down mechanisms exist is only to say that the rural economy works in such a way that a rise in agricultural production and income levels per head would lead to some decline in rural poverty. This is quite different from saying that trickle-down has worked in the sense that it has actually led to a decline in poverty over time. Such an outcome would require not only that trickle-down mechanisms exist but also that agricultural growth has been sufficiently rapid for income levels per head to rise over time. The estimated inverse relationship docs indeed suggest that trickle-down mechanisms do exist. But it is also true that growth was not fast enough to achieve the desired reduction in poverty over the period as a whole. Real agricultural income, measured in terms of net domestic product in agriculture, grew about 2 percent per year from 1956 57 to 1977 78, which was only slightly faster than rural population.10 As a result, agricultural NDP per head of the rural population showed no significant growth trend. Year-to-year fluctuations reflect the effect of weather on total agricultural production, but these variations are around a near-stationary level.

Even this interpretation of the estimated equations as indicating a limited potential for trickle-down has been challenged. Some believe that while agricultural expansion may have had strong links with income generation for the poor in the first half of the period, this linkage weakened considerably in the second half. It has been argued that agricultural growth up to the mid-sixties resulted principally from area expansion, which favored increased use of labor and therefore benefited the poor. Growth in the second period was mainly the result of higher yields, which resulted from the new technology. It is argued that adoption of this technology was associated with changes in the rural economy that limited the downward flow of benefits. The concentration of increased yields in certain regions is relevant in this context. Equally important is the fact that the new technology depends heavily upon intermediate inputs such as pump sets and tractors, which may have reduced the use of labor in agriculture. In addition, the high credit requirement may have limited benefits to smaller and marginal farmers.

The hypothesis that the linkage between higher agricultural production and the alleviation of rural poverty weakened after the mid-sixties needs to be studied intensively The case for it is certainly not established a priori. While some technological changes, such as combine harvesters, probably were labor-displacing, others were not necessarily so. The spread of irrigation, high-yield varieties, and application of fertilizers calls for a more labor-intensive production. Even the use of tractors, insofar as it permits more effective multiple cropping, is not necessarily a net displacer of labor Similarly, while it may well have been more difficult for small and marginal farmers to benefit from the new technology, there was a conscious shift of policy in the seventies aimed at overcoming these difficulties. There was a considerable expansion m rural development programs and employment-generating schemes aimed at supporting productive activity and income levels in precisely these "weaker groups.

Presents a crude test of whether the relationship between agricultural production and rural poverty weakened in the second half of the period. A dummy variable d is specified which takes the value zero for 1967-68 and is set at unity for 1968 69 and thereafter. Using this variable in conjunction with y, we can introduce the product term dy as an additional explanatory variable into the equation along with y. A significant positive coefficient on the new variable would indicate that the inverse relationship between rural poverty and income per head dampened in the second period. In no case is there a significant positive coefficient on cither d or dy, which we would expect if the trickle down mechanism had become weaker. Similar equations have been estimated using slightly different cutoff points from the dummy variable but with essentially the same results.

These results suggest that trickle down mechanisms exist in the sense defined above and also that there is no evidence that they have weakened in the later period. However, this conclusion should not be interpreted as an endorsement of trickle-down strategies to the exclusion of other policies or strategies directly aimed at helping the poor. The need for devising strategies of growth to ensure adequate flows of benefits to the poor, or more modestly, for supplementing the general strategy of raising agricultural production with more target-oriented programs aimed at the weaker sections, remains urgent. Trickle-down processes alone would probably take an inordinately long time. The estimated equations certainly bear this our. Even if we take the elasticity of our bead-count measure of poverty with respect to income per head to be 1.2 the highest level obtained in table 7.2, the objective of reducing the extent of rural poverty from 40 percent of the rural population to about 20 percent would require an increase in per capita income of about 42 percent. Since our ability to raise the rate of growth of agricultural NDP is limned, an increase of this order takes time. If agricultural NDP per head of the rural population were to rise by 1 percent per year—a modest improvement over past performance it would take 35 years to reduce the percentage of the population in poverty to 20 percent by trickle-down alone. If the growth rate were raised to 2 percent a very substantial improvement over observed rates of growth it would take 18 yean. Growth certainly makes a difference, but it must be conceded that even on optimistic assumptions, the process would be slow if we relied on growth alone.

Conclusions

The implications of my results for the important issues addressed by Dharm Narain, with their limitations and qualifications, can now be summarized. To begin with, I must put things in perspective by emphasizing that a critical limitation of my analysis is the use of a undimensional measure of poverty in terms of consumption levels. A comprehensive assessment of the living conditions of the poor, and changes over time, must encompass not only consumption levels but also health, longevity, security in both health and consumption levels, and, of course, access to public goods such as drinking water and education. Rural development policy in India has been shaped consciously to improve conditions in all these aspects, and we need to assess progress in terms of changes in these dimensions as well as changes in consumption per head. Time-series data on all of these dimensions are scarce, although the available evidence points to considerable improvement in health, longevity, and education. An interesting feature of recent experience is the establishment of institutions such as the public distribution system and rural employment programs, both of which add to the security of income and consumption by insulating the population to some extent from the wont effects of drought and inflation. Unfortunately, it is not possible to assess the impact of these developments on the living conditions of the rural population in a comprehensive manner. Therefore, the indices that we have used, although clearly inadequate, probably provide the best possible basis for studying the issues considered in this chapter.

The first issue that I have considered relates to the long-term trend in rural poverty. The NSS data permit the firm conclusion that there is no basis for the view that the incidence of rural poverty has increased over time, especially in the period after the green revolution. The data for 1956-57 to 1977-78 show no significant trend, and the data for the period after the green revolution show a more or less steady decline. The measured incidence of rural poverty in 1977-78 teems to be about the same as that observed in 1960-61 and 1961 -62, but this may be misleading because of the biases pointed out by Tyagi. These may result in understatement of the extent of poverty in 1960 61 and overstatement of it later. Whether these biases exist is far from definitely established, but it they do, the corrected long-term trend may well show a slight decline in rural poverty. What is more important, however, is whether the improvements observed in the seventies will continue. The NSS has switched from annual consumption surveys to 5-year surveys. The data for 1982-83, when they become available, will help to throw light on this all-important issue. The second issue considered in this chapter is the relationship between rural poverty and agricultural income levels per head. Three conclusions have emerged: There is fairly strong evidence of an inverse relationship between agricultural income per head and the incidence of rural poverty, especially if account is taken of lagged effects. there is no evidence that this relationship has weakened since the green revolution; and reliance on growth alone will not bring about a large reduction in the incidence of poverty in the near future . These conclusions underscore the need for rural development programs aimed especially at the rural poor. Because of the highly aggregative nature of my analysis, these conclusions must be qualified. Differences among states may arise because of variations in agricultural conditions and patterns of growth. The analysis also assumes a common structure over time in the model to be estimated. Yet it could be argued that important changes have taken place that cannot be captured in the regression equations by using dummy variables. The effect of rising agricultural production on rural poverty depends upon a very wide variety of factors. Some of these are essentially exogenous, such as developments in the land-man ratio and the nature of the technology underlying the rise in production. Others depend upon policy towards agricultural development. For example, programs designed to increase the ability of small and marginal farms to benefit from available improvements in technology and irrigation help to widen the spread of production gains.

Chapter 13

Impacts of Trade, Macroeconomic, and Price Policy on Agriculture

Introduction

Trade and macroeconomic policies are important determinants of the rate of overall economic growth. Broad-based economic growth, based on favorable trade, macroeconomic and price policies, can in turn have substantial benefits for agriculture, including the creation of domestic markets for agricultural commodities and the generation of capital for investment in agriculture. Indeed, in much of Asia, particularly East and Southeast Asia, the broad performance of macroeconomic policies, including fiscal discipline, adequate incentives for savings and investment, and an outward-looking trade policy, was overwhelmingly conducive to economic growth, at least until the early to mid-1990s.

In addition to setting the economic environment for overall growth, these policies also have a profound impact on the performance of individual sectors of the economy such as agriculture. Trade, macroeconomic, and price policies can affect agriculture by either taxing or subsidizing the sector. Trade restrictions have a direct effect on the domestic prices of tradable goods, and have an impact on the real exchange rate which, in turn, affects the domestic prices of tradable goods in relation to locally produced goods. For example, import duties and quotas raise the domestic price of import-competing production in relation to exportables (including many agricultural commodities) and therefore encourage a shift away from export production. The same policy instruments reduce the demand for imports, which lowers the price of foreign exchange so that the domestic prices of tradable goods fall in relation to nontradable goods and hence indirectly bias production incentives against both importcompeting and export goods. Protection for industrial import substitutes thus penalizes the domestic production of agricultural goods in the following ways:

- The rise in the domestic price of the protected industrial output reduces the relative price of agricultural products;
- The cost of industrial inputs (fertilizer, pesticides, and farm equipment) for agricultural production increases; and
- The induced appreciation in the real exchange rate renders agricultural exports and import-competing products less profitable than nontradable goods.

Alternatively, trade and macroeconomic policies can protect agriculture or specific commodities within the agricultural sector. Agricultural protection, by raising domestic food and agricultural prices above world prices, penalizes consumers and introduces inefficiency by attracting excess resources to production of the protected commodity or sector and by rendering unprotected sectors less competitive. Protectionist policies require large government fiscal outlays to farmers to pay price supports and subsidies and may also encourage excessive use of agricultural chemicals, thus damaging the environment. Input subsidies distort input allocation decisions and compromise scarce government resources that could be used for directly productive investments.

In many cases, agricultural protection also represents an inefficient transfer of income from consumers and taxpayers to farmers, because the fiscal costs of protection are higher than the benefits received by farmers and because income is redistributed to wealthier, large farmers, who receive the greatest share of benefits. In addition, price stabilization policies significantly have influenced agricultural production in many Asian developing economies.

Despite the high costs of either taxing or protecting agriculture through trade and macroeconomic policies, a common "developmental" path, consisting of a period of taxation of agriculture followed by increasing agricultural protection, has been adopted by most countries as they develop and industrialize. Will this historical pattern of declining taxation and increasing protection of the agriculture sector be repeated in the developing countries of Asia? What impact might present-day trade and macroeconomic policies on agricultural taxation and protection have on the playing out of this historical pattern in the Asian developing countries? Might developments in international trade negotiations and institutions or developments in the structure of agricultural trade provide countervailing forces to increasing agricultural protection?

Historical Patterns of Agricultural Protection

As economies grow, they tend to shift from taxing agriculture to protecting agriculture relative to other sectors. This shift occurs at an earlier stage the weaker an economy's comparative advantage in agriculture and more rapidly the higher an economy's growth rate and the faster the decline in its comparative advantage in agriculture. This pattern has been observed in Western Europe and North America and, more recently, in Japan; Taipei, China; and the Republic of Korea. In Japan, agricultural protection was zero or negative in the 19th century, became positive in the early years of the 20th century, and rose sharply after the 1950s. The Republic of Korea and Taipei,China have followed the Japanese pattern, but at an accelerated pace. Over a 20-year period, beginning in the early 1960s, the Republic of Korea and Taipei,China shifted from slightly taxing agriculture to heavily assisting it.

The historical rise in levels of agricultural protection in

industrializing countries is linked to the changing role of agriculture during economic growth. First, the declining importance of food in household budgets as incomes grow reduces the political pressure for low imports to variations in domestic production and prices and by forecasting errors in estimating import requirements. Both these results have often increased price variability instead of reducing it. The budgetary costs of managing public stocks and open-market operations have been very high and the lack of operational transparency has encouraged corruption and rent seeking. Public intervention in domestic markets has squeezed the normal seasonal price spreads, driving private traders from the market and reducing market efficiency.

By the late 1980s, many Asian countries were realizing that price stabilization was an ineffective and unsustainably expensive strategy for achieving stable prices. In Pakistan, the government abolished its monopoly in rice in 1988 89; in Bangladesh, the rice monopoly in external trade ended in 1992 -93. The Philippines has proceeded slowly, opening up import trade in wheat, flour, and animal feeds to the private sector, but retaining the National Food Authority monopoly on international trade in rice and maize. BULOG in Indonesia, probably the most effective public agency in Asia in stabilizing grain prices is in the process of a significant reduction in its stabilization role. In Viet Nam, a complete liberalization of prices was introduced in the agricultural sector in 1989 and restrictions on imports and exports of important products, such as rice, were relaxed. In 1997, additional implicit and explicit restrictions to internal trade were removed and export quotas were decentralized.

Trade, Macroeconomic and Price Policies in Asia

In most Asian developing countries, the indirect effects of trade and macroeconomic policies have caused overvaluation of the real exchange rate, which in turn has lowered effective agricultural prices, taxing the agricultural sector. In the Philippines, for example, overvaluation of the exchange rate arising from the protection of domestic industry lowered agricultural prices by 30 percent during the 1980s.

Policies in Pakistan, Sri Lanka, and Thailand similarly induced overvaluation of the real exchange rate by 15–25 percent during the 1980s. Nevertheless, there was a downward trend in the degree of overvaluation in the real exchange rate in most Asian countries throughout the 1980s, followed by a gradual real appreciation in the 1990s that again penalized agriculture and other tradable sectors.

To compensate at least partially for the discrimination of trade and exchange-rate policies against agricultural production, most East and Southeast Asian countries have provided subsidies for agricultural inputs fertilizer, credit, and irrigation and have targeted direct price supports to favored crops, particularly rice and wheat. These selective subsidies and price supports have fallen far short of fully offsetting the pervasive taxation caused by the trade restrictions. In addition, they distort economic incentives and penalize consumers, while imposing costs on farming activities that receive lower subsidies and on the environment, the latter by encouraging overuse of inputs. However, as David shows, there was a gradual but significant reduction in direct price support for most food crops in East and Southeast Asia after the mid-1980s: many countries reduced levels of commodity-price protection and moved toward a policy of following the long-term world price in setting domestic agricultural prices.

In Indonesia, for example, taxation of agriculture through currency overvaluation has been minimal. The average overvaluation during 1980–90 was about 7 percent, and when overvaluation reached higher levels the rupiah was devalued to restore balance. The slight overvaluation was balanced by heavy fertilizer subsidies that kept fertilizer prices at about one half of world prices; by moderate direct price protection of rice and other food crops; and by heavy price protection for favored commercial crops such as sugar, soybeans, and milk and dairy products in order to promote crop-diversification strategies. Beginning in the mid-1980s, policies shifted toward a gradual reduction of fertilizer subsidies and agricultural price protection. By 1994, nominal protection rates were low for virtually all agricultural commodities, estimated at -5 percent for rice, 5 percent for corn and soybeans, -2 percent for cassava, 20 percent for milk, 14 percent for poultry products, 1 percent for beef, and 5 percent for other livestock products. The reduction in protection of rice led to the elimination of producer subsidies for rice farmers. The annual value of subsidies to rice production peaked at $1.1 billion in 1985 and was -$71 million in 1990.

Compared to other Southeast Asian countries, Malaysia's trade and macroeconomic policies have been relatively neutral toward agriculture, with the exception of rice, which has been highly protected. Exchange-rate distortions due to trade and macroeconomic policy have been minimal, with overvaluation averaging only 6 percent from 1980 to 1990 before the beginning of the real appreciation in the 1990s due to massive short-term capital inflows. In contrast, direct rice-price interventions to support farm income and encourage production have resulted in nominal protection rates in excess of 100 percent. Important export crops such as rubber and palm oil, on the other hand, have been subject to export taxes to generate government revenues and to finance research, marketing, and replanting programs. The level of taxation, however, has declined from 25-30 percent in the early 1980s to 5-10 percent in the 1990s.

In the Philippines providing income support to producers and maintaining affordable prices to consumers were primary objectives of direct price policy. The policy was intended to prevent or smooth out sharp changes in food prices in response to changes either in world prices or domestic supplies. Low and stable rice prices were considered important for keeping the rate of inflation low, for reducing upward pressure on wages, and for improving the profitability of the industrial sector. In practice price interventions have had varied impacts for different commodities. Maize has received high protection averaging 62 percent in 1990-92 through import tariffs and restrictions due to a strong emphasis on import substitution. Rice has fluctuated between being protected during periods of higher imports and being taxed during the years that rice was exported. The export crops, sugar and copra, have been highly taxed, but the level of taxation has declined somewhat since the mid-1980s. Although direct price support favored some crops, an overvalued exchange rate implemented in support of import-substituting industrialization heavily taxed the agricultural sector. The Philippine exchange rate was overvalued by about 25 percent in the early 1980s, but trade policy reforms implemented after 1986 significantly reduced the overvaluation to around 10 percent in late 1990. In Thailand, while maintenance of low and stable food prices for civil servants and the urban poor was considered important, the primary objective of price policy was to maximize foreign-exchange earnings from agricultural exports by maintaining a high and stable export price. Before the early 1980s, therefore, price interventions followed the classic pattern of taxation of major export commodities, including rice, rubber, and cassava, and protection of crops targeted for import substitution, including cotton, soybeans, and palm oil. Trade liberalization beginning in the early 1980s, however, has essentially eliminated the taxation of rice, rubber, and maize and has greatly reduced the protection for other crops such as sugar, for which the nominal protection rate declined from over 90 percent in 1985 to –8 percent in 1990. Exchange-rate policies in Thailand resulted in an average overvaluation and taxation of agriculture of about 20 percent during 1980–84, but improvements in current-account balances reduced the overvaluation to about 10 percent in the late 1980s. Before the PRC began its economic transition process in 1978, the chief role of agriculture was to provide cheap food, capital, and labor for industrial development. Agricultural products were priced below international market prices, thus transferring rents from agriculture to the industrial sector. The implicit taxation of agriculture was enforced by mandatory procurement quotas, a state grain monopoly, strict foodgrain acreage controls, administrative prescription of agricultural inputs, restrictions on nonagricultural activities, and prevention of rural-urban migration. This strategy of squeezing the agriculture sector failed, however, due to the cumulative misallocation of resources and low productivity in agriculture.

Since 1978, the PRC has been in transition between taxing and subsidizing agricultural production. During the first reform period of 1978–84, state procurement prices for agricultural products were raised and rural markets were opened; the household responsibility system was also introduced. Interregional trade was authorized in 1984. In the second phase of reforms, during 1985–93, the agricultural pricing and marketing systems were liberalized and rural offfarm activities were encouraged. By 1993, more than 90 percent of all agricultural produce was sold at market-determined prices. The average nominal rate of protection during 1978–93 ranged from –27 to –68 percent for wheat, from –11 to –56 percent for rice, and from –21 to –57 percent for maize, based on a comparison of quota prices with international prices. Since 1994, however, this high taxation has dropped substantially. Recently, in the face of rising grain prices, declines in production, and increasing inflationary pressure, there have been some signs that the government, at least at the provincial level, is attempting to regain control. In 1995, the governor's responsibility system was introduced, whereby provincial governors are responsible for balancing grain supply and demand and stabilizing grain prices. So far there is no clear indication of a shift to increasingly protectionist policies.

Compared to the more export-oriented growth model of East and Southeast Asia, most of South Asia has pursued a strategy emphasizing import substitution and self-sufficiency in capital-goods production and neglect of agriculture and exports. Direct agricultural-price policies have often compounded the negative impacts of indirect trade and macroeconomic policies in this region, with the result that agriculture has been much more heavily taxed than in Southeast Asia. In Pakistan, for example, some protection was provided by direct price supports for wheat, ordinary rice, and cotton in the 1960s, but the overvaluation of the rupee outweighed the direct protection of these crops, while increasing the priceinduced taxation of basmati rice. In the 1970s and early 1980s, direct effects of trade policies turned negative and became the dominant form of taxation for wheat, basmati rice, and ordinary rice, because the exchange-rate effect the distortion caused by the appreciation of the real exchange rate was smaller than in the 1960s. For cotton, trade policies had only a small direct effect on domestic prices, but domestic prices remained significantly lower than equilibrium free-trade prices because of the indirect effect of exchange-rate appreciation and overall trade policy.

Beginning in the mid-1980s, large declines in the world prices of cotton and rice resulted in significant reductions in implicit taxation, because domestic prices of these commodities were not allowed to fall precipitously. Thus, the five major agricultural products in Pakistan wheat, basmati rice, ordinary rice, cotton, and sugarcane were consistently taxed from the 1960s to the mid-1980s. Dorosh and Valdés estimate that the combined effect of trade and exchange-rate policies and agricultural-price policies reduced wheat production by 24 percent and basmati rice production by 52 percent during 1983- 87 compared to what they would have been without government intervention. In the absence of direct and indirect price interventions, farm incomes from these five major crops would have been 40 percent higher during that period. Import substitution policies became the cornerstone of Bangladesh's development policy and remained so until the onset of policy reforms in the 1980s. High export taxes and export restrictions, as well as fixed and multiple exchange rates, characterized the external trade regime. The importcontrol regime and the exchange-rate policy combined to cause an overvalued exchange rate until the mid-1980s, imposing an implicit tax on exportables. The reform process that started in the 1980s included the gradual removal of trade distortions, the introduction of a flexible exchange rate, and the elimination of agricultural input subsidies. Appreciation of the exchange rate during the second half of the 1980s offset the protection provided by direct trade policies for wheat, cotton, and potatoes and increased the implicit taxation of rice, lentils, jute, and tea.

Nevertheless, the overall degree of taxation of the agricultural sector had declined by early 1990s compared to the late 1970s. The implicit protection rate of the agriculture sector as a whole averaged –18.1 percent between 1986-87 and 1990 91. Average nominal protection of rice ranged from –26.3 percent during 1976 77–1980 81 to –0.5 percent during 1981 82–1985-86 to –10.3 percent during 1986 87–1990 91. The total nominal protection rate for wheat declined sharply from –21 percent during 1981 82–1985 86 to –0.3 percent in 1986 87.

In India, agriculture has been heavily taxed through both direct and indirect price policies, with only partial compensation through input subsidies that have introduced additional distortions in production incentives. Protection of industry and overvaluation of exchange rates have taxed agriculture and export restrictions on agricultural commodities kept domestic agricultural prices below world prices. Overall taxation of the agricultural sector was estimated at 30 percent during 1970–84. Even in the state of Punjab, which received substantial input subsidies, Bhalla and Singh estimate aggregate measures of support of -32.64 percent for the period of 1981 2 to 1992 3.

India instituted economic reforms during 1991 that were necessitated by an unmanageable fiscal deficit and a balanceof-payments crisis. These reforms included liberalization of industrial and trade policy, relaxation of foreign-exchange controls, and reduced trade- and investment-licensing requirements. The reforms were concentrated in the nonagricultural sector, but the liberalization had a positive effect on agriculture by reducing the anti-agricultural bias of protectionist industrial policies. Overall net taxation of agriculture has been cut to just above 9 percent during the postreform period, although important crops, such as rice, still face taxation rates in excess of 30 percent. In addition, state trading in agricultural commodities is still pervasive.

The Indian government has attempted to compensate farmers for high taxation through indirect and direct price policy by heavy subsidies to fertilizer, power, credit, and irrigation. Total input subsidies grew dramatically starting in the early 1980s, although fertilizer subsidies were reduced during the economic reform process initiated in 1991. Input subsidies were equivalent to 53 percent of plan expenditure in 1982 83, and 131 percent in 1992-93. Very conservative estimates of losses due to subsidies in 1989-90 range from 0.5 percent of GDP for irrigation; 1 percent of GDP for electricity; and nearly 1 percent of GDP for fertilizers . By 1995 96, following the introduction of economic reforms, fertilizer subsidies dropped to 0.6 percent of GDP. The record of trade and macroeconomic policies and their impact on the agricultural sector in Asia has thus been highly complex. Policymakers have pursued inherently conflicting objectives, such as maintaining high prices for farmers and low prices for consumers, and have simultaneously taxed and protected agriculture. On balance, trade and macroeconomic policies have until recently produced a substantial bias against agriculture, with the degree of taxation higher in South Asia than in East and Southeast Asia. Economic reforms since the mid-1980s have significantly reduced this bias, however. The evolution in policies can best be described as being toward a reduction in distortions and toward increased liberalization in both direct and indirect policies, rather than the shift from taxation to protection that is implied by the historical pattern of agricultural policies. Developments in international trade institutions and structural changes in international trade also appear to lead to continued liberalization of policies rather than increased protectionism, as seen below.

Gatt and WTO

The General Agreement on Tariffs and Trade served as the multilateral framework for international trade relations for nearly fifty years, following the decision of the United States not to ratify the charter of the International Trade Organization that was proposed at the Havana conference of 1947–1948. Although technically the GATT was not an organization but a multilateral agreement, it nonetheless succeeded in substantially reducing barriers to world trade through eight successive rounds of multilateral negotiations held under its auspices. As a result of the Uruguay Round agreement in December 1993, the World Trade Organization a formal international organization, subsumed the GATT. As of September 1997, the WTO had 132 member countries and 34 observer countries, all but four of which have applied to join the organization. The Kyrgyz Republic became the 133rd member of the WTO in December 1998. The PRC; Taipei,China; and the Russian Federation are the largest trading countries that are still negotiating accession. In addition to creating the WTO framework for the long-term reform of agricultural trade and domestic policies, to achieve increased market orientation in agricultural trade, and to strengthen the rules governing agricultural trade in order to improve predictability and stability for both importing and exporting countries. The most important component of the agricultural agreement is the requirement that all nontariff border measures be replaced by tariffs that initially provide the same level of protection. Tariffs resulting from this "tariffication" process and other agricultural tariffs are to be reduced for developed and developing countries over a period of 6 and 10 years, respectively, by an average of 36 percent and 24 percent, with minimum reductions for each tariff line of at least 15 percent and 10 percent. Many loopholes and exemptions limit the scope of agricultural trade liberalization under the UR agreements, however. For example, loopholes in the process of tariffication have allowed countries to bind tariffs at levels well above the existing average tariff so-called "dirty tariffication". Countries are also allowed to retain import restrictions until the end of the implementation period under certain circumstances. Developing countries are afforded special treatment through the "rice clause" negotiated by Japan and the Republic of Korea to continue managed rice imports that in effect exempts those countries from the liberalization of agricultural commodities that are predominant staples in their traditional diet. The UR on agriculture also restrains domestic subsidies to agriculture, but measures that have a "minimal" impact on trade (so-called "green box" policies), such as income support to agricultural producers that is decoupled from production, are permitted to continue.

Agricultural research, disease control, infrastructure, and foodsecurity policies are also among the green box policies. The main farm programs of the United States and the European Union were exempted and Japan was allowed to increase its direct payments to farmers. Moreover, developing countries were exempted from commitments to reduce input subsidies provided to "low-income or resource-poor producers." Again, these significant exemptions will limit the immediate effectiveness of subsidy-reducing policies. Given the high levels of bound or base-level tariffs resulting from dirty tariffication, the fairly long implementation periods, the permitted exemptions, and the exclusion of some trade-distorting policies from elimination, it is likely that the extent of liberalization of agriculture under existing rules will be small. Indeed, available quantitative estimates of the growth in trade and in incomes with full implementation of the liberalization agreed to in the UR show notable but modest benefits. Hertel et al. estimate global welfare gains from UR agreements on agriculture and manufacturing of $260 billion per year, or 0.4 percent of global GDP, by 2005. The largest gains are for developing countries, particularly those that are more open or that liberalize to a greater extent. The East and Southeast Asian developing countries are therefore projected to be substantial gainers, with an increase in GDP of 4.7 percent by 2005. Francois, McDonald, and Nordstrom also find that Asian developing countries will benefit significantly more from the UR agreements than other regions, with the PRC receiving a boost in GDP annually of 4.0 percent, other developing East and Southeast Asian countries receiving a 3.2 percent increase, and South Asia receiving a 3.1 percent increase, based on 1992 real prices. Despite the modest quantitative benefits estimated by modeling, integration of agricultural trade into the WTO is a major achievement and the most significant benefits cannot be captured in quantitative models. The dynamic gains to developing countries in Asia are likely to be substantial, including the improvement of access to international technology and capital; strengthening of investor confidence, employment and productivity growth; and encouragement to unilateral trade liberalization programs. The political benefits in Asia and elsewhere may be especially large, because the UR agreements will help to break up the existing constellation of political forces that, as described above, has tended to make increasing agricultural protection an inevitable part of economic growth.

Anderson argues that multilateral trade agreements can alter the political equilibrium in favor of more open trading policies. A country that reduces trade barriers and allows more imports may harm its import-competing producers, but if its trading partners simultaneously lower their barriers to the first country's exports, the producers of those exports will benefit. Exporters may benefit more than the importcompeting industries lose, so that the liberalizing politicians also become net gainers in terms of electoral support in both countries.

Political gains from trade negotiations involving exchange of market access will tend to be greater, the larger the number of countries involved and the broader the products and issues coverage of the negotiations. Expansion of membership in the WTO compared to the GATT has dramatically increased the scope for exchange of market access among countries. In addition, it is easier for politicians to placate those harmed by reform when similar producers in other countries are being simultaneously asked to make sacrifices. This has been especially important in the case of farm-policy reforms during the UR.

Thus, the inclusion of agriculture under the GATT WTO umbrella is a major step forward, but the limited degree of real agricultural liberalization leaves much to be done in the years ahead. Governing rules should be tightened by reducing or eliminating the special and differential treatment given to both developed countries and to developing countries in Asia and elsewhere. Special exemptions weaken the political benefits of the WTO, because they reduce the scope for governments to use the agreements to justify domestically the adoption of politically unpopular but economically desirable reforms. Elimination of farm-export subsidies should be considered in the next comprehensive round, to bring agriculture into line with nonfarm products, for which export subsidies are banned under the GATT.

Dirty tariffication, which set bound tariffs well above actual tariffs, could permit protection levels to be raised considerably, if countries should choose to use tariffs to insulate their domestic markets from fluctuations in international markets. The next multilateral negotiations should aim to bring those bound tariffs down at least to applied rates.

The long and often frustrating UR negotiation, culminating at one point in the collapse of the "final" negotiating session in Brussels in December 1990, was a significant factor in the revival of interest in regional trade agreements that seek to liberalize trade among countries within a region. Prominent RTAs include the North American Free Trade Agreement (NAFTA) and the Southern Common Market in the southern cone of South America. Negotiations have begun to develop a free (or at least liberalized) Asia-Pacific trade area based on the Asia Pacific Economic Cooperation forum. In Asia, ASEAN formed the AFTA in 1992 and the member states of SAARC signed a framework agreement for SAPTA in 1993.

Policy Reforms in Developed-Country Agriculture

In addition to progress on multilateral and regional trade negotiations, fundamental changes in the structure of agricultural trade will influence trade and macroeconomic policies in the Asian economies and the impact of these policies on agriculture. The United States and Western Europe have historically provided large subsidies and high levels of protection to agriculture. However, unilateral agricultural policy reform that has been completed in the United States and is under negotiation in the European Union will fundamentally change developed-country farm policies, moving them away from the paradigm of market intervention and price manipulation in favor of direct payments to farmers tied less to output.

In the United States, the Federal Agriculture Improvement and Reform Act of 1996 dramatically altered the support system that US producers had relied upon since the Great Depression. The Act replaces the long-standing, crop-linked, deficiency-payment supply-management program that covered wheat, rice, feedgrains, and upland cotton with a program of fully decoupled, temporary contract payments based on land acreage. Payments are capped at about $36 billion over 1996– 2002 and are scheduled to decline over the 7-year period. The FAIR Act also eliminates the Acreage Reduction Program, gradually eliminates dairy-price supports, and modifies US peanut and sugar programs.

During 1993–95, the Common Agricultural Policy of the European Union went through significant reforms that initiated a shift from direct price supports to decoupled income supports by lowering intervention prices. In July 1997, the European Commission initiated Agenda 2000, which seeks to broaden the shift from price supports to income supports under the CAP, to continue the reduction in intervention prices, and to reduce export subsidies on agricultural products. These policy reforms in previously highly protected agricultural markets should reduce tensions in international markets and encourage the development of a more liberalized agricultural trade system.

Changes in the Nature of Agricultural Trade

Josling, Tangerman, and Warley note that the nature of trade in agricultural goods is also changing over time, in ways that tend to expand its importance in the multilateral trade system and to increase the relative political strength of interests that favor liberalized trade policy. Agricultural trade has historically been dominated by bulk products, such as cereals, milk, meat, and sugar. Trade in bulk commodities is still based largely on comparative advantage and policy-induced distortions and these bulk products have not generally attracted international investment.

But the share in world trade of differentiated products with higher value added such as processed foods, including fruits and vegetables, is now becoming much larger in both developed and developing countries. Producers of these goods can develop comparative advantage by investment from abroad and can build markets through quality and name recognition. Government price-support policy has traditionally been less important in this trade and is in fact often detrimental to processors who have to deal with high-priced raw materials. Government regulations regarding quality and food-safety standards are more significant.

Growing mobility of technology, management, and marketing skills is making it possible to develop the agricultural and food sector through international investment. Foreign processing firms are searching for reliable sources of raw materials at low cost and are increasingly looking abroad. Changing consumer tastes, developed through urbanization and contact with other cultures or introduced by immigrants, have expanded markets for commodities previously considered nontradable. All of these developments point to the globalization and further liberalization of agricultural trade.

International Price Variability

What will be the impact of the agricultural trade liberalization and the changing structure of agricultural trade on international price variability? Some observers have argued that the increasing openness of trade regimes could usher in a period of increasing price variability that could destabilize farm incomes and harm poor consumers who still spend a large share of income on food. But with the changing structure of international agricultural trade, a number of countervailing forces will come into play that on balance could actually reduce international price variability.

Policy reforms in North America and Western Europe may indeed have increased the likelihood of increased variability in international prices. Until recently, the developed countries have borne most of the costs of maintaining food stocks, largely as a byproduct of domestic farm-support programs. However, as North American and European governments scale back pricesupport programs in favor of direct payments to farmers, they no longer need to buy and hold large reserves. In 1996, the United States and European Union together held less than one half the stocks they held in 1993. This policy-induced reduction in stocks could mean larger price fluctuations in the future, because fewer supplies may be available to the market to dampen price changes when production varies and privatesector stocks may not make up for the difference in reduced public stocks.

Given that the lack of transparency and consistency in government stockholding and trade policies were often sources of instability in the past, however, a reduced involvement by governments in stock management and a more transparent trade policy could contribute to increased stability in the future. Moreover, market liberalization initiatives including those completed under the UR agreements and those resulting from future multilateral trade negotiations, regional trading arrangements, and other unilateral initiatives—should contribute to stability in international markets by inducing greater adjustments to demand supply shocks in domestic markets. Protectionist policies in the past shifted the impact of fluctuations in domestic production to the world market, increasing international price variability and insulating the domestic market from external fluctuations. The elimination or reduction of protectionist policies is therefore expected to help reduce price instability in the world market. Improved market integration should also smoothe the effect of international trade on available supplies: the elasticity of demand facing any group of producers would increase, as would the supply elasticity facing any group of consumers. Increased stability should follow in an economy that responded faster and more strongly to shocks as consumers and producers made rational decisions aided by improved information and price transparency.

Although it is too soon to assess the full impact of trade liberalization and structural change on international price variability, an analysis by Sarris of inter-year price variability of cereals from 1972 to 1996 concluded that no increase in interyear variability in world cereal markets had taken place. Recent price changes do not appear to herald anything unusual and are not outside the range of normal annual variations. Furthermore, analysis of the intrayear cereal price variability showed that there does not seem to be a tendency for the coefficients of variation of monthly seasonal prices to increase over time; if any, the tendency is towards a decline in variability. It is unlikely that international price instability will cause significant problems for the continuation of the trade liberalization process.

Conclusion

In much of Asia, gradual reform in the mid-1980s and early 1990s of trade and macroeconomic policy regimes that have historically penalized agriculture have recently improved its competitive position. This long-term policy evolution was temporarily interrupted in the early 1990s, when the competitive position of agriculture and other tradable sectors began to erode due to the dramatic appreciation in real exchange rates in East and Southeast Asia (and a significant but smaller appreciation in

South Asia; this erosion resulted from macroeconomic policies and the massive influx of short-term foreign capital. The sharp depreciation of currencies in several countries in East and Southeast Asia during the financial and economic crisis that began in 1997 eliminated effective taxation of agriculture caused by real exchange-rate overvaluation. This development should provide a significant stimulus to agriculture in these countries.

Chapter 14

Bringing Agriculture to the Market

Far-reaching changes in domestic and global markets are creating big opportunities for farmers and agribusiness entrepreneurs. The demand for high-value primary and processed products is rapidly increasing, driven by rising incomes, faster urbanization, liberalized trade, foreign investment, and advancing technology. These developments are expanding market opportunities, which is important for faster agricultural and nonfarm growth and for greater employment and rural incomes. But the new markets demand quality, timely deliveries, and economies of scale, posing special challenges for smallholders. Still in many agriculture-based and transforming countries, food staples remain a mainstay for a major share of households, many of them poor. But the performance of food staple markets is often hampered by poor infrastructure, inadequate support services, and weak institutions, pushing up transaction costs and price volatility. How markets for food staples function thus affects livelihoods, welfare, and food security, especially for poor households. Well-functioning agricultural marketing systems can reduce the cost of food and the uncertainty of supply, improving the food security of poor and nonpoor households. By linking farmers more closely to consumers, these marketing systems transmit signals to farmers on new market opportunities and guide their production to meet changing consumer preferences for quantity, quality, variety, and food safety. Effi cient markets require good governance and public policy—infrastructure, institutions, and services that provide market information, establish grades and standards, manage risks, and enforce contracts a continuing challenge in many countries. However, efficient markets alone do not promote equitable outcomes. So smallholders may need to build their bargaining power through their producer organizations, assisted by public policy. The nature and pace of market development differs across food staples (cereals), traditional bulk export commodities coffee, cocoa, tea, cotton, and higher-value products for domestic and export markets (dairy, meat, fruits, vegetables). This chapter examines the new opportunities and challenges for smallholders in the markets for each of these important commodity groups. It highlights the broad array of private, public, and civil society initiatives that have been pursued to make markets work better for development and poverty reduction.

Food staples: improving commodity trading and risk management

The market for food staples remains by far the most important in many agriculturebased and transforming countries, because staples take up a major share of household food expenditures and account for the bulk of agricultural gross domestic product. Growing populations sustain demand, supplemented by the rapidly growing demand for livestock feed in middleincome countries. Inhibiting the market for food staples are high transaction costs, product wastage and losses, wide marketing margins, poor market integration, limited access to trade fi nance, and weak regulatory institutions. Better markets for food staples have broad implications for agricultural growth because they raise farmgate prices, build the confi dence of farmers in their reliability, and allow farmers to diversify to higher-value products.

In agriculture-based and transforming countries, small and medium-size traders and layers of intermediaries are common in the marketing of food staples and other agricultural commodities. Often one-person businesses dealing in several commodities, the traders and intermediaries are mainly self-funded because of limited access to credit. They maximize the returns on their working capital by rapidly turning over small quantities, with little storage. Quality grades are rarely standardized, nor are weights and measures, making personal inspection by buyers essential. This requires that traders travel extensively, increasing transaction costs. Improving and modernizing the marketing system can increase market effi - ciency, foster competitiveness with imports, and reduce losses and risks. Market modernization, beyond improving basic transport, includes marketing information systems, commodity exchanges, and price-risk management.

Poor road connections

Inadequate transport infrastructure and services in rural areas push up marketing costs, undermining local markets and exports. This is particularly the case in Africa, where less than 50 percent of the rural population lives close to an all-season road. Trader surveys in Benin, Madagascar, and Malawi fi nd that transport costs account for 50–60 percent of total marketing costs.1 Improving road connections is thus critical to strengthening the links of farmers and the rural economy to local, regional, and international markets.

Market information systems

Market information keeps farmers and traders attuned to the demands and changing preferences of consumers, guiding farming, marketing, and investing. Market information encompasses timely and accurate prices, buyer contacts, distribution channels, buyer and producer trends, import regulations, competitor profi les, grade and standards specifi cations, postharvest handling advice, and storage and transport recommendations.

Public market information systems have often been disappointing, with information disseminated too slowly, in the wrong form, or too infrequently to be of real use to market participants.3 Several innovative approaches are being piloted in different parts of the world, building on advances in communications technology (radio, cell phone, television, Internet) and the liberalization of telecommunications and broadcasting. In India, the Ministry of Agriculture operates AgMark Net, which collects price information from wholesale markets nationwide and disseminates it through the Internet. The private sector in India is investing in telecommunications infrastructure, such as mobile phone networks and Internet-linked rural kiosks, which aid in strengthening market information, extension, and other services to farmers. In West Africa, a publicprivate partnership set up TradeNet, a trading platform that allows sellers and buyers to get into contact over the Internet and by cell phones.

Market information systems also disseminate price information in Kenya, Mozambique, and Senegal, using a mix of Internet, short message service (SMS), voicemail, radio, and market chalkboards. Local FM radio broadcasts market information in Mali and Uganda. It is still too early to judge the long-term viability and impact, but anecdotal evidence points to the interest of farmers and the willingness of mobile phone companies to invest in these systems, supported by initial donor funding. The new systems have the potential to signifi cantly reduce transaction costs, especially search and transport costs, and warrant continued investment and evaluation.

Commodity exchanges: fast and low cost

Commodity exchanges offer a fast and low-cost mechanism for discovering prices, trading, and resolving contractual disputes. Rural road development has the potential to reduce transport costs and generate market activity. In Vietnam, road rehabilitation increased the variety of goods that households sold in the market—primary fruits, vegetables, and meat—and encouraged greater participation in trade and services. In Georgia, the construction and rehabilitation of roads increased the opportunities for off-farm and female employment. In Madagascar, simulations suggest that a 50 percent reduction in travel time per kilometer on roads would increase rice production by 1 percent. However, these effects will be mediated by specifi c geographic, political, and economic settings. Complementary inputs and policies may be required to achieve the full benefi ts from improved roads. Even if aggregate output gains are forthcoming, there will almost certainly be losers too. How one weighs the gains and losses and whether poverty falls is ultimately an empirical question. Recent work using impact evaluation methods shows mixed results, suggesting that to be effective, rural road policy needs to adapt to context and setting.

Policy should focus more on the complementary role of rural roads. Past policy has fi xated on the supply of rural roads as a catalyst to development and market activity. Poor road conditions often coincide with a number of other bottlenecks inhibiting agricultural productivity and economic development, including poor agroclimatic endowments, low population density, no transport services, low education levels, a lack of electricity, and risk, credit, and other market failures. Road benefi ts depend heavily on interactions with other infrastructure and geographical, community, and household characteristics. For example, one study in Vietnam found that four to six years after road rehabilitation, road transport services were more likely to respond where markets were already established and natural disasters were relatively infrequent. Policy needs to consider more than the absence or dire condition of a road before deciding that a new road is critical. In each specifi c case, policy should ask whether roads are the right instrument for overcoming the constraints to a given welfare outcome and if so, what other policy initiatives and investments are needed. Heterogeneities across households will determine who gains and who loses. Holding community characteristics constant, some households will be better placed to take advantage of a new road, based on their endowments and the nature of their occupations. Households differ in what they buy and sell and hence how much they will gain or lose from the changes in prices induced by better roads. Poor households are more likely to rely on the production of nontraded goods and services that may actually be displaced by better roads fomenting increased competition. On the other hand, road improvement has a general income effect that could generate demand for services from poor providers. The net effect is an empirical question. The picture that emerges from recent, more methodologically rigorous impact evaluations is a complex one. In Nepal, better road access benefi ted the poor and the nonpoor, but the proportionate gains were higher for the nonpoor. Dercon and others fi nd that access to all-weather roads in 15 villages in Ethiopia reduced the incidence of poverty by 6.7 percent. Given the heterogeneity of impacts, more attention needs to go to benefi ciary selection, recognizing that tradeoffs exist. Moreover, roads may need to be provided as part of a package of interventions that helps certain groups benefi t more than they would have and that protects or compensates those who may lose. The governance and institutional settings are also important in determining impacts.

Road project funds may not end up funding what was intended and hence have no impact. Infrastructure expenditures present opportunities for graft and the diversion of resources. This can change when incentives change. One study found that the threat of an audit on road projects in Indonesia signifi cantly increased the actual amounts spent on labor and building materials for roads, thereby bringing the quality of the roads nearer to that originally intended. Fungibility can also dull impacts, as aid or central government funding for road projects may substitute for local government infrastructure spending. Finally, the lack of funding and institutional arrangements for routine maintenance can signifi cantly reduce the impacts of newly improved roads. How much roads matter depends on a range of factors. Of course, roads matter to economic development, but how much they matter depends on a number of other factors.

Comprehensive approaches are needed that are compatible with how local institutions work in practice, including what they are capable of delivering. This may require fashioning a whole package of cross-sectoral investments (roads *and* complementary investments) and policy changes that will ensure a higher effi ciency impact, as well as more desirable poverty and equity outcomes.

India's commodity futures exchanges expanded rapidly after the government eliminated the ban on their operations in 2004.[7] Three national electronic and 21 regional futures exchanges trade contracts for cereals, sugar, cotton, potatoes, oilseeds, and spices.8 The fortnightly turnover totaled $8.7 billion on the three national exchanges in a two-week period in September 2005. The South Africa Futures Exchange offers futures contracts on white and yellow maize, wheat, sunfl ower, and soybeans, and it traded more than 1.9 million contracts in 2006. Traders throughout southern Africa use SAFEX as a benchmark for pricing physical trades. In 2006 the government of Malawi used a SAFEX-based call option to protect itself from the risk of international price increases when a bad harvest would require signifi cant imports.

Futures trading requires good fi nancial and legal structures and supportive government policies. The benefi ts diminish if the markets for smallholders are separated from the exchange by high transport and transaction costs or by quality differences. Establishing exchanges in Africa is challenging because of continuing government intervention in grain markets, small markets, and weak systems for warehouse receipts and grades and standards.

Price-risk management: a role for governments

Because of the vulnerability of poor producers and consumers to price shocks for food staples, governments often seek to stabilize prices, countering efforts to liberalize markets. The variability in world grain prices remains signifi cant, with coeffi cients of variation 20–30 percent for rice, wheat, and white maize. Domestic price instability tends to be high in Africa, especially in land-locked countries (such as Ethiopia), where the wedge between the export and import parity price is large and drought increases the impact of domestic shocks. The appropriate role of government in managing food-price risk continues to be debated. Opponents of government intervention note that price stabilization policies often lead to economically inefficient production decisions and discourage incentives to search for cost-reducing technical and institutional innovations.

TradeNet, a West African trading platform with Internet and mobile phones

TradeNet, a Ghana-based trading platform, allows users to

sign up for short message service alerts for commodities and markets of their choice and receive instant alerts for offers to buy or sell as soon as anyone else on the network has submitted an offer on their mobile phone. Users can also request and receive real-time prices for more than 80 commodities from 400 markets across West Africa. Individual users can advertise their goods and offers on free Web sites with their own Internet addresses, and farmer and trader groups can set up Web sites to manage all these services for their members.

Another view is that the nature and extent of price-stabilization interventions will depend on country-specifi c factors. Food-price stabilization is more relevant in low-income countries where food staples are a large share of the incomes of poor producers and the expenditures of poor consumers, where one food staple dominates, where domestic production is highly variable, and where poor infrastructure and location restrict tradability. Lessons over several decades suggest that the design of food-price risk interventions should be part of a long-term strategy that emphasizes measures to raise productivity of food staples, improve the effi ciency of markets (infrastructure, market information, grades and standards, warehouse receipts), and minimize the impact of price shocks weather-based insurance and safety nets. Liberalizing trade, especially by promoting regional trade, can be a source of "quick wins" for reducing price volatility, especially in small and mediumsize countries.

Many developing countries have agencies to maintain publicly owned strategic reserves that aim to reduce price instability, but the agencies instead often destabilize prices through unpredictable market interventions, border closings, and poorly timed imports.16 Safeguards are needed to prevent this. They include arm's length, central bank–type autonomy; highly professional management and analytical capacity; strict rule-based and transparent market operations to meet a narrowly defi ned objective; and tendering procurement and storage to the private sector.

Traditional bulk export commodities: maintaining international competitiveness

Maintaining international competitiveness in bulk agricultural commodity exports is a major challenge for many low-income countries, especially in Africa. Competitiveness is important, because exports of coffee, cocoa, tea, cotton, and other bulk commodities are their main source of foreign exchange. For Benin, Burkina Faso, Burundi, and Mali, one such commodity accounts for more than half of the value of total exports.

Producers of these commodities, however, have faced a long-term downward trend in prices as global supply outpaced demand. Productivity increased among traditional producers and exporters, and new players, such as Vietnam in coffee and tea, further expanded supply. Increasing productivity to cope with declining prices helped some countries in the short term but added to the long-term downward pressure on world prices, with consumption stagnating in the major markets (Western countries) and growth limited in the "new" markets (Eastern Europe, the Middle East, and the former Soviet Union).19 Cotton subsidies in member countries of the Organisation for Economic Co-operation and Development further depressed prices. Projections for coffee, cocoa, and tea indicate continuing price declines.

And the technology advances in roasting lower-quality robusta coffee allow its substitution for higher-quality arabica. Changing consumer preferences, such as the shift toward instant and fl avored coffees and convenience teas, further shift demand toward lower-quality products. Cotton is the exception, where the importance attached to lint quality has risen in recent years with the widespread use of high-speed spinning machines with demanding quality requirements. Specialty markets organic, gourmet, Fair Trade offer an alternative higherpriced market, but they account for only a small share of the global market. Currently, the specialty coffee sector accounts for only about 6–8 percent of global consumption. Many countries, such as Tanzania and its Kilimanjaro specialty coffee or KILLICAFE initiative, are targeting these markets to expand export markets and increase revenues.

Different paths to liberalizing domestic markets

Bulk export commodity markets in Africa were traditionally controlled by parastatal agencies, which often had monopoly powers in domestic marketing, exporting, and providing inputs to farmers (seeds, fertilizer, credit, extension services). The parastatals also aimed to stabilize prices received by farmers. In many instances the vertical coordination arrangements in production and marketing enabled farmers to overcome market failures in the input, credit, and insurance markets. They also ensured a steady supply of products of assured quality for export. But the agencies were widely criticized for ineffi ciencies and mismanagement that lowered the prices paid to farmers and raised the fi scal costs to government. To redress these failures, the bulk commodity markets in many countries in Africa were liberalized in the 1980s and 1990s, and many parastatal agencies were abolished or restructured.

African countries that restructured their bulk commodity markets followed different paths, ranging from restructuring the parastatal ownership to include the private sector and farmers to market zoning to full market liberalization.

Overall the liberalization programs generated immediate benefi ts: an infl ux of private capital, management, and marketing expertise; and market competition reducing transaction costs, increasing prices received by farmers and typically leading to prompter payment for crops purchased.

One study found that 85 percent of coffee producers in Tanzania were better off as the gains from higher producer prices more than offset the loss from reduced access to credit through public sources.

After liberalizing: addressing second-generation problems

In many countries, the restructuring of the market brought second-generation problems, aptly illustrated by cotton in major producing countries in Africa. The absence of a clear legal and regulatory framework to guide private sector and farmer behavior in the context of free market competition or weak contract enforcement created confusion and allowed some malpractices to persist. To help private traders enforce contracts, Côte d'Ivoire and Zambia adopted zoning arrangements to regulate cotton marketing that have worked reasonably well.28 However, competition from new buyers in Zimbabwe and Tanzania weakened quality enforcement.

What contributed to these secondgeneration problems? The weaknesses and lack of credibility of public institutions to enforce appropriate rules of behavior for the private sector is part of it. Public intervention in grades and standards and in contract enforcement is essential to ensure that private markets work. Liberalization also exposed the underdevelopment of rural fi nancial systems, which need to be addressed. The African experience also highlights the potential for associations and professional organizations (farmer groups in Tanzania) to overcome the shortsightedness of individual farmers and buyers.30 Partial privatization in Burkina Faso has given farmers more ownership, but it led to heavy fi scal outlays (box 5.4).

Higher-value urban markets: linking producers to modern supply chains

Rising incomes, urbanization, greater female participation in the workforce, wider media penetration all are driving the demand for higher-value products, semiprocessed and processed products, and convenience foods. They are also increasing consumer attention to food quality and safety. Diets are globalizing too, with local consumer preferences infl uenced by international tastes. These trends open new markets for a wide range of higher-value agricultural products and propel the evolution of the marketing system in many developing countries, with the entry and rapid growth of supermarket chains and the food processing and food service industries.

For many developing countries, the supermarket revolution began in the early to mid-1990s. By the early 2000s, retail food sales in supermarkets exceeded 50 percent of total retail food sales in many countries in Latin America and in major urban centers elsewhere. Accelerating the expansion: signifi cant foreign direct investment by multinational supermarket chains in developing countries, either directly or through joint ventures with local fi rms. Changing consumer demand is also driving the growth of the food processing and food service industries. Processed foods account for about 80 percent of global food sales, estimated at $3.2 trillion in 2002.31 Although spending on processed foods is still low in developing countries ($143 per capita per year in lower-middleincome countries and $63 per capita in low-income countries), it is growing fastest in these countries 28 percent a year in lower-middle-income countries and 13 percent a year in low-income countries.

"Eating out" is also becoming popular. For example, spending on food services now accounts for 22 percent of food budgets in Brazil and Indonesia and 15 percent of urban food spending in China.

Infrastructure impediments

The perishability of most high-value agricultural products requires careful handling, special facilities packhouses, cold storage, and refrigerated transport, and rapid delivery to consumers to maintain quality and reduce physical and nutritional losses. In many developing countries, the long supply chain, poor access to roads and electricity, and inadequate infrastructure and services in physical markets add to the transaction costs and cause quality deterioration and high spoilage losses. In India it is estimated that fruit and vegetable postharvest losses amount to about 40 percent of total annual production, equal to a year's consumption in the United Kingdom.

Market infrastructure and facilities in developing countries are often limited and congested, increasing the diffi culty of trading perishable goods. A survey of wholesale markets handling fresh produce in four states in India found that 17 percent had no covered shops, about half did not have paved roads in the market yard, about 40 percent of the shops had no electricity, and only 6 percent of the markets had a coldstorage facility. In Tamil Nadu, India, a related study found that wealthier farmers tend to capture a disproportionate share of the benefi ts of faciiities in congested wholesale markets.34 Nonetheless, investments in market facilities would be pro-poor because sales by poorer farmers would increase proportionally more than those by the wealthy farmers.

Modern procurement systems

Supermarket growth in most countries follows similar diffusion patterns across space, consumer segments, and product categories. From a base in large cities, supermarkets initially spread to intermediate cities and towns, and later to small towns in rural areas—in response to market competition and saturation. They often fi rst target the upper-income consumer (national and expatriate), followed by the middle class and later the urban lowerincome households.

Dominating the supermarket's product selection in the early stages are processed foods (canned, dry, and packaged food items), motivated by èconomies of scale in procurement and direct relations with processed-food manufacturers. Product selection gradually expands to semiprocessed foods (dairy, meat, and fruit products). The last category to be added is fresh fruits and vegetables, as consumer preference for fresh produce and the proximity and convenience of small produce shops and wet markets offer a competitive alternative. Fresh fruits and vegetables generally account for the lowest share in supermarket sales, and small shops and wet markets will likely remain important marketing channels for these products for years to come.

Signifi cant ineffi ciencies in the traditional wholesale marketing systems and competition encourage supermarkets, food processors, and food service providers to use supply chains to reduce coordination costs, capture economies of scale, and increase food safety and quality. This is 1profoundly changing the structure of production and wholesale marketing in many developing countries. Recent studies show that procurement systems change earliest for processed foods, meat, and dairy products, eventually extending to fresh fruits and vegetables.

Procurement takes many forms, varying by supermarket chain, product, and country. It can involve centralized procurement, which shifts from fragmented per-store purchases to operating a distribution center catering to a district as in China , the whole country or whole region. It can also involve shifting from purchases in traditional spot wholesale markets to relying on specialized or dedicated wholesalers and logistics firms (as in Central America and East Asia) or to direct contracting to cut transaction, coordination, and search costs and ensure greater control over quality and consistency of supply.

Modern procurement can also involve contracting with processors and farmers or using preferred-supplier lists. This is often done where farmers or processors are grouped or are individually large. The contracts are incentives for suppliers to stay with the buyer and invest in assets that fit the retailer's specifi cations for products. The arrangements may include direct or indirect assistance for farmers to invest in training, management, inputs, and basic equipment. Modern procurement also often involves private standards and their enforcement—standards that serve two main functions. They help coordinate supply chains by standardizing product requirements for suppliers over many regions or countries, enhancing effi ciency and lowering transaction costs. And they help ensure that public food-safety standards are met in all markets served by the retail chain or food-processing firm, distinguishing one's products from competitors through signaling. As these private standards are more widely adopted, there is growing concern about the capacity of small farmers to meet them.

Impact on smallholders and retailers

The modernization of procurement systems affects farmers differently across countries and products. Some recent studies of selected commodities fi nd that the modern procurement systems exclude asset-poor farmers. Supermarket buying agents prefer to source from large and medium-size farmers if they can (for example, for tomatoes in Mexico and potatoes in Indonesia); if large and medium-size farmers have suffi cient quantities, smallholders are not included. Where small farms are the dominant structure, supermarkets have no choice but to source their produce from them. Supermarkets may also rely on small farmers to satisfy consumers' demand for specialty or niche products that only small farmers with abundant labor produce. Sometimes supermarkets need an advertising tool to promote sales with socially conscious consumers: "buying local, from smallholders."

The most important determinant of small farmers' participation is not always farm size. Instead, it can be access to physical, human, and social assets: to education, irrigation, transport, roads, and such other physical assets as wells, cold chains, greenhouses, good quality irrigation water (free of contaminants), vehicles, and packing sheds.

An effective producer organization another major asset can also help small farmers enter the high-value supply chains. Most farmers lacking these assets are excluded. In Guatemala, lettuce farmers participating in modern supply chains have twice the farm size (two hectares versus one) and 40 percent more education than nonparticipating farmers, and are nearly twice as likely to have irrigation, four times as likely to have a truck, and twice as likely to be close to paved roads and be in a farmer organization. Participating farmers use much more labor-intensive practices because of requirements for fi eld practices, sorting, and packing. Because they are more likely to double-crop over the year, participating farmers hire 2.5 times more labor typically from local asset-poor households. So even if small farmers do not participate directly, they can benefit through farm employment. Studies of tomato growers in Indonesia and kale growers in Kenya fi nd similar results. Participation in modern supply chains can increase farmer income by 10 to 100 percent. Indonesia, Kenya. Recent studies of contract farmers show that they have signifi cantly higher incomes than other farmers. Because participating farmers tend to reap substantial benefits, the payoff from assisting farmers to make the necessary "threshold investments" can be high.

Some studies have found that smaller processing fi rms were left out of the supply chain, with medium-size and large processors preferred for long-term contracts. The number of small retail stores often declined with rising market share for supermarkets with implications for employment.

In urban Argentina, from 1984 to 1993, the most intense period of supermarket takeoff, the number of small food shops declined from 209,000 to 145,000.51 But the competition is also driving some small retail stores and processors to grow and upgrade their services as in India.

Helping smallholders keep up with the requirements

The government and the private sector can help smallholders expand and upgrade their range of assets and practices to meet the new requirements of supermarkets and other coordinated supply chains. The options include public good investments to increase farmers' productivity and connectivity to markets, policy changes to facilitate trade and market development, and publicprivate efforts to promote collective action and build the technical capacity of farmers to meet the new standards.

Some supermarkets and processors or their agents help farmers overcome their asset constraints and improve their business image by providing technical assistance, in some instances through publicprivate partnerships. Examples include joint extension by supermarket fi eld staff and government extension offi cers, technical assistance to acquire inputs and obtain certifi cation, and training to improve product quality and food safety.

Other supermarkets and processors enter into production contracts, which sometimes include the supply of inputs, credit, and extension services for example, in Madagascar and Slovakia For many small farmers, these contracts are the only means to acquire inputs and use support services. By supplying inputs and providing assured markets and prices, contracting fi rms share production and marketing risks with farmers. Reducing these risks helps stabilize farmers' incomes, critical in the absence of insurance markets. The technical assistance to farmers also generates indirect benefi ts, as farmers apply the improved farm practices for the contract crops to other crops, increasing their productivity. Supermarkets also procure through preferred suppliers or wholesalers that contract with producer organizations or commercial farmer "leaders" that supplement their own production with that from individual small farmers. The producer organizations or farmer leaders provide technical assistance to ensure quality, quantity, and timing of delivery. In addition, the preferred supplier or wholesaler often expects the producer organizations or farmer leaders to assemble the products washing, sorting, grading, packaging, and labeling, ready to be placed on supermarket shelves.

Conclusion

Markets are good for effi ciency, and much progress has been made in market development, especially under private sector leadership. But further effi ciency gains will require public sector support to deliver the necessary public goods, foster institutional innovation, and secure competitiveness. Because effi cient markets do not always secure socially desirable outcomes, complementary policies are often needed to ensure smallholder participation. A large agenda remains in improving the performance of the marketing systems in developing countries. Public investments to expand access to rural infrastructure and services such as rural roads and transport services, physical markets, telecommunications, and electricity will be critical to reducing transaction costs and physical losses and to enhancing transparency and competitiveness in traditional markets. Technical and institutional innovations reducing transaction costs and risks also show promise, especially the wider use of information technologies mobile phones, the Internet, and commodity exchanges and vertical coordination arrangements with individual farmers or producer organizations.

Bibliography

Abbott, J.C. (1987). Agricultural Marketing Enterprises for the Developing World with Case Studies of Indigenous Private, Transnational, co-operative and Parastatal Enterprises. Cambridge: Cambridge University Press.

Brake, J. et al. (1972), "The NAtional Agricultural Cooperatives Federation: An Appraisal", Korean Agricultural Sector Study (KASS), Special Report 1, Mechigan State University, East Lansing.

CAD (1991). Annual Report on Financial Statistics : Agricultural Land Reform Cooperatives. Bangkok : Ministry of Agriculture and Cooperatives.

Chowdhury, PK.; Huq, MA.; Rahman, SA. (1987). Cooperatives as institutions for development of the rural poor. Kotbari: Academy for Rural Development

Bangladesh; Community Development Library.

Duelfer, Eberhard (1994) and Jahani Laurinkari [Eds]. The International Handbook of Cooperative Organizations. Goettingen: Vandenhoeck und Ruprecht, 961 pages.

Ergstrom, Lee (1994). Make No Small Plans: A Cooperative Revival for Rural America. Rochester, Minnesota: Lone Oak Press Ltd., 294 pages.

Gehres, Donald J. (1968). Report on Cooperatives in Guatemala. A report prepared for US-AID, Guatemala, May.

FAO (1986). Profile of Agricultural Cooperatives in Selected Asian Countries. Bangkok: FAO Regional Office for Asia and Pacific.

Hazell, Peter B.R. and Sidney Hoos (1962), "Cooperative Enterprise and Organization Theory", Journal of Farm Econoics, 44, pp.275-290.

Korovkin,T.(1988). The politics of agricultural cooperativism:Peru, Dissertation Abstracts International, A Humanities and Social Sciences. 48: 12, p.3188; Diss., York University, Canada, 1986.

Kulkarni, R. and Krishna Rao (1956). Agricultural Marketing in India, with Special reference to Coopertive Marketings of Agricultural Produce in India. Bombay: Cooperators Book.

Larson, Adlowe (1969). "Universalities of Cooperation" in Anschel et al. [eds], Agricultural Cooperatives and Markets in Developing Countries. New York: Praeger.

Patwardhan, V.S. (1969). "Distribution of consumer goods by co-operatives in rural areas". Economic and Political Weekly, 4, pp. 361-370.

Roy, Ewell Paul (1964). Cooperatives: Today and Tomorrow. Danville: The Interstate Printers and Publishers.

Sando,RA.(1986). Implications of development policies for agriculture in Taiwan. Practicing development anthropology [edited by Green,E. C.]. 195-210. Boulder, Colorado : Westview Press.

Singh, Mohinder (1970). Co-operatives in Asia. New York: Praeger.

Svsrdsrum, K.F. (1969). Agricultural Marketing for Co-operators. Bombay: Allied Publishers.

Texier,J.M.(1978). The Promotion of Cooperatives in Traditional Rural Societies. In Policy and Practice in Rural Development (Edited by Guy Hunter, A. Hugh Bunting, Anthony Bottrall), p.215. London:Croom Helm Ltd.

Thompson, David (n.d.). Weavers of Dreams. [Authors address for copies: David Thompson, 516 Rutgers Drive, Davis CA 95616, USA]

Umeki,T.(1989). Marketing of processed farm products of agricultural cooperatives. Marketing farm products in Asia and the Pacific. pp.149-159, Tokyo: Asian Productivity Organization.

Won, HS.(1989). The agricultural co-operative movement in Korea. Review of International Co-operation. 82: 4, pp.65-74.

Young, Kun Shim (1989). Korea Republic. Marketing farm products in Asia and the Pacific. pp. 257-271; Tokyo:Asian Productivity Organization.

Index

I

K

M

N

O

P

Q

R

S

T

U

V

W

Z